Q: Skills for Success

LISTENING AND SPEAKING

4

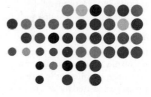

Robert Freire

Tamara Jones

SERIES CONSULTANTS

Marguerite Ann Snow

Lawrence J. Zwier

VOCABULARY CONSULTANT

Cheryl Boyd Zimmerman

OXFORD

UNIVERSITY PRESS

OXFORD
UNIVERSITY PRESS

198 Madison Avenue
New York, NY 10016 USA

Great Clarendon Street, Oxford OX2 6DP UK

Oxford University Press is a department of the University of Oxford.
It furthers the University's objective of excellence in research, scholarship,
and education by publishing worldwide in

Oxford New York

Auckland Cape Town Dar es Salaam Hong Kong Karachi
Kuala Lumpur Madrid Melbourne Mexico City Nairobi
New Delhi Shanghai Taipei Toronto

With offices in

Argentina Austria Brazil Chile Czech Republic France Greece
Guatemala Hungary Italy Japan Poland Portugal Singapore
South Korea Switzerland Thailand Turkey Ukraine Vietnam

OXFORD and OXFORD ENGLISH are registered trademarks of
Oxford University Press in certain countries.

© Oxford University Press 2011

Database right Oxford University Press (maker)

General Manager, American ELT: Laura Pearson
Publisher: Stephanie Karras
Associate Publishing Manager: Sharon Sargent
Development Editor: Brandon Lord
Associate Development Editors: Rebecca Mostov, Keyana Shaw
Director, ADP: Susan Sanguily
Executive Design Manager: Maj-Britt Hagsted
Associate Design Manager: Michael Steinhofer
Electronic Production Manager: Julie Armstrong
Production Artist: Elissa Santos
Cover Design: Molly Scanlon
Image Manager: Trisha Masterson
Image Editors: Robin Fadool and Liaht Pashayan
Production Coordinator: Elizabeth Matsumoto

ISBN: 978-0-19-475613-6 Listening Speaking 4 Student Book Pack
ISBN: 978-0-19-475603-7 Listening Speaking 4 Student Book
ISBN: 978-0-19-475621-1 Q Online Practice Student Access Code Card

Printed in China

This book is printed on paper from certified and well-managed sources.

10 9 8 7 6 5 4 3 2 1

ACKNOWLEDGMENTS

*The publisher would like to thank the following for their permission to reproduce copyrighted
material:* p. 6 "The Best of Both Worlds?" by Tara Weiss. Reproduced by Permission of
Forbes.com. © 2009 Forbes LLC; p. 11 "Myths of Effective Leadership," from Center
for Creative Leadership *Leading Effectively* Podcast Series, www.ccl.org. Used by
permission of Center for Creative Leadership; p. 46 "Generation Next" from the
series *Generation X.* Used by permission of BBC Worldwide Americas; p. 68 "Vacation,
Adventure, and Surgery?" from "Medical Tourism," *60 Minutes*, www.cbsnews.com.
Used by permission of CBS News Archives; p. 95 "Thomas Kinkade" from "Kinkade,"
60 Minutes, www.cbsnews.com. Used by permission of CBS News Archives;
p. 112 "Food Additive Linked to Hyperactivity in Kids" from "Food additives may
cause hyperactivity: study" by Maggie Fox, September 5, 2007, Reuters. All rights
reserved. Republication or redistribution of Thomson Reuters content, including
by framing or similar means, is expressly prohibited without the prior written
consent of Thomson Reuters. Thomson Reuters and its logo are registered
trademarks or trademarks of the Thomson Reuters group of companies around
the world.© Thomson Reuters 2009. Thomson Reuters journalists are subject to
an Editorial Handbook which requires fair presentation and disclosure of relevant
interests; p. 117 "The 'Flavr Savr' Tomato," *The World at Six*, July 4, 1994, www.cbc.ca.
© Canadian Broadcasting Corporation. All rights reserved. Used by permission;
p. 136 "Life Experience Before College" from "'Gap Year' Before College Slowly
Catches On With U.S. Students," *CBS The Early Show*, June 2, 2003, www.cbsnews.com.
Used by permission of CBS News Archives; p. 154 "The Power of Serendipity" from
CBS Sunday Morning, Oct. 7, 2007, www.cbsnews.com. Used by permission of CBS
News Archives; p. 159 "Against All Odds, Twin Girls Reunited" from CBS The Early
Show, April 12, 2006, www.cbsnews.com. Used by permission of CBS News Archives.

*The publishers would like to thank the following for their kind permission to reproduce
photographs:* Cover John Giustina/Iconica/Getty Images; Sean Justice/Riser/Getty
Images; Kirsty Pargeter/iStockphoto; Leontura/iStockphoto; Illustrious/iStockphoto;
vi Marcin Krygier/iStockphoto; xii Rüstem GÜRLER/iStockphoto; p. 2 JEWEL SAMAD/
AFP/Getty Images; p. 4 Dennis MacDonald/Alamy (coach); Alaska Stock/age fotostock
(hike); p. 6 Image Source/Getty Images; p. 8 Photodisc/Oxford University Press;
p. 11 Jon Feingersh Photography Inc/Getty Images; p. 15 Radius Images/Alamy;
p. 22 Glowimages RM/age fotostock; p. 24 Kablonk/SuperStock (business);
Westend61 GmbH/Alamy (casual); Blend Images/SuperStock (uniform); p. 27 Patti
McConville/Alamy; p. 30 Stockbyte/Getty Images (Man with tie); Fancy/Alamy
(casual); Yukmin/Getty Images (corporate); p. 35 Jan Greune/Getty Images (casual);
Asia Images/Masterfile (business); p. 39 Image Source/Alamy; p. 42 Masterfile;
p. 44 Masterfile (driver); blueking/Shutterstock (cap); Rebecca Photography/
Shutterstock (cake); Cheryl A. Meyer/Shutterstock (house); p. 46 Blend Images/
Oxford University Press; p. 49 Digital Vision/Getty Images; p. 50 Jupiterimages/Getty
Images; p. 51 Masterfile; p. 57 Food and Drink/SuperStock; p. 64 Jeff Greenberg/
Alamy; p. 68 Masterfile; p. 71 Image Source/Oxford University Press; p. 72 Digital
Vision/Oxford University Press; p. 73 I Dream Stock/Masterfile (stethoscope); NOAH
SEELAM/AFP/Getty Images (emergency room); p. 78 roberto benzi/age fotostock;
p. 86 Juergen Hasenkopf/Alamy; p. 88 whitefoxphoto/Alamy (food); Ingolf Pompe/
age fotostock (museum); ELENA PALM/AFP/Getty Images (hair); p. 90 Kyodo via AP
Images (artist); AP Photo/Eckehard Schulz (comic); p. 95 photooiasson/Shutterstock
(palette); ©1997 Thomas Kinkade (Twilight Cottage); p. 98 ©The Thomas Kinkade
Company, LLC; p. 100 Pepeira Tom/Photolibrary; p. 104 Tomas Abad/Alamy;
p. 108 John Innes Centre UK via Getty Images; p. 112 DUSAN ZIDAR/Shutterstock
(cereal); Reflexstock/Blend RM/Klaus Tiedge (scientist); Tobias Titz/Getty Images
(sports drink); p. 116 TOPIC PHOTO AGENCY/age fotostock; p. 117 Jerry Horbert/
Shutterstock; p. 121 Roy Morsch/Photolibrary (canned tomatoes); Laurie Rubin/
Masterfile (vine tomatoes); p. 125 Cordelia Molloy/Photo Researchers, Inc.
(strawberries); Food and Drink/SuperStock (normal chicken); Michael Blann/Getty
Images (modified chicken); p. 128 Oote Boe Photography 3/Alamy; p. 130 Barros &
Barros/Getty Images (raise hand); Yuri Tutov/AFP/Getty Images (vet); Clive Sawyer
PCL/SuperStock (airport); p. 132 Photodisc/Getty Images; p. 136 RAW FILE/Masterfile;
p. 140 Reflexstock/Cultura RM/yellowdog; p. 143 Olivier Goujon/SuperStock;
p. 144 Jeff Greenberg/Alamy; p. 150 Pascal Goetgheluck/Photo Researchers, Inc.;
p. 152 Jim Barber/Shutterstock (x-ray); IndexStock/SuperStock (potato chips); Sam
P.S. II/Alamy (dynamite); Cordelia Molloy/Photo Researchers, Inc. (penicillin); GK
Hart/Vicky Hart/Getty Images (microwave); Martyn F. Chillmaid/Photo Researchers,
Inc. (plastics); p. 154 Science Faction/SuperStock; p. 157 David J. Green - technology/
Alamy; p. 158 Guy Grenier/Masterfile; p. 159 Masterfile; p. 163 Reflexstock/
PhotoNonStop/Nicolas Thibaut/Photononstop; p. 168 age fotostock/SuperStock;
p. 173 Norbert Rosing/Getty Images; p. 176 Bruce & Jan Lichtenberger/SuperStock;
p. 179 age fotostock/SuperStock; p. 181 Etienne Girardet/Photolibrary; p. 182 AP
Photo/Jack Smith; p. 185 Ben Seelt/Masterfile; p. 187 Niebrugge Images/Alamy;
p. 192 SIMON MAINA/AFP/Getty Images; p. 193 Jeff Greenberg/Alamy; p. 198 AP
Photo/Gene J. Puskar; p. 200 Elvele Images Ltd/Alamy (runner); Michael Ventura/
Alamy (karate); Russell Sadur/Getty Images (soccer); p. 202 KAZUHIRO NOGI/AFP/
Getty Images; p. 205 Stephen Simpson/Getty Images; p. 207 Masterfile; p. 208 i love
images/Alamy; p. 212 Will Iredale/Shutterstock; p. 216 AP Photo/Mike Wintroath.

Illustrations by: p. 4 Bill Smith Group; p. 44 Claudia Carlson; p. 59 Greg Paprocki;
p. 66 Karen Minot; p. 88 Bill Smith Group; p. 90 Grace Chen; p. 110 Barb Bastian;
p. 130 Bill Smith Group; p. 146 Barb Bastian; p. 174 Claudia Carlson; p. 200 Bill
Smith Group.

ACKNOWLEDGEMENTS

Authors

Robert Freire holds an M.A. in Applied Linguistics from Montclair State University in New Jersey. He is a teacher and materials developer with more than ten years of ELT experience. He presently teaches ESL and linguistics at Montclair State University.

Tamara Jones holds an M.Ed. from the University of Sheffield in the United Kingdom and is currently pursuing her Ph.D. in Education. She has taught in Russia, Korea, the United Kingdom, the United States, and Belgium. She is currently an instructor at the SHAPE Language Center in Belgium. She specializes in the areas of pronunciation, conversation, and test preparation.

Series Consultants

Marguerite Ann Snow holds a Ph.D. in Applied Linguistics from UCLA. She is a professor in the Charter College of Education at California State University, Los Angeles where she teaches in the TESOL M.A. program. She has published in *TESOL Quarterly*, *Applied Linguistics*, and *The Modern Language Journal*. She has been a Fulbright scholar in Hong Kong and Cyprus. In 2006, she received the President's Distinguished Professor award at Cal State L.A. In addition to working closely with ESL and mainstream public school teachers in the United States, she has trained EFL teachers in Algeria, Argentina, Brazil, Egypt, Japan, Morocco, Pakistan, Spain, and Turkey. Her main interests are integrated content and language instruction, English for Academic Purposes, and standards for English teaching and learning.

Lawrence J. Zwier holds an M.A. in TESL from the University of Minnesota. He is currently the Associate Director for Curriculum Development at the English Language Center at Michigan State University in East Lansing. He has taught ESL/EFL in the United States, Saudi Arabia, Malaysia, Japan, and Singapore. He is a frequent TESOL conference presenter and has published many ESL/EFL books in the areas of test-preparation, vocabulary, and reading, including *Inside Reading 2* for Oxford University Press.

Vocabulary Consultant

Cheryl Boyd Zimmerman is Associate Professor of TESOL at California State University, Fullerton. She specializes in second-language vocabulary acquisition, an area in which she is widely published. She teaches graduate courses on second-language acquisition, culture, vocabulary, and the fundamentals of TESOL and is a frequent invited speaker on topics related to vocabulary teaching and learning. She is the author of *Word Knowledge: A Vocabulary Teacher's Handbook*, and Series Director of *Inside Reading*, both published by Oxford University Press.

REVIEWERS

We would like to acknowledge the advice of teachers from all over the world who participated in online reviews, focus groups, and editorial reviews. We relied heavily on teacher input throughout the extensive development process of the Q series, and many of the features in the series came directly from feedback we gathered from teachers in the classroom. We are grateful to all who helped.

UNITED STATES Marcarena Aguilar, North Harris College, TX; **Deborah Anholt**, Lewis and Clark College, OR; **Robert Anzelde**, Oakton Community College, IL; **Arlys Arnold**, University of Minnesota, MN; **Marcia Arthur**, Renton Technical College, WA; **Anne Bachmann**, Clackamas Community College, OR; **Ron Balsamo**, Santa Rosa Junior College, CA; **Lori Barkley**, Portland State University, OR; **Eileen Barlow**, SUNY Albany, NY; **Sue Bartch**, Cuyahoga Community College, OH; **Lora Bates**, Oakton High School, VA; **Nancy Baum**, University of Texas at Arlington, TX; **Linda Berendsen**, Oakton Community College, IL; **Jennifer Binckes Lee**, Howard Community College, MD; **Grace Bishop**, Houston Community College, TX; **Jean W. Bodman**, Union County College, NJ; **Virginia Bouchard**, George Mason University, VA; **Kimberley Briesch Sumner**, University of Southern California, CA; **Gabriela Cambiasso**, Harold Washington College, IL; **Jackie Campbell**, Capistrano Unified School District, CA; **Adele C. Camus**, George Mason University, VA; **Laura Chason**, Savannah College, GA; **Kerry Linder Catana**, Language Studies International, NY; **An Cheng**, Oklahoma State University, OK; **Carole Collins**, North Hampton Community College, PA; **Betty R. Compton**, Intercultural Communications College, HI; **Pamela Couch**, Boston University, MA; **Fernanda Crowe**, Intrax International Institute, CA; **Margo Czinski**, Washtenaw Community College, MI; **David Dahnke**, Lone Star College, TX; **Gillian M. Dale**, CA; **L. Dalgish**, Concordia College, MN; **Christopher Davis**, John Jay College, NY; **Sonia Delgadillo**, Sierra College, CA; **Marta O. Dmytrenko-Ahrabian**, Wayne State University, MI; **Javier Dominguez**, Central High School, SC; **Jo Ellen Downey-Greer**, Lansing Community College, MI; **Jennifer Duclos**, Boston University, MA; **Yvonne Duncan**, City College of San Francisco, CA; **Jennie Farnell**, University of Connecticut, CT; **Susan Fedors**, Howard Community College, MD; **Matthew Florence**, Intrax International Institute, CA; **Kathleen Flynn**, Glendale College, CA; **Eve Fonseca**, St. Louis Community College, MO; **Elizabeth Foss**, Washtenaw Community College, MI; **Duff C. Galda**, Pima Community College, AZ; **Christiane Galvani**, Houston Community College, TX; **Gretchen Gerber**, Howard Community College, MD; **Ray Gonzalez**, Montgomery College, MD; **Alyona Gorokhova**, Grossmont College, CA; **John Graney**, Santa Fe College, FL; **Kathleen Green**, Central High School, AZ; **Webb Hamilton**, De Anza College, San Jose City College, CA; **Janet Harclerode**, Santa Monica Community College, CA; **Sandra Hartmann**, Language and Culture Center, TX; **Kathy Haven**, Mission College, CA; **Adam Henricksen**, University of Maryland, MD; **Peter Hoffman**, LaGuardia Community College, NY; **Linda Holden**, College of Lake County, IL; **Jana Holt**, Lake Washington Technical College, WA; **Gail Ibele**, University of Wisconsin, WI; **Mandy Kama**, Georgetown University, Washington, DC; **Stephanie Kasuboski**, Cuyahoga Community College, OH; **Chigusa Katoku**, Mission College, CA; **Sandra Kawamura**, Sacramento City College, CA; **Gail Kellersberger**, University of Houston–Downtown, TX; **Jane Kelly**, Durham Technical Community College, NC; **Julie Park Kim**, George Mason University, VA; **Lisa Kovacs-Morgan** University of California, San Diego, CA; **Claudia Kupiec**, DePaul University, IL; **Renee La Rue**, Lone Star College-Montgomery, TX; **Janet Langon**, Glendale College, CA; **Lawrence Lawson**, Palomar College, CA; **Rachele Lawton**, The Community College of Baltimore County, MD; **Alice Lee**, Richland College, TX; **Cherie Lenz-Hackett**, University of Washington, WA; **Joy Leventhal**, Cuyahoga Community College, OH; **Candace Lynch-Thompson**, North Orange County Community College District, CA; **Thi Thi Ma**, City College of San Francisco, CA; **Denise Maduli-Williams**, City College of San Francisco, CA; **Eileen Mahoney**, Camelback High School, AZ; **Brigitte Maronde**, Harold Washington College, IL; **Keith Maurice**, University of Texas at Arlington, TX; **Nancy Mayer**, University of Missouri-St. Louis, MO; **Karen Merritt**, Glendale Union High School District, AZ; **Holly Milkowart**, Johnson County Community College, KS; **Eric Moyer**, Intrax International Institute, CA; **Gino Muzzatti**, Santa Rosa Junior College, CA; **William Nedrow**, Triton College, IL; **Eric Nelson**, University of Minnesota, MN; **Rhony Ory**, Ygnacio Valley High School, CA; **Paul Parent**, Montgomery College, MD; **Oscar Pedroso**, Miami Dade College, FL; **Robin Persiani**, Sierra College, CA; **Patricia Prenz-Belkin**, Hostos Community College, NY; **Jim Ranalli**, Iowa State University, IA; **Toni R. Randall**, Santa Monica College, CA; **Vidya Rangachari**, Mission College, CA; **Elizabeth Rasmussen**, Northern Virginia Community College, VA; **Lara Ravitch**, Truman College, IL; **Deborah Repasz**, San Jacinto College, TX; **Andrey Reznikov**, Black Hills State University, SD; **Alison Rice**, Hunter College, NY; **Jennifer Robles**, Ventura Unified School District, CA; **Priscilla Rocha**, Clark County School District, NV; **Dzidra Rodins**, DePaul University IL; **Maria Rodriguez**, Central High School, AZ; **Maria Ruiz**, Victor Valley College, CA; **Kimberly Russell**, Clark College, WA; **Irene Sakk**, Northwestern University, IL; **Shaeley Santiago**, Ames High School, IA; **Peg Sarosy**, San Francisco State University, CA; **Alice Savage**, North Harris College, TX; **Donna Schaeffer**, University of Washington, WA; **Carol Schinger**, Northern Virginia Community College, VA; **Robert Scott**, Kansas State University, KS; **Suell Scott**, Sheridan Technical Center, FL; **Shira Seaman**, Global English Academy, NY; **Richard Seltzer**, Glendale Community College, CA; **Kathy Sherak**, San Francisco State University, CA; **German Silva**, Miami Dade College, FL; **Andrea Spector**, Santa Monica Community College, CA; **Karen Stanely**, Central Piedmont Community College, NC; **Ayse Stromsdorfer**, Soldan I.S.H.S., MO; **Yilin Sun**, South Seattle Community College, WA; **Thomas Swietlik**, Intrax International Institute, IL; **Judith Tanka**, UCLA Extension–American Language Center, CA; **Priscilla Taylor**, University of Southern California, CA; **Ilene Teixeira**, Fairfax County Public Schools, VA; **Shirl H. Terrell**, Collin College, TX; **Marya Teutsch-Dwyer**, St. Cloud State University, MN; **Stephen Thergesen**, ELS Language Centers, CO; **Christine Tierney**, Houston Community College, TX; **Arlene Turini**, North Moore High School, NC; **Suzanne Van Der Valk**, Iowa State University, IA; **Nathan D. Vasarhely**, Ygnacio Valley High School, CA; **Naomi S. Verratti**, Howard Community College, MD; **Hollyahna Vettori**, Santa Rosa Junior College, CA; **Laura Walsh**, City College of San Francisco, CA; **Andrew J. Watson**, The English Bakery; **Donald Weasenforth**, Collin College, TX; **Juliane Widner**, Sheepshead Bay High School, NY; **Lynne Wilkins**, Mills College, CA; **Dolores "Lorrie" Winter**, California State University at Fullerton, CA; **Jody Yamamoto**, Kapi'olani Community College, HI; **Ellen L. Yaniv**, Boston University, MA; **Norman Yoshida**, Lewis & Clark College, OR; **Joanna Zadra**, American River College, CA; **Florence Zysman**, Santiago Canyon College, CA;

ASIA Rabiatu Abubakar, Eton Language Centre, Malaysia; **Wiwik Andreani**, Bina Nusantara University, Indonesia; **Mike Baker**, Kosei Junior High School, Japan; **Leonard Barrow**, Kanto Junior College, Japan; **Herman Bartelen**, Japan; **Siren Betty**, Fooyin University, Kaohsiung; **Thomas E. Bieri**, Nagoya College, Japan; **Natalie Brezden**, Global English House, Japan; **MK Brooks**, Mukogawa Women's University, Japan; **Truong Ngoc Buu**, The Youth Language School, Vietnam; **Charles Cabell**, Toyo University, Japan; **Fred Carruth**, Matsumoto University, Japan; **Frances Causer**, Seijo University, Japan; **Deborah Chang**, Wenzao Ursuline College of Languages, Kaohsiung; **David Chatham**, Ritsumeikan University, Japan; **Andrew Chih Hong Chen**, National Sun Yat-sen University, Kaohsiung; **Christina Chen**, Yu-Tsai Bilingual Elementary School, Taipei; **Jason Jeffree Cole**, Coto College, Japan; **Le Minh Cong**, Vungtau Tourism Vocational College, Vietnam; **Todd Cooper**, Toyama National College of Technology, Japan; **Marie Cosgrove**, Daito Bunka University, Japan; **Tony Cripps**, Ritsumeikan University, Japan; **Daniel Cussen**, Takushoku University, Japan; **Le Dan**, Ho Chi Minh City Electric Power College, Vietnam; **Simon Daykin**, Banghwa-dong Community Centre, South Korea; **Aimee Denham**, ILA, Vietnam; **Bryan Dickson**, David's English Center, Taipei; **Nathan Ducker**, Japan University, Japan; **Ian Duncan**, Simul International Corporate Training, Japan; **Nguyen Thi Kieu Dung**, Thang Long University, Vietnam; **Nguyen Thi Thuy Duong**, Vietnamese American Vocational Training College, Vietnam; **Wong Tuck Ee**, Raja Tun Azlan Science Secondary School, Malaysia; **Emilia Effendy**, International Islamic University Malaysia, Malaysia; **Robert Eva**, Kaisei Girls High School, Japan; **Jim George**, Luna International Language School, Japan; **Jurgen Germeys**, Silk Road Language Center, South Korea; **Wong Ai Gnoh**, SMJK Chung Hwa Confucian, Malaysia; **Peter Goosselink**, Hokkai High School,

Japan; **Wendy M. Gough**, St. Mary College/Nunoike Gaigo Senmon Gakko, Japan; **Tim Grose**, Sapporo Gakuin University, Japan; **Pham Thu Ha**, Le Van Tam Primary School, Vietnam; **Ann-Marie Hadzima**, Taipei; **Troy Hammond**, Tokyo Gakugei University International Secondary School, Japan; **Robiatul 'Adawiah Binti Hamzah**, SMK Putrajaya Precinct 8(1), Malaysia; **Tran Thi Thuy Hang**, Ho Chi Minh City Banking University, Vietnam; **To Thi Hong Hanh**, CEFALT, Vietnam; **Janis Hearn**, Hongik University, South Korea; **David Hindman**, Sejong University, South Korea; **Nahn Cam Hoa**, Ho Chi Minh City University of Technology, Vietnam; **Jana Holt**, Korea University, South Korea; **Jason Hollowell**, Nihon University, Japan; **F. N. (Zoe) Hsu**, National Tainan University, Yong Kang; **Wenhua Hsu**, I-Shou University, Kaohsiung; **Luu Nguyen Quoc Hung**, Cantho University, Vietnam ; **Cecile Hwang**, Changwon National University, South Korea; **Ainol Haryati Ibrahim**, Universiti Malaysia Pahang, Malaysia; **Robert Jeens**, Yonsei University, South Korea; **Linda M. Joyce**, Kyushu Sangyo University, Japan; **Dr. Nisai Kaewsanchai**, English Square Kanchanaburi, Thailand; **Aniza Kamarulzaman**, Sabah Science Secondary School, Malaysia; **Ikuko Kashiwabara**, Osaka Electro-Communication University, Japan; **Gurmit Kaur**, INTI College, Malaysia; **Nick Keane**, Japan; **Ward Ketcheson**, Aomori University, Japan; **Montchatry Ketmuni**, Rajamangala University of Technology, Thailand; **Dinh Viet Khanh**, Vietnam; **Seonok Kim**, Kangsu Jongro Language School, South Korea; **Kelly P. Kimura**, Soka University, Japan; **Stan Kirk**, Konan University, Japan; **Donald Knight**, Nan Hua/Fu Li Junior High Schools, Hsinchu; **Kari J. Kostiainen**, Nagoya City University, Japan; **Pattri Kuanpulpol**, Silpakorn University, Thailand; **Ha Thi Lan**, Thai Binh Teacher Training College, Vietnam; **Eric Edwin Larson**, Miyazaki Prefectural Nursing University, Japan; **Richard S. Lavin**, Prefectural University of Kumamoto, Japan; **Shirley Leane**, Chugoku Junior College, Japan; **Tae Lee**, Yonsei University, South Korea; **Lys Yongsoon Lee**, Reading Town Geumcheon, South Korea; **Mallory Leece**, Sun Moon University, South Korea; **Dang Hong Lien**, Tan Lam Upper Secondary School, Vietnam; **Huang Li-Han**, Rebecca Education Institute, Taipei; **Sovannarith Lim**, Royal University of Phnom Penh, Cambodia; **Ginger Lin**, National Kaohsiung Hospitality College, Kaohsiung; **Noel Lineker**, New Zealand/Japan; **Tran Dang Khanh Linh**, Nha Trang Teachers' Training College, Vietnam; **Daphne Liu**, Buliton English School, Taipei; **S. F. Josephine Liu**, Tien-Mu Elementary School, Taipei ; **Caroline Luo**, Tunghai University, Taichung; **Jeng-Jia Luo**, Tunghai University, Taichung; **Laura MacGregor**, Gakushuin University, Japan; **Amir Madani**, Visuttharangsi School, Thailand; **Elena Maeda**, Sacred Heart Professional Training College, Japan; **Vu Thi Thanh Mai**, Hoang Gia Education Center, Vietnam; **Kimura Masakazu**, Kato Gakuen Gyoshu High School, Japan; **Susumu Matsuhashi**, Net Link English School, Japan; **James McCrostie**, Daito Bunka University, Japan; **Joel McKee**, Inha University, South Korea; **Colin McKenzie**, Wachirawit Primary School, Thailand; **William K. Moore**, Hiroshima Kokusai Gakuin University, Japan; **Hudson Murrell**, Baiko Gakuin University, Japan; **Frances Namba**, Senri International School of Kwansei Gakuin, Japan; **Keiichi Narita**, Niigata University, Japan; **Kim Chung Nguyen**, Ho Chi Minh University of Industry, Vietnam; **Do Thi Thanh Nhan**, Hanoi University, Vietnam; **Dale Kazuo Nishi**, Aoyama English Conversation School, Japan; **Louise Ohashi**, Shukutoku University, Japan; **Virginia Peng**, Ritsumeikan University, Japan; **Suangkanok Piboonthamnont**, Rajamangala University of Technology, Thailand; **Simon Pitcher**, Business English Teaching Services, Japan; **John C. Probert**, New Education Worldwide, Thailand; **Do Thi Hoa Quyen**, Ton Duc Thang University, Vietnam; **John P. Racine**, Dokkyo University, Japan; **Kevin Ramsden**, Kyoto University of Foreign Studies, Japan; **Luis Rappaport**, Cung Thieu Nha Ha Noi, Vietnam; **Lisa Reshad**, Konan Daigaku Hyogo, Japan; **Peter Riley**, Taisho University, Japan; **Thomas N. Robb**, Kyoto Sangyo University, Japan; **Maria Feti Rosyani**, Universitas Kristen Indonesia, Indonesia; **Greg Rouault**, Konan University, Japan; **Chris Ruddenklau**, Kindai University, Japan; **Hans-Gustav Schwartz**, Thailand; **Mary-Jane Scott**, Soongsil University, South Korea; **Jenay Seymour**, Hongik University, South Korea; **James Sherlock**, A.P.W. Angthong, Thailand; **Yuko Shimizu**, Ritsumeikan University, Japan; **Suzila Mohd Shukor**, Universiti Sains Malaysia, Malaysia; **Stephen E. Smith**, Mahidol University, Thailand; **Mi-young Song**, Kyungwon University, South Korea; **Jason Stewart**, Taejon International Language School, South Korea; **Brian A. Stokes**, Korea University, South Korea; **Mulder Su**, Shih-Chien University, Kaohsiung;

Yoomi Suh, English Plus, South Korea; **Yun-Fang Sun**, Wenzao Ursuline College of Languages, Kaohsiung; **Richard Swingle**, Kansai Gaidai University, Japan; **Tran Hoang Tan**, School of International Training, Vietnam; **Takako Tanaka**, Doshisha University, Japan; **Jeffrey Taschner**, American University Alumni Language Center, Thailand ; **Michael Taylor**, International Pioneers School, Thailand; **Tran Duong The**, Sao Mai Language Center, Vietnam; **Tran Dinh Tho**, Duc Tri Secondary School, Vietnam; **Huynh Thi Anh Thu**, Nhatrang College of Culture Arts and Tourism, Vietnam; **Peter Timmins**, Peter's English School, Japan; **Fumie Togano**, Hosei Daini High School, Japan; **F. Sigmund Topor**, Keio University Language School, Japan; **Yen-Cheng Tseng**, Chang-Jung Christian University, Tainan; **Hajime Uematsu**, Hirosaki University, Japan; **Rachel Um**, Mok-dong Oedae English School, South Korea; **David Underhill**, EEExpress, Japan; **Siriluck Usaha**, Sripatum University, Thailand; **Tyas Budi Utami**, Indonesia; **Nguyen Thi Van**, Far East International School, Vietnam; **Stephan Van Eycken**, Kosei Gakuen Girls High School, Japan; **Zisa Velasquez**, Taihu International School/Semarang International School, China/Indonesia; **Jeffery Walter**, Sangji University, South Korea; **Bill White**, Kinki University, Japan; **Yohanes De Deo Widyastoko**, Xaverius Senior High School, Indonesia; **Greg Chung-Hsien Wu**, Providence University, Taichung; **Hui-Lien Yeh**, Chai Nan University of Pharmacy and Science, Tainan; **Sittiporn Yodnil**, Huachiew Chalermprakiet University, Thailand; **Ming-Yu Li**, Chang Jung Christian University, Tainan; **Shamshul Helmy Zambahari**, Universiti Teknologi Malaysia, Malaysia; **Aimin Fadhlee bin Mahmud Zuhodi**, Kuala Terengganu Science School, Malaysia;

TURKEY **Gül Akkoç**, Boğaziçi University; **Seval Akmeşe**, Haliç University; **Deniz Balım**, Haliç University; **Robert Ledbury**, Izmir University of Economics; **Oya Özağaç**, Boğaziçi University;

THE MIDDLE EAST **Amina Saif Mohammed Al Hashamia**, Nizwa College of Applied Sciences, Oman; **Sharon Ruth Devaneson**, Ibri College of Technology, Oman; **Hanaa El-Deeb**, Canadian International College, Egypt; **Brian Gay**, Sultan Qaboos University, Oman; **Gail Al-Hafidh**, Sharjah Higher Colleges of Technology, U.A.E.; **Jonathan Hastings**, American Language Center, Jordan; **Sian Khoury**, Fujairah Women's College (HCT), U.A.E.; **Jessica March**, American University of Sharjah, U.A.E.; **Neil McBeath**, Sultan Qaboos University, Oman;

LATIN AMERICA **Aldana Aguirre**, Argentina; **Claudia Almeida**, Coordenação de Idiomas, Brazil; **Cláudia Arias**, Brazil; **Maria de los Angeles Barba**, FES Acatlan UNAM, Mexico; **Lilia Barrios**, Universidad Autónoma de Tamaulipas, Mexico; **Adán Beristain**, UAEM, Mexico; **Ricardo Böck**, Manoel Ribas, Brazil; **Edson Braga**, CNA, Brazil; **Marli Buttelli**, Mater et Magistra, Brazil; **Alessandra Campos**, Inova Centro de Linguas, Brazil; **Priscila Catta Preta Ribeiro**, Brazil; **Gustavo Cestari**, Access International School, Brazil; **Walter D'Alessandro**, Virginia Language Center, Brazil; **Lilian De Gennaro**, Argentina; **Mônica De Stefani**, Quality Centro de Idiomas, Brazil; **Julio Alejandro Flores**, BUAP, Mexico; **Mirian Freire**, CNA Vila Guilherme, Brazil; **Francisco Garcia**, Colegio Lestonnac de San Angel, Mexico; **Miriam Giovanardi**, Brazil; **Darlene Gonzalez Miy**, ITESM CCV, Mexico; **Maria Laura Grimaldi**, Argentina; **Luz Dary Guzmán**, IMPAHU, Colombia; **Carmen Koppe**, Brazil; **Monica Krutzler**, Brazil; **Marcus Murilo Lacerda**, Seven Idiomas, Brazil; **Nancy Lake**, CEL-LEP, Brazil; **Cris Lazzerini**, Brazil; **Sandra Luna**, Argentina; **Ricardo Luvisan**, Brazil; **Jorge Murilo Menezes**, ACBEU, Brazil; **Monica Navarro**, Instituto Cultural A. C., Mexico; **Joacyr Oliveira**, Faculdades Metropolitanas Unidas and Summit School for Teachers, Brazil; **Ayrton Cesar Oliveira de Araujo**, E&A English Classes, Brazil; **Ana Laura Oriente**, Seven Idiomas, Brazil; **Adelia Peña Clavel**, CELE UNAM, Mexico; **Beatriz Pereira**, Summit School, Brazil; **Miguel Perez**, Instituto Cultural Mexico; **Cristiane Perone**, Associação Cultura Inglesa, Brazil; **Pamela Claudia Pogré**, Colegio Integral Caballito/Universidad de Flores, Argentina; **Dalva Prates**, Brazil; **Marianne Rampaso**, Iowa Idiomas, Brazil; **Daniela Rutolo**, Instituto Superior Cultural Británico, Argentina; **Maione Sampaio**, Maione Carrijo Consultoria em Inglês Ltda, Brazil; **Elaine Santesso**, TS Escola de Idiomas, Brazil; **Camila Francisco Santos**, UNS Idiomas, Brazil; **Lucia Silva**, Cooplem Idiomas, Brazil; **Maria Adela Sorzio**, Instituto Superior Santa Cecilia, Argentina; **Elcio Souza**, Unibero, Brazil; **Willie Thomas**, Rainbw Idiomas, Brazil; **Sandra Villegas**, Instituto Humberto de Paolis, Argentina; **John Whelan**, La Universidad Nacional Autonoma de Mexico, Mexico

WELCOME TO Q:Skills for Success

Q: Skills for Success is a six-level series with two strands, *Reading and Writing* and *Listening and Speaking*.

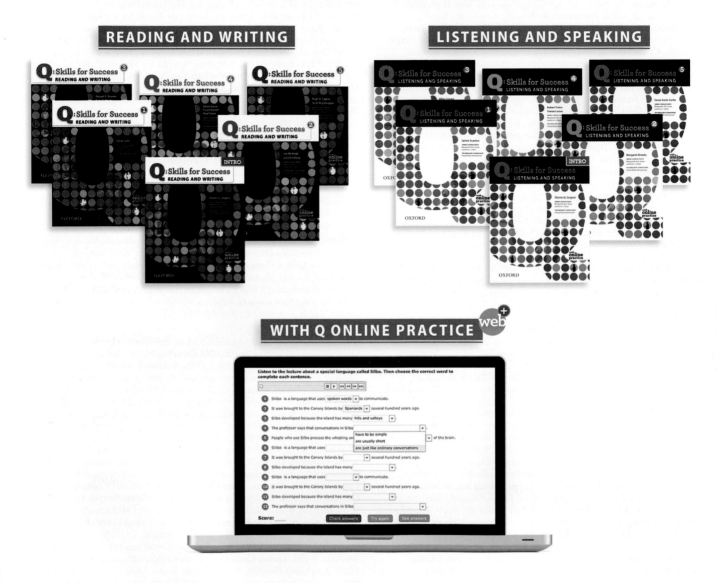

READING AND WRITING

LISTENING AND SPEAKING

WITH Q ONLINE PRACTICE

STUDENT AND TEACHER INFORMED

Q: Skills for Success is the result of an extensive development process involving thousands of teachers and hundreds of students around the world. Their views and opinions helped shape the content of the series. *Q* is grounded in teaching theory as well as real-world classroom practice, making it the most learner-centered series available.

CONTENTS

Quick Guide	viii	
Scope and Sequence	xiv	

Unit 1 **Q: How does power affect leaders?** 2
Listening 1: Best of Both Worlds?
Listening 2: Myths of Effective Leadership
webQ Online Practice Listening: Are Leaders Born or Made?

Unit 2 **Q: How does appearance affect our success?** 22
Listening 1: A Perfect Mess
Listening 2: The Changing Business Dress Code
webQ Online Practice Listening: Appearances Matter in the Animal World

Unit 3 **Q: When does a child become an adult?** 42
Listening 1: Generation Next
Listening 2: Growing Up Quickly
webQ Online Practice Listening: Child Prodigies

Unit 4 **Q: How is health care changing?** 64
Listening 1: Vacation, Adventure, and Surgery?
Listening 2: Medical Travel Can Create Problems
webQ Online Practice Listening: A Doctor's Journey

Unit 5 **Q: What makes a work of art popular?** 86
Listening 1: Manga's New Popularity
Listening 2: Thomas Kinkade
webQ Online Practice Listening: Progressive Art Education

Unit 6 **Q: How has science changed the food we eat?** 108
Listening 1: Food Additives Linked to Hyperactivity in Kids
Listening 2: The "Flavr Savr" Tomato
webQ Online Practice Listening: Superfoods

Unit 7 **Q: Is one road to success better than another?** 128
Listening 1: Changing Ways to Climb the Ladder
Listening 2: Life Experience Before College
webQ Online Practice Listening: Is Popular Culture Making Us Smarter?

Unit 8 **Q: How can chance discoveries affect our lives?** 150
Listening 1: The Power of Serendipity
Listening 2: Against All Odds, Twin Girls Reunited
webQ Online Practice Listening: An Unlikely Discovery

Unit 9 **Q: How can we maintain a balance with nature?** 172
Listening 1: Polar Bears at Risk
Listening 2: The Effects of Oil Spills
webQ Online Practice Listening: Swimming for Mother Earth

Unit 10 **Q: Is athletic competition good for children?** 198
Listening 1: Training Chinese Athletes
Listening 2: *Until It Hurts* Discusses Youth Sports Obsession
webQ Online Practice Listening: A Child's Dream Helps a Village

Audioscript 220

Q connects critical thinking, language skills, and learning outcomes.

LANGUAGE SKILLS

Explicit skills instruction enables students to meet their academic and professional goals.

LEARNING OUTCOMES

Clearly identified **learning outcomes** focus students on the goal of their instruction.

UNIT **6**
The Science of Food

LISTENING	● understanding bias in a presentation
VOCABULARY	● prefixes and suffixes
GRAMMAR	● comparative forms of adjectives and adverbs
PRONUNCIATION	● common intonation patterns
SPEAKING	● expressing interest during a conversation

LEARNING OUTCOME ●

Participate in a debate on food science, stating and supporting your opinions about food modification.

Q

Unit QUESTION

How has science changed the food we eat?

PREVIEW THE UNIT

Ⓐ Discuss these questions with your classmates.

Which is more important in the food you choose: flavor, cost, or nutrition? Why?

Scientists have developed ways to genetically modify plants. What do you know about genetically modified food?

Look at the photo. How have the tomatoes been modified? Would you want to try them?

Ⓑ Discuss the Unit Question with your classmates.

◉ Listen to *The Q Classroom*, Track 24 on CD 2, to hear other answers.

108 UNIT 6

109

CRITICAL THINKING

Thought-provoking **unit questions** engage students with the topic and provide a **critical thinking framework** for the unit.

Having the learning outcome is important because it gives students and teachers a clear idea of what the point of each task/activity in the unit is.
Lawrence Lawson, Palomar College, California

PREVIEW LISTENING 1

LANGUAGE SKILLS

Two listening texts provide input on the unit question and give **exposure to academic content.**

Food Additives Linked to Hyperactivity in Kids

You are going to listen to a radio report about food chemicals and their effects on children's behavior.

Work with a partner. Why might chemicals in food affect a child's behavior? Give reasons for your answer.

Q WHAT DO YOU THINK?

CRITICAL THINKING

Students **discuss** their opinions of each listening text and **analyze** how it changes their perspective on the unit question.

A. Discuss the questions in a group.

1. Some genetically altered plants need less water to grow, are resistant to insects, or are more nutritious. Farmers may be able to feed more people by growing genetically modified crops. Do the benefits of growing genetically modified crops outweigh possible risks? Give reasons for your answer.

2. In some countries, genetically altered foods must have a label explaining that they are altered. Is this law a good idea? Why or why not?

B. Think about both Listening 1 and Listening 2 as you discuss the questions.

Do you know if any foods you eat have been genetically modified? Do you know which foods contain additives? How can you find out? How will this information affect what you buy?

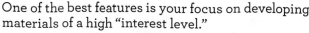

> One of the best features is your focus on developing materials of a high "interest level."
>
> *Troy Hammond, Tokyo Gakugei University,*
> *International Secondary School, Japan*

Explicit skills instruction prepares students for academic success.

LANGUAGE SKILLS

Explicit instruction and practice in listening, speaking, grammar, pronunciation, and vocabulary skills **help students achieve language proficiency.**

LEARNING OUTCOMES

Practice activities allow students to **master the skills** before they are evaluated at the end of the unit.

Listening Skill | Understanding bias in a presentation

Bias is a strong feeling for or against something. Understanding the bias in a presentation is important. Speakers may express biases even when they're trying to sound objective. In Listening 1, the speaker presents research both for and against a link between food additives and hyperactivity, but the speaker's bias appears to be against food additives.

There are several clues to help you understand the bias of a presentation.

Title: Listening 1 is "Food Additives Linked to Hyperactivity in Kids." This is a negative idea, and it sounds very definite. This probably means the speaker agrees with the research in the report. A different title, such as "Some Researchers Believe Food Additives May Affect Hyperactivity" does not show such a strong bias.

Introduction: Pay attention to how a speaker introduces a topic. For example, if a speaker starts with, *I'm going to talk about the negative effects of food additives on children's behavior,* that statement alone tells you the speaker's bias.

Imbalance: Reports with a bias usually report on both sides of the issue, but the information is not balanced well. In Listening 1, most of the report is about the research results that show a link between additives and hyperactivity, and only a small part of the report is about research that doesn't show any link.

Information source: Consider who is providing the information. For example, suppose a company that sells chocolate presents research that shows eating chocolate is good for you. Knowing the company sells chocolate can help you decide how much to trust the information.

CD 2 Track 27   **A. Listen to the short report. Then answer the questions.**

1. Check (✓) the clues you hear that tell you the bias.

   ☐ Title
   ☐ Introduction
   ☐ Imbalance
   ☐ Information source

2. Is the speaker against organic food or in favor of organic food?

   _____

CD 2 Track 28   **B. Listen to excerpts from four news reports. What bias is being shown in each report? Circle the correct answer.**

Excerpt 1

a. Some scientists believe there are many causes of obesity.

b. Some scientists believe fast food is the main cause of obesity.

114   **UNIT 6** | How has science changed the food we eat?

Tip for Success

When you listen to the radio, focus on the speakers' intonation. Pay attention to how they use their voices to express ideas and emotions.

B. Work with a partner. Take turns asking and answering the questions. Ask follow-up questions if needed. Focus on using the correct intonation.

1. What are your favorite foods?

2. What is the strangest food you have ever eaten?

3. What are three foods you would never try?

4. Who usually cooks at your house?

Speaking Skill | Expressing interest during a conversation

Expressing interest during a conversation shows the speaker you are paying attention. There are several ways to express interest in the speaker's ideas. In addition to leaning forward and making eye contact, you can use special words and phrases to show you are interested.

Encouraging words: Yeah. / Wow! / Mm-hmm. / Cool!
Comments: How interesting! / That's amazing!
Emphasis questions: Really?
Repeating words: Speaker: I went to Paris. You: Oh, Paris!

It is not necessary to wait until the speaker has finished talking to use these words and phrases. You can use them throughout the conversation, whenever the speaker completes a thought.

CD 2 Track 33   **A. Listen to the conversation between two students who are eating lunch. Fill in the blanks with the words in the box. Then practice the conversation with a partner.**

mm-hmm	that's interesting	wow
really	every day	yeah

Noriko: Hey, Marc. Is this seat free? Do you mind if I sit here?

Marc: Not at all. How are you doing?

Noriko: I'm absolutely starving!

Marc: _____? Why?

Noriko: I went to the gym this morning before school, and by 11:00, my stomach was growling in class.

Marc: _____, that had to be embarrassing.

| Listening and Speaking   **123**

" The tasks are simple, accessible, user-friendly, and very useful.
Jessica March, American University of Sharjah, U.A.E. "

Q Online Practice provides all new content for additional practice in an easy-to-use online workbook. Every student book includes a *Q Online Practice access code card*. Use the access code to register for your *Q Online Practice* account at www.Qonlinepractice.com.

| Vocabulary Skill | Using the dictionary |  |

There are many words that have similar meanings but are not exactly the same. For example, in Listening 1, the speakers use the words *adolescence* and *youth* for the time between childhood and adulthood. Read the following definitions.

ad·o·les·cence /ˌædl'esns/ *noun* [U] the time in a person's life when he or she develops from a child into an adult **SYN** PUBERTY ➷ collocations at AGE

youth 🔑 /yuθ/ *noun* (*pl.* **youths** /yuðz; yuθs/)
1 [U] the time of life when a person is young, especially the time before a child becomes an adult: *He had been a talented musician in his youth.*

The dictionary definitions show that although the words are very similar, *adolescence* describes a more specific time period, while *youth* is more general.

Checking the definitions of similar words can help you determine which word is appropriate in a context.

All dictionary entries are taken from the *Oxford Advanced American Dictionary for learners of English.*

LANGUAGE SKILLS

A **research-based vocabulary program** focuses students on the words they need to know academically and professionally, using skill strategies based on the same research as the Oxford dictionaries.

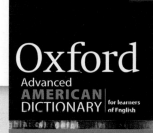

All dictionary entries are taken from the *Oxford Advanced American Dictionary for learners of English.*

The *Oxford Advanced American Dictionary for learners of English* was developed with English learners in mind, and provides extra learning tools for pronunciation, verb types, basic grammar structures, and more.

The Oxford 3000™ 🔑
The Oxford 3000 encompasses **the 3000 most important words to learn in English.** It is based on a comprehensive analysis of the Oxford English Corpus, a two-billion word collection of English text, and on extensive research with both language and pedagogical experts.

The Academic Word List AWL
The Academic Word List was created by Averil Coxhead and contains **570 words that are commonly used in academic English,** such as in textbooks or articles across a wide range of academic subject areas. These words are a great place to start if you are studying English for academic purposes.

Clear learning outcomes focus students on the goals of instruction.

QUICK GUIDE

LEARNING OUTCOMES

A culminating unit assignment evaluates the students' **mastery of the learning outcome.**

Unit Assignment	Persuade a group

In this section, you are going to present your opinion to persuade a group of people. As you prepare your presentation, think about the Unit Question, "How can we maintain a balance with nature?" and refer to the Self-Assessment checklist on page 196.

For alternative unit assignments, see the Q: Skills for Success Teacher's Handbook.

CONSIDER THE IDEAS

CD 4
Track 11

A. Listen to a news report about the situation in a small town. Think about the questions as you listen.

1. Why does Spring Hill need to develop the land near the lake?

2. What are the concerns about developing the land?

3. What outcome does the mayor hope the town hall meeting will produce?

LEARNER CENTERED

Track Your Success allows students to **assess their own progress** and provides guidance on remediation.

Check (✓) the skills you learned. If you need more work on a skill, refer to the page(s) in parentheses.

LISTENING ●	I can understand bias in a presentation. (p. 114)
VOCABULARY ●	I can recognize and use prefixes and suffixes. (pp. 118–119)
GRAMMAR ●	I can use comparative forms of adjectives and adverbs. (p. 120)
PRONUNCIATION ●	I can use common intonation patterns. (p. 122)
SPEAKING ●	I can express interest during a conversation. (p. 123)
LEARNING OUTCOME ●	I can participate in a debate on food science, stating and supporting my opinions about food modification.

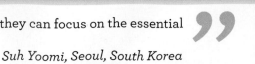

“ Students can check their learning ... and they can focus on the essential points when they study. ”

Suh Yoomi, Seoul, South Korea

Q Online Practice

For the student

- **Easy-to-use:** a simple interface allows students to focus on enhancing their speaking and listening skills, not learning a new software program
- **Flexible:** for use anywhere there's an Internet connection
- **Access code card:** a *Q Online Practice* access code is included with this book—use the access code to register for *Q Online Practice* at www.Qonlinepractice.com

For the teacher

- **Simple yet powerful:** automatically grades student exercises and tracks progress
- **Straightforward:** online management system to review, print, or export reports
- **Flexible:** for use in the classroom or easily assigned as homework
- **Access code card:** contact your sales rep for your *Q Online Practice* teacher's access code

Teacher Resources

Q Teacher's Handbook gives strategic support through:
- specific teaching notes for each activity
- ideas for ensuring student participation
- multilevel strategies and expansion activities
- the answer key
- special sections on 21st century skills and critical thinking
- a *Testing Program CD-ROM* with a customizable test for each unit

For additional resources visit the
Q: Skills for Success companion website at
www.oup.com/elt/teacher/Qskillsforsuccess

Q Class Audio includes:
- listening texts
- pronunciation presentations and exercises
- *The Q Classroom*

> "It's an interesting, engaging series which provides plenty of materials that are easy to use in class, as well as instructionally promising."
> *Donald Weasenforth, Collin College, Texas*

UNIT	LISTENING	SPEAKING	VOCABULARY
1 **Power and Responsibility** Q **How does power affect leaders?** **LISTENING 1: Best of Both Worlds?** A Report (Business Management) **LISTENING 2: Myths of Effective Leadership** A Lecture (Human Resources Management)	• Listen for expressions that announce a topic to anticipate what you will hear • Listen to results of a study in order to understand evidence • Distinguish stressed and unstressed syllables to better identify words in speech • Predict content • Listen for main ideas • Listen for details	• Use repetition and signal words to draw attention to main ideas • Discuss a reading with group members to analyze the author's points • Take notes to prepare for a presentation or group discussion	• Understand the meaning of new vocabulary from context
2 **Appearances** Q **How does appearance affect our success?** **LISTENING 1: A Perfect Mess** A Book Review (Psychology) **LISTENING 2: The Changing Business Dress Code** An Interview (Fashion design)	• Identify new and previously known information to focus on important details • Decide which information to take notes on so note-taking is efficient • Listen for unstressed vowels to recognize individual words in speech • Predict content • Listen for main ideas • Listen for details	• Confirm that you understand what another has said • Give another person advice to help handle a difficult situation • Take notes to prepare for a presentation or group discussion	• Find the relevant definition for a multi-meaning word in the dictionary • Assess your prior knowledge of vocabulary
3 **Growing Up** Q **When does a child become an adult?** **LISTENING 1: Generation Next** A Radio Report (Cultural Anthropology) **LISTENING 2: Growing Up Quickly** A Lecture (Developmental Psychology)	• Pay attention to titles, previous experience, etc. to anticipate information • Listen for key words to understand who is performing an action • Predict content • Listen for main ideas • Listen for details	• Give individual and small-group presentations to define a term and explain it • Stress important words in speech to communicate important information • Brainstorm ideas to prepare for presentations • Take notes to prepare for a presentation or group discussion	• Use the dictionary to distinguish between words with similar meanings • Assess your prior knowledge of vocabulary

GRAMMAR	PRONUNCIATION	CRITICAL THINKING	UNIT OUTCOME
• Gerunds and infinitives	• Syllable stress	• Examine personal attitudes toward leadership • Distinguish between truth and myths • Discuss research findings and evidence • Assess your prior knowledge of content • Relate personal experiences to listening topics • Integrate information from multiple sources	• Give a presentation about effective leadership and how to avoid the negative effects of power.
• Subjunctive verbs for suggestions	• Syllables with unstressed vowels (represented by the schwa)	• Examine factors involved in personal success • Formulate advice for others • Infer meaning from photographs • Assess your prior knowledge of content • Relate personal experiences to listening topics • Integrate information from multiple sources	• Role-play a conversation offering advice to help someone become better organized.
• Transitive and intransitive phrasal verbs	• Patterns of stress in sentences	• Become aware of personal behavior in social contexts • Apply criteria to classify individual circumstances • Identify cultural norms and compare them with those of other eras • Assess your prior knowledge of content • Relate personal experiences to listening topics • Integrate information from multiple sources	• Present a personal story describing an important event in your life that made you feel like an adult.

UNIT	LISTENING	SPEAKING	VOCABULARY
4 Health Care **Q** How is health care changing? **LISTENING 1:** Vacation, Adventure, and Surgery? A News Report (Public Health) **LISTENING 2:** Medical Travel Can Create Problems A Report (Public Policy)	• Listen for reasons to better understand the views and actions of others • Listen for numbers to better understand circumstances • Distinguish between similar-sounding words to understand exactly what a speaker says • Predict content • Listen for main ideas • Listen for details	• Ask open-ended and follow-up questions to get information and to keep a conversation going • Interview others to discover widespread trends • Take notes to prepare for a presentation or group discussion	• Learn and remember collocations of verbs with nouns • Assess your prior knowledge of vocabulary
5 Art Today **Q** What makes a work of art popular? **LISTENING 1:** Manga's New Popularity A Radio Report (Art) **LISTENING 2:** Thomas Kinkade A Report (Aesthetics)	• Make inferences to more fully understand what someone says • Recognize the meaning of speed, pitch, and tone • Predict content • Listen for main ideas • Listen for details	• Avoid answering questions to keep certain information out of a conversation • Take notes to prepare for a presentation or group discussion	• Recognize and produce word forms for different parts of speech • Assess your prior knowledge of vocabulary
6 The Science of Food **Q** How has science changed the food we eat? **LISTENING 1:** Food Additives Linked to Hyperactivity in Kids A Radio Report (Nutrition) **LISTENING 2:** The "Flavr Savr" Tomato A News Report (Agriculture and Genetics)	• Understand a speaker's bias to put information into perspective • Listen for examples to better understand general statements • Predict content • Listen for main ideas • Listen for details	• Express interest during a conversation to encourage the speaker to continue • Use rising intonation to indicate attitudes and purposes • Take notes to prepare for a presentation or group discussion	• Understand prefixes and suffixes • Assess your prior knowledge of vocabulary
7 From School to Work **Q** Is one road to success better than another? **LISTENING 1:** Changing Ways to Climb the Ladder A College Lecture (Business Management) **LISTENING 2:** Life Experience Before College A Radio Program (Career Counseling)	• Listen for contrasts to understand relationships of ideas • Listen for specific words or phrases to complete a transcript • Predict content • Listen for main ideas • Listen for details	• Change the topic to move a conversation into a comfortable area • Talk about real and unreal conditions to speculate about choices • Take notes to prepare for a presentation or group discussion	• Use the dictionary to determine how formal or informal a vocabulary item is • Assess your prior knowledge of vocabulary

GRAMMAR	PRONUNCIATION	CRITICAL THINKING	UNIT OUTCOME
• Past unreal conditionals	• *Can* and *can't*	• Identify desirable characteristics for professionals • Evaluate possible courses of action • Speculate about what might have happened under certain conditions • Assess your prior knowledge of content • Relate personal experiences to listening topics • Integrate information from multiple sources	• Participate in an interview about the advantages and disadvantages of medical tourism.
• Present perfect and present perfect continuous	• Basic intonation patterns	• Contrast individuals' tastes • Infer meanings from what a speaker chooses not to say • Judge the truth and relevance of traditional wisdom • Assess your prior knowledge of content • Relate personal experiences to listening topics • Integrate information from multiple sources	• Role-play a conversation expressing personal opinions about what makes art popular.
• Comparative forms of adjectives and adverbs	• More intonation patterns	• Describe personal tastes and habits • Integrate ideas from several sources • Examine the implications of scientific achievements • Show polite interest in a conversation • Assess your prior knowledge of content • Relate personal experiences to listening topics • Integrate information from multiple sources	• Participate in a debate on food science, stating and supporting your opinions about food modification.
• Simple, compound, and complex sentences	• Stress to highlight important words	• Match personal qualities with career requirements • Evaluate alternative paths for personal growth • Classify information • Assess your prior knowledge of content • Relate personal experiences to listening topics • Integrate information from multiple sources	• Participate in a group discussion about qualifications of job applicants and arrive at a hiring decision.

UNIT	LISTENING	SPEAKING	VOCABULARY
8 Discovery **Q How can chance discoveries affect our lives?** **LISTENING 1: The Power of Serendipity** A Report (History of Science) **LISTENING 2: Against All Odds, Twin Girls Reunited** A Report (Psychology)	• Listen for signal words and phrases to understand the structure of a listening passage • Listen for reasons and methods to understand a narrative • Recognize vowel linkages to distinguish words a speaker uses • Predict content • Listen for main ideas • Listen for details	• Use questions to maintain listener interest • Use direct and indirect quotations to report information from sources • Take notes to prepare for a presentation or group discussion	• Learn and remember collocations involving prepositions • Assess your prior knowledge of vocabulary
9 Humans and Nature **Q How can we maintain a balance with nature?** **LISTENING 1: Polar Bears at Risk** A Report (Ecology) **LISTENING 2: The Effects of Oil Spills** A Lecture (Climatology)	• Listen carefully to an introduction to prepare for upcoming information • Recognize vocabulary patterns in a listening passage • Listen for specific words and phrases to complete a transcript • Predict content • Listen for main ideas • Listen for details	• Use persuasive language to encourage positive attitudes toward your positions • Use reduced forms of pronouns and verbs to achieve a proper tone • Take notes to prepare for a presentation or group discussion	• Add suffixes to change word forms • Assess your prior knowledge of vocabulary
10 Child's Play **Q Is athletic competition good for children?** **LISTENING 1: Training Chinese Athletes** An Interview (Child Development) **LISTENING 2: *Until It Hurts* Discusses Youth Sports Obsession** A Book Discussion (Sports Medicine)	• Listen for causes and effects to understand relationships among ideas • Listen for opinions to match them with the people who hold them • Recognize idioms to understand a speaker's true meaning • Predict content • Listen for main ideas • Listen for details	• Add to a speaker's comments to become an active conversation partner • Use thought groups to segment sentences into understandable pieces • Take notes to prepare for a presentation or group discussion	• Understand idioms to avoid confusion about a speaker's true meaning • Assess your prior knowledge of vocabulary

GRAMMAR	PRONUNCIATION	CRITICAL THINKING	UNIT OUTCOME
• Structures for indirect speech	• Linked words with vowels	• Trace the origins of familiar objects • Examine the role of chance in daily events • Assess the significance of an item's characteristics • Assess your prior knowledge of content • Relate personal experiences to listening topics • Integrate information from multiple sources	• Recount the events involved in a personal discovery you made accidently and tell how it affected you.
• Relative clauses	• Reduced forms	• Determine causes and effects • Apply information about distant events to your own circumstances • Assess your prior knowledge of content • Relate personal experiences to listening topics • Integrate information from multiple sources	• Role-play a meeting in which you present and defend an opinion in order to persuade others.
• Real conditionals	• Thought groups	• Compare cultural approaches to personal development • Associate causes with effects • Evaluate the effectiveness of different training regimens • Assess your prior knowledge of content • Relate personal experiences to listening topics • Integrate information from multiple sources	• Participate in a group discussion about how to encourage children to exhibit good sportsmanship.

UNIT 1

Power and Responsibility

LISTENING	●	listening for main ideas
VOCABULARY	●	meaning from context
GRAMMAR	●	gerunds and infinitives
PRONUNCIATION	●	syllable stress
SPEAKING	●	checking for understanding

NATIONAL
PARK
SERVICE

LEARNING OUTCOME ●

Give a presentation about effective leadership and how to avoid the negative effects of power.

Unit QUESTION

How does power affect leaders?

PREVIEW THE UNIT

A Discuss these questions with your classmates.

Have you ever been a leader? For example, have you ever been in charge of a group at school or been the captain of a sports team? If so, what challenges did you face as a leader?

Think of a leader you admire. What makes this person a good leader?

Look at the photo. What different images do you see that show leadership?

B Discuss the Unit Question above with your classmates.

🔊 Listen to *The Q Classroom*, Track 2 on CD 1, to hear other answers.

C Think about some important characteristics of a leader. Check (✓) the three characteristics you think are most important. Compare your answers with a partner.

Important Leadership Characteristics

- ☐ intelligent
- ☐ independent
- ☐ considerate
- ☐ courageous
- ☐ patient
- ☐ honest
- ☐ kind
- ☐ confident

D Discuss these questions in a group.

1. What kinds of people become leaders?

2. What are some characteristics of people who are not good leaders?

3. Abraham Lincoln, president of the United States from 1861–1865, once wrote, "If you want to test a man's character, give him power." What do you think he meant?

LISTENING 1 | Best of Both Worlds?

VOCABULARY

Here are some words from Listening 1. Read the definitions. Then complete each sentence with the correct word.

> **acknowledge** (*v.*) to accept that something is true
> **address** (*v.*) to think about a problem or a situation and decide how to deal with it
> **aspect** (*n.*) a particular part or feature of a situation, idea, or problem
> **criticism** (*n.*) the act of expressing disapproval of someone or something
> **exemplify** (*v.*) to be an example of something
> **expert** (*n.*) a person with special knowledge, skill, or training in something
> **favoritism** (*n.*) giving unfair advantages to the people who you like best
> **issue** (*n.*) an important topic that people discuss or argue about
> **negotiate** (*v.*) to try to reach an agreement by formal discussion
> **outline** (*v.*) to give the most important facts or ideas about something
> **potential** (*n.*) the possibility of happening or becoming something
> **staff** (*n.*) the group of people who work for an organization

1. Good employees take ___criticism___ well. They hear what they are doing wrong, and they make appropriate changes to their work.

2. Bob showed ___favoritism___ when he promoted Hwa-jeong. They are friends, so Hwa-jeong got the job instead of Laura.

3. I ___acknowledge___ that I made a mistake on the report. I take responsibility, and I will correct it.

4. The new employee has a lot of ___potential___. She knows a lot about our business. I'm sure she'll be promoted soon.

5. The new plan gives employees more vacation time. That's one ___aspect___ of the plan I really like!

6. Tom is a(n) ___expert___ at this computer program. He worked with it for many years, and he teaches classes about it.

7. The manager told the ___Staff___ that an important customer was pleased with their work. Everyone thought that was great news.

8. I know we don't agree on this subject, but I'm sure we can ___negotiate___ a solution that we both like.

9. The project is very complex, so I'll ___outline___ the basic problems we are trying to fix.

10. I'd like to ___address___ one of the main questions that people ask in meetings. Together we can find an answer.

11. David and Ernesto are always on time, and they work well with others. I think they ___exemplify___ good employees.

12. We need to settle this ___issue___. Arguing about it will not help us solve the problem.

PREVIEW LISTENING 1

Best of Both Worlds?

You are going to listen to a report that discusses the challenges of being your friend's boss.

Discuss this question with a partner. If someone becomes the boss of a friend, can they continue to be friends? Why or why not?

Can a boss be a friend?

LISTEN FOR MAIN IDEAS

CD 1
Track 3

Read the statements. Then listen to the report. Write *T* (true) or *F* (false).

___F___ 1. It is important to bring personal issues into business relationships.

___T___ 2. A manager must outline for a friend what is expected at work.

___F___ 3. A good boss should always try to show favoritism.

___T___ 4. The key to working with friends is developing rules and boundaries.

LISTEN FOR DETAILS

Read the sentences. Then listen again. Circle the answer that best completes each statement.

1. When Ginny Pitcher offered Kate Massey a job, Kate Massey ____.
   a. rejected the offer
   b. hesitated before accepting the offer
   c. quickly accepted the offer

2. According to Ginny Pitcher, one benefit of hiring close friends is that ____.
   a. you know their personality
   b. you know that you can trust them
   c. you know if they are qualified for the job

3. Carly Drum hired a friend who ____.
   a. expected more money
   b. allowed her problems to affect her work
   c. soon quit

4. Tory Delany worked at a restaurant in Manhattan where she ____.
   a. worked for a friend
   b. had to fire a friend
   c. managed friends

WHAT DO YOU THINK?

Discuss the questions in a group.

1. What do you think are the main advantages of hiring a friend?

2. If you were a small business owner, would you consider hiring your closest friend to work for you? Why or why not?

3. If your closest friend became your boss, how would this affect your relationship? How do you think your friend might change?

When listening to a presentation, it is difficult to remember every piece of information you hear. Instead of trying to remember every detail, it is more important to identify the speaker's **main ideas**. These are the most important ideas that the speaker wants you to understand and remember.

A speaker often states the main idea as part of the introduction. Here are some signal phrases used to introduce main ideas.

> Today <u>we'll focus on</u> . . .
> This morning <u>we'll consider</u> . . .
> Today <u>I'm going to talk about</u> . . .
> For today's lecture, <u>we're going to look at</u> . . .

Main ideas are often repeated or rephrased during a presentation, especially at the end.

After you listen and take notes, review your notes. Notice which ideas are repeated or described in greater detail. This will help you decide what the main ideas are.

A. Read the introduction to each presentation. Circle the option that best describes the main idea of each presentation.

1. For most people, business meetings are boring, but they don't have to be that way. Today I'm going to give you a few tips on how to run an effective business meeting. Although every tip might not work for you, meetings don't have to put everyone in the room to sleep.

   a. Business meetings are often boring because they're too long and waste too much time.

   b. Business meetings are often boring, but there are ways to make them worthwhile.

   c. Business meetings are often boring, so we should find ways to eliminate them.

2. Hiring the right employees can be a real challenge. Many managers add a new person to their staff who is not a good choice. Let's consider some techniques to evaluate potential employees and explore ways to successfully pick the best people to hire.

   a. Many people hire employees for the wrong reasons. Soon they regret their hiring decisions.

   b. It is important that managers learn to recognize that someone is not a good hiring choice.

   c. Hiring employees can be difficult, but this presentation will teach skills for choosing the best possible employees.

3. There are many job-finding tools available online. For instance, some websites tell job searchers about positions that are available, while others give tips on writing a resume or answering questions in a job interview. Today I'd like to focus on how to make the best use of these online tools. Online job resources are valuable, but they won't help us much if we don't know the best ways to use them.

   a. Job searchers should learn how to answer interview questions and write resumes.

   b. Job searchers should learn how to use online job-finding tools effectively.

   c. Job searchers should go online to find out about available jobs.

CD 1 Track 5

B. Listen to a short presentation. As you listen, take notes in the chart.

Topic	How to make a successful business
Most important factor	People
First characteristic mentioned	Share your vision
Second characteristic mentioned	Creative
Last characteristic mentioned	Hard working

LISTENING 2 | Myths of Effective Leadership

VOCABULARY

Here are some words from Listening 2. Read the definitions. Then complete each sentence with the correct word.

> **advance** (v.) to make progress in a career
>
> **assess** (v.) to make a judgment about someone or something
>
> **capable** (adj.) having the ability or qualities necessary to do something
>
> **contact** (n.) a person that you know, especially somebody who can be helpful to you in your work
>
> **effective** (adj.) producing the result that is wanted or intended
>
> **ethical** (adj.) morally good or correct
>
> **executive** (n.) a person who has an important job as a manager of a company or organization
>
> **perspective** (n.) a way of thinking about something
>
> **style** (n.) the way in which something is done
>
> **title** (n.) a word or phrase that shows a person's rank, profession, or status

1. We need to hire a more ___capable___ office assistant. The current assistant doesn't have enough experience and isn't highly skilled.

2. My management ___style___ is very different from Roger's. I prefer to lead by example. He prefers to give detailed instructions to employees.

3. I'm nervous about the meeting with my manager next Monday. She is going to ___assess___ my performance for this year.

4. Blake joined the company in 2000. Within five years he was able to ___advance___ to the position of vice president.

5. Please tell me what you think about this design. I'm interested in hearing your ___perspective___ on it.

6. Anne knows a lot of people in our industry. She has a good business ___contact___ at the London office who can help us.

7. I am concerned that our company is not making _____ethical_____ decisions. Our factory creates more pollution and waste than it needs to.

8. We created a plan to save the company. Unfortunately, it was not as _____effective_____ as we had hoped, and the company was forced to close last month.

9. I called her *Mrs. Rodgers*, but later I learned that her _____title_____ is actually *Doctor*.

10. Emma only recently started working for the company, but her goal is to become a(n) _____executive_____ there someday. I think she will make a good manager.

PREVIEW LISTENING 2

| Myths of Effective Leadership

You are going to listen to a lecture about some of the negative ways in which successful executives can change and what they can do about those changes.

List two ways that you think people tend to change negatively when they become leaders.

1. _____Power_____

2. _____money_____

LISTEN FOR MAIN IDEAS

 CD 1 Track 6

A. Listen to the podcast lecture. Then answer the questions.

1. According to a study by the Center for Creative Leadership, how do many powerful executives see themselves?

   _____more intelligent and more capable and more ethical_____

2. What do many powerful executives think about people who disagree with them?

   _____less intelligent and less capable and less ethical_____

3. How do employees begin to react to these executives?

   _____they have taken their ideas with them_____

LISTEN FOR DETAILS

CD 1
Track 7

A. Read the statements. Then listen again. Write _T_ (true) or _F_ (false).

_T_ 1. Many executives forget the skills that helped them become successful.

_T_ 2. An effective executive must know the difference between power and leadership.

_F_ 3. A study shows that most executives respect employees who disagree with them.

_T_ 4. Many executives begin to believe they are more powerful than they really are.

_F_ 5. It is impossible to learn the skills necessary for effective leadership.

_T_ 6. To become an effective leader, you must view yourself through the eyes of your team members.

B. What three final pieces of advice does the speaker offer to executives? Check (✓) the boxes.

☐ Take a vacation at least twice a year.

☑ Find and listen to new ideas and perspectives.

☐ Have meetings with your staff every week.

☑ Find someone who is willing to disagree with you.

☑ Get some feedback that assesses your leadership style.

Q WHAT DO YOU THINK?

A. Discuss the questions in a group.

1. The speaker states that leadership and power are not the same. What do you think are some differences between leadership and power?

2. According to the lecture, some successful executives begin to "blur the lines" between leadership and power. They act as if leadership and power are the same thing. Why do you think this happens?

B. Think about both Listening 1 and Listening 2 as you discuss the questions.

1. Power can affect relationships and individuals in a negative way. What are some positive effects power may have?

2. Both Listenings offer advice to bosses. Which advice do you think is the most valuable? Is there any advice that you disagree with? Why?

One way to figure out the meaning of a word is from the **context** of the sentence it is in. Use the words around the unknown word to help you understand the new word.

> She started as a coat checker at Maggie's Place . . . and, after a series of <u>promotions</u>, eventually became general manager.

The speaker mentions that Ms. Delany "started" in one position and "eventually became general manager." These words describe making progress in a company over time. The context tells you that *promotion* means receiving a higher position or a more important job.

It also helps to consider the presentation as a whole, not just one sentence.

> Knowing someone will fit in doesn't <u>alleviate</u> other problems. Carly Drum had hired four trusted friends to work at her family's executive search firm. . . . One of them had great potential but was bringing her personal problems to the office. It was affecting her work.

The speaker uses several sentences to describe a problem that developed even though Carly Drum hired a friend. From this context, you may be able to figure out that to *alleviate* problems means to solve, correct, or remove the problems.

CD 1
Track 8

A. **Listen to the sentences. Use the context to match each bold word with its definition.**

___b__ 1. The job didn't pay very well, but I loved the office and my co-workers. It was a great **environment** to work in.

___c__ 2. It's impossible to **function** well when you don't get along with your co-workers. I can't work in a situation like that.

___d__ 3. I'm sure you can **resolve** the conflict with your co-worker if you listen to each other's opinions.

___a__ 4. James has great **aptitude**, but he needs more training. In a year or so, he'll probably be our best programmer.

___e__ 5. The members of Emily's group are experienced and talented, plus they **exhibit** great teamwork.

a. natural ability to do something

b. the conditions that affect a person's behavior and development

c. to work in the correct way

d. to find an acceptable solution to a problem

e. to show or display

CD 1
Track 9

B. Listen to excerpts from Listening 1 and Listening 2. Circle the correct answers.

1. **In charge of** probably means ____.
   a. meeting with
   b. working with
   c. having responsibility over

2. **Interaction** probably means ____.
   a. disagreement
   b. communication
   c. responsibility

3. **Enforcing** probably means ____.
   a. making sure that rules are obeyed
   b. changing rules occasionally
   c. explaining rules

4. **Opposing** probably means ____.
   a. smart
   b. contrasting
   c. similar

5. **Perceive** probably means ____.
   a. view
   b. enjoy
   c. dislike

C. Choose five words from Activities A and B. Write a sentence using each word. Then take turns reading your sentences aloud to a partner.

1. Rabbits live in a really nice and quite environment

2. That machine didn't function so well at the beggining

3. The captain was in charge of the whole plane and crew members

4. There was a great interaction between the two companies

5. It's good to perceive other people mistakes and reconsider it.

Grammar   Gerunds and infinitives   web⁺

> **Gerunds (verb + –ing)** are often used as the subject of a sentence.
>
> ⌐ **Leading** your team members is a tough job.
>
> Gerunds are also used after prepositions, such as *about*, *of*, *in*, *for*, and *against*, and after certain verbs, such as *consider*, *suggest*, and *recommend*.
>
> ⌐ Jae thought **about accepting** the promotion.
> └ **I considered voting** for her.
>
> **Infinitives (*to* + verb)** are often used after the adjective phrase *be* + adjective.
>
> ⌐ It **is important to respect** your employees.
>
> Infinitives are also used after certain verbs, such as *want*, *decide*, *try*, *hope*, *need*, *expect*, *agree*, and *learn*.
>
> ⌐ She **hopes to become** president one day.

A. Read the sentences. Underline each gerund or infinitive.

1. When Ginny Pitcher needed to hire a director of business development, she turned to her closest friend, Kate Massey. *Infinitive*

2. As for the subordinate, he or she needs to understand that the boss can't show any favoritism. *Infinitive*

3. Knowing someone will fit in doesn't alleviate other problems. *Gerund*

4. Managing friends isn't always a choice. *Gerund*

5. Gena Cox . . . suggests saying something like this: "I still want us to be friends." *Gerund*

6. Say something like this: "I still want to be friends." *Gerund*

7. "I didn't jump on it immediately," says Massey. "I thought about taking the job for a while." *Gerund*

B. Complete each sentence with the gerund or infinitive form of the verb in parentheses. (In some sentences, either form is correct.) Then practice saying the sentences with a partner.

1. Song Min expects ___to finish___ (finish) business school in June.

2. This book recommends ___hiring___ (hire) people you already know.

3. ___Working___ (work) for the government has been a great learning experience.

4. It is difficult ___to work___ (work) while you go to school.

5. Although it took me several months, I finally learned ___to communicate___ (communicate) effectively with my manager.

6. I suggest ___discussing___ (discuss) this with your partner before you make a final decision.

7. We need ___to discuss___ (discuss) this problem immediately.

8. Derek was interested in ___moving___ (move) to Hong Kong, but he decided ___to wait___ (wait) until next year.

Pronunciation	Syllable stress	web

CD 1
Track 10

Every word with more than one **syllable** has a syllable that is **stressed** more than the others. That stressed syllable is longer, and it has a change in pitch.

Listen to the word *negotiate*. Then repeat it.

　　negotiate

The second syllable (-*go*-) is stressed. The vowel in this syllable is extra long, and it has a change in pitch.

CD 1
Track 10

Listen to the word again and practice saying it, stressing the second syllable.

　　negotiate

Every word has its own stress pattern. Using correct word stress will make your speech clearer and easier to understand. When you learn a new word, also take note of the correct stress pattern for that word.

CD 1
Track 11

A. Listen to the words. Which syllable is stressed? Circle each stressed syllable.

Tip for Success

Many dictionaries show a pronunciation guide for each entry. The pronunciation guide shows the correct syllable stress. Use a dictionary regularly to learn the stress patterns of new words.

1. excerpt

2. aspect

3. enforce

4. effective

5. leadership

6. acknowledge

7. perspective

8. opposing

9. promotion

10. interaction

 CD 1
Track 12

B. Listen again. Then practice with a partner. Take turns saying the words.

| Speaking Skill | Checking for understanding | web+ |

When you're giving a presentation or having a conversation, occasionally check that you are clearly communicating your ideas. To check that your listeners understand your main point(s), you can use phrases like these.

> Do you know what I mean?
> Does that make sense?
> Do you understand?
> Are you following me?
> Any questions (so far)?

A. Listen to a manager giving instructions to her staff. Check (✓) the phrases she uses to check for understanding.

- ☑ Do you know what I mean?
- ☐ Do you know what I'm saying?
- ☐ Does that make sense?
- ☑ Does everyone understand?
- ☑ Are you following me?
- ☐ Are you with me so far?
- ☐ Have you got it?
- ☑ Any questions?
- ☑ Got it?

Tip Critical Thinking

Activity B asks you to **summarize** the main points the speaker wants to communicate. When you summarize, you give a shorter version of what you heard or read, including only the main points. Summarizing shows you understand the material.

CD 1
Track 14

B. Listen again. Then work with a partner. In your notebook, summarize the main points the manager wants to communicate.

Unit Assignment | Offer advice on how to be an effective leader

In this assignment, you are going to give a short presentation about how to be an effective leader. As you prepare your presentation, think about the Unit Question, "How does power affect leaders?" and refer to the Self-Assessment checklist on page 20.

For alternative unit assignments, see the *Q: Skills for Success Teacher's Handbook*.

CONSIDER THE IDEAS

Read about a paradox, a situation that has two opposite qualities at the same time. In a group, discuss what the author means by a *power paradox*.

The Power Paradox

The best leaders understand the needs and goals of the people they lead. They are careful thinkers who understand the challenges they face. They have the ability to make intelligent choices about how to address those challenges. Great leaders are also communicators. They can explain both problems and solutions to people in a way that everyone can understand.

These abilities are not common, and when we recognize them in someone—in the business world or some other field—we are inspired to say, "That's someone I can trust! That's someone I can follow!" Unfortunately, these abilities also tend to disappear once a person actually takes on a position of leadership.

The British historian Lord Acton once said, "Power tends to corrupt, and absolute power corrupts absolutely." Researchers are now finding scientific support for Acton's claim. Many studies have shown that power can lead people to act without thinking carefully about their decisions. It can also lead people to ignore or misunderstand other people's feelings and desires.

Researchers have created experiments to see how people react when they are given power. The people who were given power over others were more likely to make risky choices, to act aggressively, to speak rudely, and to behave in ways that made others feel scared and uncomfortable. They were also more likely to tease their colleagues.

This is why we call it the *power paradox*. Power is given to people who show an ability to understand, guide, and communicate with others. But, unfortunately, once they become leaders, their power has the potential to make them rude and insensitive. In other words, what people respect and want most from leaders is often what can be damaged when someone has power.

PREPARE AND SPEAK

A. GATHER IDEAS Review the information in "The Power Paradox" about how power can affect people. Then think about the information you learned in this unit about people in positions of power.

What are some important skills and qualities of a leader?

_____

_____

_____

_____

What are negative effects that come from having power?

_____

_____

_____

_____

_____

B. **ORGANIZE IDEAS** Choose two qualities and two problems from Activity A that you think are most important. Place these ideas in the chart. Then suggest ways to develop those qualities and avoid the negative effects.

Important leadership qualities	Ways to develop these qualities
Negative effects of power that leaders can develop	Ways to avoid these effects

C. **SPEAK** Present your advice to the class. As you speak, check that your classmates understand the ideas you are trying to communicate. Refer to the Self-Assessment checklist below before you begin.

CHECK AND REFLECT

A. **CHECK** Think about the Unit Assignment as you complete the Self-Assessment checklist.

SELF-ASSESSMENT		
Yes	No	
☐	☐	I was able to speak easily about the topic.
☐	☐	My partner, group, and class understood me.
☐	☐	I understood meaning from context.
☐	☐	I used vocabulary from the unit.
☐	☐	I checked for understanding.
☐	☐	I used correct syllable stress.

B. **REFLECT** Discuss these questions with a partner.

What is something new you learned in this unit?

 Look back at the Unit Question. Is your answer different now than when you started this unit? If yes, how is it different? Why?

Track Your Success

Circle the words you learned in this unit.

Nouns
aspect 🔑 AWL
contact 🔑 AWL
criticism 🔑
executive 🔑
expert 🔑 AWL
favoritism
issue 🔑 AWL
perspective 🔑 AWL
potential 🔑 AWL
staff 🔑
style 🔑 AWL
title 🔑

Verbs
acknowledge 🔑 AWL
address 🔑
advance 🔑
assess AWL
exemplify
negotiate
outline 🔑

Adjectives
capable 🔑 AWL
effective 🔑
ethical AWL

🔑 Oxford 3000™ words
AWL Academic Word List
For more information on the Oxford 3000™ and the AWL, see page xi.

Check (✓) the skills you learned. If you need more work on a skill, refer to the page(s) in parentheses.

LISTENING	●	I can listen for main ideas. (p. 8)
VOCABULARY	●	I can understand meaning from context. (p. 13)
GRAMMAR	●	I can use gerunds and infinitives. (p. 15)
PRONUNCIATION	●	I can use syllable stress. (p. 16)
SPEAKING	●	I can check for understanding. (p. 17)
LEARNING OUTCOME	●	I can give a presentation about effective leadership and how to avoid the negative effects of power.

UNIT 2

Appearances

LISTENING	●	identifying details
VOCABULARY	●	using the dictionary
GRAMMAR	●	the subjunctive for suggestions
PRONUNCIATION	●	unstressed syllables
SPEAKING	●	confirming understanding

LEARNING OUTCOME ●

Role-play a conversation offering advice to help someone become better organized.

Unit QUESTION

How does appearance affect our success?

PREVIEW THE UNIT

A Discuss these questions with your classmates.

When you are at work or school, is the space around you usually neat or messy? What does a messy desk tell you about the owner's personality?

Think about some successful people. How would you describe each person's appearance?

Look at the photo. Do you think a suit makes a person appear successful? Why or why not?

B Discuss the Unit Question above with your classmates.

🔊 Listen to *The Q Classroom*, Track 15 on CD 1, to hear other answers.

PREVIEW THE UNIT

C What is your first impression of the people in the pictures below? Discuss the questions with a partner.

1. Which person would you most like to work with? Why?

2. How would you describe each person's character?

3. Which person do you think you have the most in common with?

D Look at the behaviors in the chart. Check (✓) if each one would help, hurt, or have no effect on someone's success in the workplace. Compare answers with a partner.

	Help	Hurt	Have no effect
dress like other people in the workplace	☐	☐	☑
dress differently to be noticed	☐	☐	☑
eat at one's desk while working	☐	☑	☐
eat with one's co-workers	☐	☑	☐
play sports on the company team	☑	☐	☐
keep one's work space neat	☑	☐	☐
be well-groomed	☑	☐	☐
display one's degrees and professional certificates	☑	☐	☐
have personal pictures at one's desk	☐	☐	☑

LISTENING 1 | A Perfect Mess

VOCABULARY

Here are some words from Listening 1. Read the sentences. Circle the answer that best matches the meaning of each bold word or phrase.

1. We hope everyone will **embrace** our new plan for the class trip. We think you will really like the new destination!
    a. to be unwilling to accept
    b. to accept an idea with enthusiasm
    c. to be concerned about

2. I don't want to **stifle** your creativity, but your ideas for the brochure are too complicated. Let's try to make it very simple.
    a. to let go of something
    b. to prevent something from happening
    c. to support something strongly

3. A mother often has a **bias** toward her own children. She sometimes thinks they are better than other children.
    a. hope for
    b. thoughts about
    c. preference for

4. You need to **point out** in your job application why you think you are qualified for the job. It's important that the interviewer understand your skills and experience.
    a. to look at something carefully
    b. to make something clear
    c. to consider someone's ideas

5. The student was **moderately** successful last semester. He didn't fail any classes, but he didn't get excellent grades, either.
    a. not at all
    b. fairly, but not very
    c. extremely

6. I couldn't find my book, and then I happened to **stumble upon** it at my friend's house. It was there the whole time!
    a. find by accident
    b. hit quickly
    c. damage

7. We worked hard all week, but finally we had to **recognize** that we weren't going to finish the project on time.
   a. acknowledge
   b. discourage
   c. ignore

8. The museum was **stimulating**. I was so excited about what I saw that I went back the next day.
   a. expensive
   b. boring
   c. interesting

9. I was worried, but I think the party will **turn out** fine. It looks like everyone is having a good time.
   a. increase to a new level
   b. change direction quickly
   c. happen with a particular result

10. I am an **open-minded** person. Just because something is different doesn't mean I won't like it.
    a. afraid of trying new things
    b. careless with someone's property
    c. willing to accept new ideas or opinions

11. The chef is very **inflexible**. He always uses the same recipes. He does not like to try new ideas.
    a. unfriendly to others
    b. unsure of the answer
    c. unwilling to change

12. The little boy's room was complete **chaos**. Books, clothes, and games were scattered all over the floor.
    a. a big mess
    b. orderly and neat
    c. well-organized

PREVIEW LISTENING 1

A Perfect Mess

You are going to listen to a review of a book about mess. The book compares people who are neat to people who aren't. It explores who is more successful. The reviewer will discuss what the book has to say about people and the condition of their desks, homes, and other spaces.

Look at the statements below. Check (✓) the statements you agree with.

☐ Messy people are never very organized.
☐ Children should not focus too much on neatness.
☐ Neatness is required to work effectively.
☐ It is OK to be a little messy at home.

LISTEN FOR MAIN IDEAS

CD 1
Track 16

Read the statements. Then listen to the review. Write T (true) or F (false).

_T_ 1. Moderate messiness seems to be good for people.

_F_ 2. Messy homes are cold and impersonal.

_F_ 3. Messy environments are not stimulating enough for children.

_T_ 4. Messy people tend to be more creative and open-minded.

LISTEN FOR DETAILS

CD 1
Track 17

Read the sentences. Then listen again. Circle the answer that best completes each statement.

1. ____ was a very messy but open-minded musician.
   a. Albert Einstein
   b. Leon Heppel
   c. Johann Sebastian Bach

2. Keeping a house ____ can be bad for a child's health.
   a. too clean
   b. too dirty
   c. too stimulating

3. A messy desk helped ____ two researchers' work.
   a. cause confusion about
   b. show a connection between
   c. find errors in

4. No one at the NAPO conference could answer the question ___.
   a. "Why are people fined at work?"
   b. "What's wrong with being messy?"
   c. "Why is there a bias toward neatness?"

Q WHAT DO YOU THINK?

Discuss the questions in a group.

1. How messy are you? Do you agree with the authors of *A Perfect Mess* about the benefits of being a bit messy? Why or why not?

2. How much freedom to be messy should workers have in their work space?

3. When you were a child, were you neat or messy? Have you changed at all as you have gotten older? How?

| Listening Skill | Identifying details | |

When you listen to a long presentation or lecture, it's difficult to take notes on everything. It's important to focus on details that support the main ideas you hear. Ask yourself three questions as you listen.

> Is this new information?
> Does this information support the main idea?
> Is this information repeated or rephrased?

If you answer yes to any of these questions, the detail may be important to remember.

CD 1
Track 18

A. Listen to a short lecture about three strategies for being more organized. Complete the chart with important details about each strategy.

Tip for Success

Use abbreviations and symbols when you take notes. This will make it easier to take notes quickly. Then review your notes to make sure your ideas are clear.

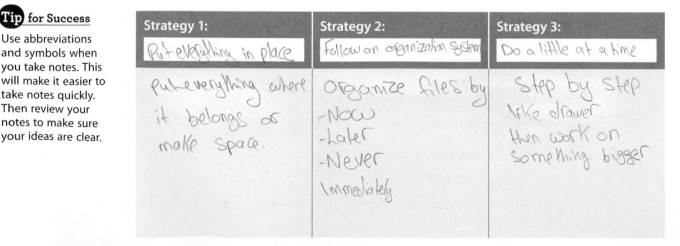

Strategy 1: Put everything in place	Strategy 2: Follow an organization system	Strategy 3: Do a little at a time
Put everything where it belongs or make space.	Organize files by -Now -Later -Never Immediately	Step by step like drawer then work on something bigger

B. Work with a partner. Compare your notes. Ask each other the following questions. If you answer *no* to a question, revise your notes.

1. Does this information support the main idea?

2. Is this information repeated or rephrased?

LISTENING 2 | The Changing Business Dress Code

VOCABULARY

Here are some words you will hear in Listening 2. Read the definitions. Then complete each sentence with the correct word.

> **anecdote** (*n.*) a short, interesting story about a real person or event
> **appropriate** (*adj.*) right for the particular situation
> **associate** (*v.*) to make a connection in your mind
> **cautious** (*adj.*) careful about what you say or do
> **conduct** (*v.*) to organize and do something
> **cycle** (*n.*) a series of events that always repeat in the same order
> **enthusiasm** (*n.*) a strong feeling of excitement and interest in something
> **investor** (*n.*) a person who puts money into a company to make a profit
> **morale** (*n.*) the way a group feels at a particular time
> **norm** (*n.*) a situation or pattern of behavior that is normal
> **reward** (*n.*) something that is given to someone for doing a good job
> **trend** (*n.*) a general change or development

1. Andrew knew first impressions are important. He thought about what would be most ____appropriate____ to wear for his job interview.

2. When the team lost its tenth game in a row, ____morale____ among the players and the fans was very low. Everyone seemed sad.

3. In the past, many people worked for large companies. Now there is a ____trend____ toward more people working for small businesses.

4. The employees at our office usually work long hours. I'd say the ____norm____ is about 60 hours a week.

5. Ming gave us a lot of money to open our new store. She is our most important ____investor____.

Tip for Success

To really learn a word, most people need to see and use the word many times. Making flashcards with new words and studying them often is a good way to review the words.

6. The employees worked hard to finish the project on time. As a _____ reward _____, their boss gave them an extra day off.

7. Clothing style goes in a _____ cycle _____. Something becomes popular. Then it's out of style, and then it's in style again.

8. My grandfather once told me a(n) _____ anecdote _____ about what he did when he was a little boy.

9. I always _____ associate _____ that book with my senior year in high school. I remember reading it in class.

10. The government decided to _____ conduct _____ a study on the effects of caffeine.

11. My uncle enjoyed playing soccer his whole life. He never lost his _____ enthusiasm _____ for it.

12. The woman was _____ cautious _____ as she walked down the icy stairs. She was concerned that she might fall and get hurt.

PREVIEW LISTENING 2

The Changing Business Dress Code

You are going to listen to an interview in which two experts discuss dressing for work. The experts focus on how appearance can affect success in the corporate world in the United States, and how fashion trends are changing.

Work with a partner. Discuss these questions.

How does your appearance at work affect how you feel? Does it affect the way you do your job? Why or why not?

LISTEN FOR MAIN IDEAS

CD 1
Track 19

Listen to the radio program. Circle the correct answer.

1. According to Andrew Park, what is the current trend for business dress codes?
   a. Casual dress is becoming the norm.
   b. More formal dress is becoming popular again.
   c. Employees can dress however they want to dress.

2. How has casual dress affected some businesses?
   a. It has had a negative effect on the way clients see them.
   b. It has had a negative effect on the employees' morale.
   c. It has had a negative effect on CEOs' productivity.

3. What does Andrew Park say about fashion in the workplace?
   a. Older people will always dress more formally than young people.
   b. Fashion trends go in cycles, from formal to informal and back again.
   c. CEOs dress more formally than their employees.

4. According to the speakers, what does the way we dress tell other people?
   a. It tells people how fashion moves in cycles.
   b. It tells people where we work.
   c. It tells people who we are.

LISTEN FOR DETAILS

CD 1
Track 20

Listen again and take notes. Then use your notes to answer the questions.

1. Why did executives think casual dress would be a good idea when it started?
   They think it will increase

2. Why are investors more cautious about casually dressed business executives?
   Because they look for a sign of proffesional

3. What is casual or sloppy dress sometimes associated with?
   Careless work

4. What type of dress do many young people now wear at work?
   more professional, more formal

Q WHAT DO YOU THINK?

A. Discuss the questions in a group.

1. If you were a manager, how would appearance affect an employee's chance for promotion?

2. Have you ever worn a uniform for work or school? Did you like it? What are some advantages and disadvantages of wearing a uniform?

B. Think about both Listening 1 and Listening 2 as you discuss the questions.

1. How much do a person's clothing and organizational skills affect your first impression of him or her?

2. Think about a time that you judged someone based on how he or she looked or organized things. Was your first impression right or wrong? Why?

Vocabulary Skill	Using the dictionary	web+

When you look a word up in the dictionary, there are often several different **definitions** given. You must consider the context of the word to choose the correct definition.

Decide what part of speech the word is in that context—for example, a *noun* or a *verb*. When you look up the word, you can then quickly eliminate a form or use of the word not appropriate to the context.

> In many places, casual Fridays are starting to **fade**, and there's a move toward "dress-up" or "formal" Thursdays or Mondays.

fade /feɪd/ *verb* **1** [I, T] to become, or to make something become, paler or less bright: *The curtains had faded in the sun.* ◆ **~ from sth** *All color had faded from her face.* ◆ **~ sth** *The sun had faded the curtains.* ◆ *He was wearing faded blue jeans.* **2** [I] to disappear gradually: *Her smile faded.* ◆ **~ away** *Hopes of reaching an agreement seem to be fading away.* ◆ *The laughter faded away.* ◆ **~ to/into sth** *His voice faded to a whisper* (= gradually became quieter). ◆ *All other issues* **fade into insignificance** *compared with the struggle for survival.* **3** [I] if a sports player, team, actor, etc. **fades**, they stop playing or performing as well as they did before: *Black faded on the final bend.* **IDM** see WOODWORK

Read all of the definitions before you make the choice. By thinking about the context of the report, you can conclude that the first definition of *fade* is not correct in this context.

All dictionary entries are from the *Oxford Advanced American Dictionary for learners of English* © Oxford University Press 2011.

A. Read each sentence. Then circle the correct definition of each bold word.

1. Employees were allowed to **ditch** their suits and ties and formal skirts and blouses.

> **ditch** /dɪtʃ/ *noun, verb*
> • **noun** a long channel dug at the side of a field or road, to hold or take away water
> • **verb 1** [T] ~ sth/sb (*informal*) to get rid of something or someone because you no longer want or need it/them: *The new road building program has been ditched.* ◆ *He ditched his girlfriend.* **2** [T, I] ~ (sth) if a pilot **ditches** an aircraft, or if it **ditches**, it lands in the ocean in an emergency **3** [T] ~ **school** (*informal*) to stay away from school without permission

2. A very neat home can be impersonal and **cold**. A messy house can show your personality.

> **cold** /koʊld/ *adj., noun, adv.*
> • **adj.** (**cold·er, cold·est**)
> ➤ LOW TEMPERATURE **1** having a lower than usual temperature; having a temperature lower than the human body: *I'm cold. Turn the heat up.* ◆ *to feel/look cold* ◆ *cold hands and feet* ◆ *a cold room/house* ◆ *Isn't it cold today?* ◆ *It's freezing cold.* ◆ *to get/turn colder* ◆ *bitterly cold weather* ◆ *the coldest May on record*
> ➤ FOOD/DRINKS **2** not heated; cooled after being cooked: *a cold drink* ◆ *Hot and cold food is available in the cafeteria.* ◆ *cold chicken for lunch*
> ➤ UNFRIENDLY **3** (of a person) without emotion; unfriendly: *to give someone a cold look/stare/welcome* ◆ *Her manner was cold and distant.* ◆ *He was staring at her with cold eyes.*

B. Read each sentence. Then look up the definition of the bold word. Write the correct definition for the context of each bold word.

1. I found out how **deep** the world's bias toward neatness and order is.

   Very intense or extreme

2. The woman received a **fine** of more than two thousand dollars at work.

   Sum of money exacted as a penalty

3. They're looking for a **sign** that people are professional.

   An action or fact that shows something exists

4. I have been messy since I was old enough to **dress** myself.

   To put clothes on yourself

Grammar | **The subjunctive for suggestions**

The **subjunctive** is the simple or base form of a verb—for example "go" or "try."

You can use the subjunctive to talk about events that you want to happen or hope will happen. You also use it to make a strong suggestion about something that you think should happen.

This structure is formed in two ways.

1. **suggesting verb** + ~~**indirect object (IO)**~~ + **base form of verb**
2. **suggesting expression** + **indirect object (IO)** + **base form of verb**

His boss recommended that he wear a suit for the meeting tomorrow.
suggesting verb — ~~IO~~ base form of verb

It is important that employees be professional at all times.
suggesting expresssion — ~~IO~~ — base form of verb

The subjunctive doesn't change form according to the person.

I recommend that **you work** harder.
I recommend that **he work** harder.
I recommend that **they work** harder.

It also doesn't change tense when the main verb is in the past tense.

I recommend**ed** that he **work** harder.

To make a negative suggestion, insert *not* between the indirect object and the base form of the verb.

It's essential that employees **not** show up late for meetings.

Certain verbs and certain expressions are often used with the subjunctive to make suggestions and recommendations. The word *that* is always optional.

Some verbs followed by the subjunctive	Some expressions followed by the subjunctive
to advise (that)	It's best (that)
to ask (that)	It's desirable (that)
to desire (that)	It's essential (that)
to insist (that)	It's important (that)
to recommend (that)	It's recommended (that)
to request (that)	It's a good idea (that)
to suggest (that)	It's preferred (that)

A. Rewrite the sentences. Use the subjunctive.

1. Customers expect sales reps to dress more formally.

   Customers demand that sales reps _dress more formally_.

2. Employees should try to avoid looking sloppy at work.

   It is recommended that employees _avoid looking sloppy at work_.

3. When CEOs pose for a work-related picture, they should not wear shorts and sandals.

   When posing for a work-related picture, it's a good idea that CEOs _not wear shorts and sandals_.

4. Some executives want their employees to ditch their casual clothes.

   Some executives advise that employees _ditch their casual clothes_.

5. Some experts say that managers should offer a "dress-up Monday" option.

   Some experts suggest that managers _offer a "dress-up Monday" option_.

6. I think that people dressing more formally at work is a good idea.

   It's a good idea that people _dress more formally at work_.

B. Look at the pictures. Write advice for each person on how to dress. Use the subjunctive. Then share your advice with a partner.

Picture A

Picture B

Picture A: This man just started working in a very formal office.

1. _It is best that he shave his beard_

2. _I suggest the he dress up formally_

Picture B: This woman is going to start working in a casual office.

1. _I recommend that she wear casual clothes_
2. _It is preferred that she tie her hair_

Vowels in stressed syllables are long and clear. In contrast, vowels in unstressed syllables are often reduced to a short sound called a *schwa* (/ə/). It is the most common vowel sound.

**CD 1
Track 21**

Listen to this word.

appearances

The stressed syllable is the second syllable: *ap-PEAR-an-ces*. The vowel sounds in the unstressed syllables are pronounced /ə/.

/ə•pɪr•ən•səz/

To make the /ə/ sound, drop your jaw a little and relax your tongue. It is a very short, "lazy" sound.

**CD 1
Track 22**

A. Listen to the words. Which syllables are unstressed? Cross out the unstressed syllables in each word.

1. pleasure
2. forgotten
3. successful
4. habit
5. business
6. allow
7. cautious
8. professional

Tip for Success

Some online dictionaries have word pronunciations that you can click on. This is a good way to quickly learn the unstressed syllables in new words.

**CD 1
Track 23**

B. Listen again. Repeat the words. Focus on the unstressed syllables.

Sometimes you might think that you understand what someone is saying, but you are not exactly sure. These are ways you can check your understanding.

Tip Critical Thinking

In the Speaking Skill activities, you practice restating what a speaker has said. When you **restate** information, you will understand and remember it better.

Ask a question that signals your need to confirm your understanding.

- Do you mean that . . . ?
- Excuse me, are you saying . . . ?
- Does that mean . . . ?

Restate what the speaker said in your own words.

- If I understand you, . . .
- (So) you're saying that . . .

After the speaker responds, let the speaker know that you now understand the information. You can do this by using phrases like *thanks, OK, right, I see,* or *got it.*

CD 1
Track 24

A. Listen to the conversations. Complete the conversations using expressions from the Speaking Skill box. Then practice the conversations with a partner.

1. **A:** Did you hear that starting next month there won't be a "casual Friday" anymore?

   B: What? _____So you mean that_____ they are getting rid of casual Friday completely?

   A: Yes, the email said no more casual Fridays.

   B: Oh.

2. **A:** More and more customers are looking for a sign of professionalism.

   B: _____Are you saying that_____ they prefer less casual dress?

   A: Yeah, that's right.

   B: _____Got it_____.

3. **A:** If my desk is too organized, I can't be creative.

   B: _____If I understand_____ you need to be messy to work well?

   A: Yeah, I need a little mess.

   B: Hahaha _____OK_____.

4. **A:** Most people can't get organized all at once.

   B: ___So does that mean___ it's better to work on it step by step?

   A: Yes, it does.

   B: ___I see___.

B. Work in a group. Discuss the questions. Use questions and phrases from the Speaking Skill box to confirm your understanding.

1. What connection is there between appearance and quality of work? Do you think that when people look sloppy they are less careful at work?

2. Does someone's appearance and the condition of their workspace matter if they can get the job done?

3. Do you think that schools should teach students how to be organized?

Unit Assignment | Role-play

In this assignment, you are going to role-play giving advice about appearance. As you prepare your role-play, think about the Unit Question, "How does appearance affect our success?" and refer to the Self-Assessment checklist on page 40.

For alternative unit assignments, see the *Q: Skills for Success Teacher's Handbook.*

CONSIDER THE IDEAS

In a group, make a list of situations that can create a mess at school or at work (for example, too many piles of paper, not enough storage space, too many personal belongings, etc.). Discuss ways to make the situations better.

_____

_____

_____

_____

_____

PREPARE AND SPEAK

A. GATHER IDEAS Imagine you are in a business to help clients get organized. Read about a new client. Take notes on his situation.

Name: Dan Howard

Occupation: Salesman

The Situation: A few years ago, I had the best sales record in my department. My customers respected me, and they were loyal to me. In the past couple of years, however, my sales have dropped. I was doing OK until my manager moved me into a smaller office. There is less storage space for my paperwork. Now I can't find anything. I have piles of customers' papers everywhere. I even lost my phone last week. My old customers don't ask for my help anymore. The few new customers I have don't seem to trust me. I can't blame them. I can't find anything they need. My sales are now the worst in my department. I need help!

Problems	Details

B. **ORGANIZE IDEAS** What advice would you offer to help Dan Howard? Write notes about three pieces of advice you would give him. Give details and examples to support your advice.

Advice to improve the situation	Details and examples
1.	
2.	
3.	

C. **SPEAK** Work with your partner. Role-play a conversation in which one of you gives advice and one of you is Dan Howard. The person giving advice should use the subjunctive when appropriate, and the person playing Dan Howard should confirm understanding. Present the role-play to the class. Refer to the Self-Assessment checklist below before you begin.

CHECK AND REFLECT

A. **CHECK** Think about the Unit Assignment as you complete the Self-Assessment checklist.

SELF-ASSESSMENT		
Yes	No	
☐	☐	I was able to speak easily about the topic.
☐	☐	My partner, group, class understood me.
☐	☐	I used the subjunctive.
☐	☐	I used vocabulary from the unit.
☐	☐	I confirmed understanding.
☐	☐	I pronounced unstressed syllables correctly.

B. **REFLECT** Discuss these questions with a partner.

What is something new you learned in this unit?

 Look back at the Unit Question. Is your answer different now than when you started this unit? If yes, how is it different? Why?

Track Your Success

Circle the words you learned in this unit.

Nouns
anecdote
bias AWL
chaos
cycle 🔑 AWL
enthusiasm 🔑
investor AWL
morale 🔑
norm AWL
reward 🔑
trend 🔑 AWL

Verbs
associate 🔑
conduct 🔑 AWL
embrace
recognize 🔑
stifle

Phrasal Verbs
point out
stumble upon
turn out

Adjectives
appropriate 🔑 AWL
cautious
inflexible AWL
open-minded
stimulating

Adverb
moderately

🔑 Oxford 3000™ words
AWL Academic Word List

Check (✓) the skills you learned. If you need more work on a skill, refer to the page(s) in parentheses.

LISTENING	●	I can identify details. (p. 28)
VOCABULARY	●	I can use the dictionary. (p. 32)
GRAMMAR	●	I can use the subjunctive for suggestions. (p. 34)
PRONUNCIATION	●	I can pronounce unstressed syllables correctly. (p. 36)
SPEAKING	●	I can confirm understanding. (p. 37)
LEARNING OUTCOME	●	I can role-play a conversation offering advice to help someone become better organized.

UNIT 3

Growing Up

LISTENING	●	making predictions
VOCABULARY	●	using the dictionary
GRAMMAR	●	phrasal verbs
PRONUNCIATION	●	sentence stress patterns
SPEAKING	●	giving a presentation

LEARNING OUTCOME ●

Present a personal story describing an important event in your life that made you feel like an adult.

Unit QUESTION

When does a child become an adult?

PREVIEW THE UNIT

A Discuss these questions with your classmates.

In your opinion, at what age does a person become an adult? Why?

What important events or experiences can make you feel more like an adult?

Look at the photo. Why does the boy look so happy?

B Discuss the Unit Question above with your classmates.

 Listen to *The Q Classroom*, Track 25 on CD 1, to hear other answers.

C Which experiences make someone an adult? Check (✓) your top three choices. Work with a partner to compare ideas.

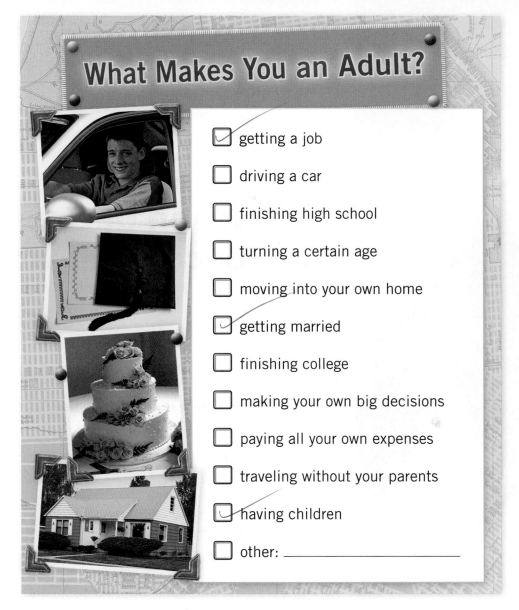

What Makes You an Adult?

- [✓] getting a job
- [ ] driving a car
- [ ] finishing high school
- [ ] turning a certain age
- [ ] moving into your own home
- [✓] getting married
- [ ] finishing college
- [ ] making your own big decisions
- [ ] paying all your own expenses
- [ ] traveling without your parents
- [✓] having children
- [ ] other: _____

D Read the statements. Do you agree or disagree with them? Why? Discuss your opinions with a partner.

Everyone is the age of their heart. (Guatemalan proverb)

Only three things in life are certain: birth, death, and change. (Arabic proverb)

A child's life is like a piece of paper on which every passerby leaves a mark. (Chinese proverb)

We start as fools and become wise through experience. (African proverb)

What is learned in youth is carved in stone. (Arabic proverb)

LISTENING 1 | Generation Next

VOCABULARY

Here are some words from Listening 1. Read the definitions. Then complete each sentence with the correct word.

> **assume** (*v.*) to think something is true although you have no proof
> **carefree** (*adj.*) happy because there are no worries or problems
> **contradiction** (*n.*) the fact of two things being opposite of each other or not matching
> **contributor** (*n.*) a person who gives to something
> **entitled** (*adj.*) given the right to have or to do something
> **initiation** (*n.*) the act of someone becoming a member of a group
> **marker** (*n.*) a sign that shows the position of something
> **milestone** (*n.*) a very important stage or event in the development of something
> **morally** (*adv.*) according to principles of good behavior and what is considered to be right or wrong
> **pinpoint** (*v.*) to find and show an exact time or place
> **run** (*v.*) to manage or control something
> **transition** (*n.*) a change from one state or condition to another

1. The ___initiation___ into the club was a secret ceremony involving the new members and the old members.

2. If you want to speak to the managers, please talk to Sergei and Liz. They ___run___ the department.

3. Some people say an important ___marker___ of maturity is the ability to balance your emotions. It tells others that you are reasonable.

4. My sixteen-year-old son says he wants to be treated like an adult, but then he acts like a child. There's a ___contradiction___ between what he says and what he does.

5. Most people consider murder to be ___morally___ wrong. It is not within the social standards for most societies.

6. I worked hard all week, so I am ___entitled___ to relax this weekend.

7. I am a proud ___contributor___ to charity. It makes me feel good to give what I can to help others.

8. If I don't come to the door when you knock, you can ___assume___ that I'm not home.

9. I like to go on vacation and be ___carefree___. It's nice not to have to deal with problems at work for a while.

10. Learning to drive, buying a home, and getting married were all big ___milestone___ in my life.

11. The ___transition___ from one job to another can be difficult, but the change might be good for your career.

12. I can't ___pinpoint___ the day I started to like cabbage, but I think it was when I was twelve.

PREVIEW LISTENING 1

| Generation Next

You are going to listen to a radio report defining the exact age or event that makes someone become an adult.

At what age do you think adulthood begins? Choose one age. Compare your answer with a partner and discuss.

☐ 16   ☑ 18   ☐ 20   ☐ 21

LISTEN FOR MAIN IDEAS

 CD 1
Track 26

Read the statements. Then listen to the radio report. Write _T_ (true) or _F_ (false).

_F_ 1. It is easy for most people to say exactly when they became an adult.

_T_ 2. We have clear ideas about childhood and adulthood, but there is confusion about the time in between.

_T_ 3. Ceremonies can help adolescents make the transition from child to adult more clearly.

_F_ 4. In many societies, the transition to adulthood takes place at age 16.

_T_ 5. In Western countries, children are often defined by emotional need.

LISTEN FOR DETAILS

Read the questions. Then listen again. Circle the correct answer.

1. When did Robin Lustig know he was an adult?
   a. when he left his parents on his eighteenth birthday
   b. when he flew a plane for the first time
   c. when he returned from teaching in Uganda

2. What event helped Lustig's daughter feel more grown up?
   a. buying a home
   b. a formal ceremony
   c. moving into a shared apartment

3. Which of the following statements is NOT true, according to Cynthia Lightfoot?
   a. Kids don't need to be responsible.
   b. Adolescents are morally independent.
   c. Adults are financially independent.

4. At what age does the United Nations consider you an adult?
   a. 16
   b. 18
   c. 20

5. How are children seen in many parts of the world outside of the West?
   a. as active contributors
   b. as morally independent
   c. as legally recognized

WHAT DO YOU THINK?

Discuss the questions in a group.

1. Robin Lustig talks about his experiences traveling. Have you ever had a travel experience that helped you to grow up? Where did you go? What happened?

2. Do you agree or disagree with the United Nations' age of adulthood? Why?

3. Do you think that there should be a formal initiation into adulthood? Why or why not?

Tip Critical Thinking

In the Listening Skill activities, you **predict** in order to anticipate new content. Predicting can help you understand new material better and be a more engaged listener.

Predictions are guesses you make based only on the information that is available. For example, you may know the title of a lecture. You can use the title to predict the topic and the ideas it might cover.

Your predictions are also based on what you already know about a topic. Background information from articles you have read, from electronic media, and from previous experiences all help prepare you to understand new information, and to predict what you are likely to hear next.

One way to make predictions is to write down the topic. Then take brief notes on the ideas and vocabulary you already know that are associated with that topic. This prepares you for the information that you will hear, so you don't have to work quite as hard to understand it.

Tip for Success

Graphic organizers work well for making predictions. Web diagrams are very useful. Write the topic in a circle in the center. Write notes about your predictions and possible vocabulary on lines coming from the center.

A. Read the lecture titles. Predict the topic of the lecture and the main ideas it might cover. Write brief notes about what you already know about the topic and five words you might expect to hear.

1. Trends in World Music (*Music Appreciation Lecture*)

   What I know about this topic: _I think this topic is about music and songs and singers_

   Five words I might hear: _Music , songs, singers, loud, classic_

2. Global Warming (*Environmental Studies*)

   What I know about this topic: _I think the topic is about the danger that the world is facing._

   Five words I might hear: _Hot, World, warm, cold, Ice_

3. Video Games in Schools (*Media Studies*)

   What I know about this topic: _I thinks its about the new technology and what most people are interested in._

Five words I might hear: __Computer, games, technology, modern, video__

 CD 1 Track 28 **B.** Read the questions. Then listen to the excerpts. Circle the correct answers.

Excerpt 1

Which of the following is most likely to be discussed in the lecture?

a. what to do when you want a promotion

(b.) how to explain your side of an argument

c. what kinds of jobs are right for you

Excerpt 2

What is Ana most likely to suggest?

a. Don't take the online class that I took.

b. You should focus on your job.

(c.) Schedule some time every night just for homework.

Excerpt 3

What is Tara most likely to say next?

(a.) "You're going to have a wonderful time."

b. "You still owe me some money."

c. "You were never very nice to me."

Excerpt 4

How will the employees most likely feel when they hear the news?

a. worried

b. confused

(c.) excited

I have some important news.

LISTENING 2 | Growing Up Quickly

VOCABULARY

Here are some words from Listening 2. Read the sentences. Then write each bold word next to the correct definition.

1. My youngest **sibling** is six years younger than I am. We still call her the "baby" of the family.

2. Taking care of my husband's elderly parents is a **burden** but also an honor. It is a lot of work, but I am happy to do it.

3. Max is **in charge of** the entire store. If anyone has a question or complaint, they go to his office.

4. I used to think children should participate in a lot of planned activities, but I decided to **reverse** my opinion. Now I think they should be free to do what they want most of the time.

5. Parents and teachers should provide **guidance** to children to help them with difficult problems.

6. My children don't always behave well, but they are **capable** of being good when they are in public.

7. We used to live on a farm far away from any town. I didn't like the **isolation**, but it was very peaceful.

8. There was some **confusion** about what was going to happen. Danielle thought I was going to the beach, and I thought she was going to the beach. Neither of us was right!

9. I **resent** Lawrence for always being late. I think it's disrespectful.

10. When the tree fell, it became a **barrier** in the road and we couldn't drive around it.

11. I felt a lot of **frustration** with my study partner. I knew we could finish our project on time if I helped him with his part, but he insisted on doing it all himself.

12. I like many things about my career, but nothing beats the **satisfaction** of a job well done.

a. ___in charge of___ (*phr.*) in control of something or someone

b. ___burden___ (*n.*) a responsibility that causes difficulty or hard work

c. ___frustration___ (*n.*) a feeling of anger or disappointment

d. ___Confusion___ (*n.*) the state of being uncertain or not clear

e. ___Sibling___ (*n.*) a brother or sister

f. ___reverse___ (*v.*) to change something to the opposite

g. ___resent___ (*v.*) to feel angry about something because you feel it is unfair

h. ___Satisfaction___ (*n.*) a feeling of pleasure when you get something you wanted

i. ___capable___ (*adj.*) able to do something

j. ___isolation___ (*n.*) the state of being separate from other people or being alone

k. ___barrier___ (*n.*) a thing or situation that makes something difficult or impossible

l. ___guidance___ (*n.*) help or advice

PREVIEW LISTENING 2

| Growing Up Quickly

You are going to listen to a lecture about children who have to act like parents.

Children with adult responsibilities might feel many emotions. Circle four emotions these children might feel because of their responsibilities. Compare your answers with a partner and discuss.

embarrassment jealousy sadness
fear   love   satisfaction
frustration   pride
happiness   regret

LISTEN FOR MAIN IDEAS

 CD 1
Track 29

Listen to the lecture. Check (✓) the main ideas the lecturer presents.

- ☑ Too much responsibility can be a burden on children.
- ☐ Many children have sick family members.
- ☑ Children often have to take on the role of parent to care for siblings.
- ☑ Some children even reverse roles with their own parents.
- ☐ Parents have to provide guidance for their children.
- ☑ Responsibilities can be barriers and cause frustration.
- ☑ Many of these children become teachers and counselors.
- ☐ Many children get satisfaction from helping others.

LISTEN FOR DETAILS

CD 1
Track 30

Read the statements. Then listen again. Write *T* (true) or *F* (false).

_F_ 1. An older sibling gave Bill some adult responsibilities.

_T_ 2. *Parentification* is when children take on the duties of parents.

_F_ 3. In a reversed role, the parents make the important decisions.

_T_ 4. The effect on a child depends on a child's personality and situation.

_F_ 5. Parentified children rarely feel confusion or isolation.

_F_ 6. Children usually experience fewer negative effects if they take on responsibilities at a younger age.

_T_ 7. Kids with adult responsibilities often care more about others.

_T_ 8. Many people in helping professions grew up having some adult responsibilities.

WHAT DO YOU THINK?

A. Discuss the questions in a group.

1. Have you or has someone you know had to take on adult responsibilities as a child? If so, what were the responsibilities?

2. Do you think that having some adult responsibility is good for an adolescent? Why or why not?

B. Think about both Listening 1 and Listening 2 as you discuss the questions.

1. What kinds of experiences cause people to grow up faster? In what ways can families and society help adolescents during this time of transition?

2. Which of the following best determine the transition from childhood to adulthood? Why?
   a. an age (like the United Nations' age of 18)
   b. an event (like graduating, getting married, or moving into your own home)
   c. responsibilities (like caring for younger siblings or helping around the house)

There are many words that have similar meanings but are not exactly the same. For example, in Listening 1, the speakers use the words *adolescence* and *youth* for the time between childhood and adulthood. Read the following definitions.

ad·o·les·cence /ˌædlˈɛsns/ *noun* [U] the time in a person's life when he or she develops from a child into an adult **SYN** PUBERTY ⊃ collocations at AGE

youth 🔑 /yuθ/ *noun* (pl. **youths** /yuðz; yuθs/) **1** [U] the time of life when a person is young, especially the time before a child becomes an adult: *He had been a talented musician in his youth.*

The dictionary definitions show that although the words are very similar, *adolescence* describes a more specific time period, while *youth* is more general.

Checking the definitions of similar words can help you determine which word is appropriate in a context.

All dictionary entries are from the *Oxford Advanced American Dictionary for learners of English* © Oxford University Press 2011.

A. Read the dictionary definitions of words from this unit and their synonyms. Complete each sentence with the correct word.

1. a. If you are having trouble managing your money, you should go to the

   bank to get some _____financial_____ advice.

   b. Countries such as India and China have experienced rapid

   _____economic_____ growth in recent years.

ec·o·nom·ic 🔑 **AWL** /ˌɛkəˈnɑmɪk; ˌikə-/ *adj.* **1** [only before noun] connected with the trade, industry, and development of wealth of a country, an area, or a society: *social, economic and political issues*

fi·nan·cial 🔑 **AWL** /fəˈnænʃl; faɪ-/ *adj.* [usually before noun] connected with money and finance: *financial services* ♦ *to give financial advice* ♦ *to be in **financial difficulties***

2. a. My whole family came to see my graduation _____ceremony_____.

   b. Before you can join a group like a fraternity, there might be some

   special initiation _____rite_____ that they will perform.

cer·e·mo·ny 🔑 /ˈsɛrəˌmoʊni/ *noun* (pl. **cer·e·mo·nies**) **1** [C] a public or religious occasion that includes a series of formal or traditional actions: *an award/opening ceremony* ♦ *a wedding/marriage ceremony* ⊃ collocations at MARRIAGE

rite /raɪt/ *noun* a ceremony performed by a particular group of people, often for religious purposes: *funeral rites*

3. a. The lawyer can _demonstrate_ that the man is guilty of the crime by recreating the events of the day.

    b. The report _shows_ us that there is still a lot of work to do.

dem·on·strate 🔑 **AWL** /'dɛmən,streɪt/ verb
1 [T] to show something clearly by giving proof or evidence: **~ that...** *These results demonstrate convincingly that our campaign is working.* ◆ **~ sth (to sb)** *Let me demonstrate to you some of the difficulties we are facing.*

show 🔑 /ʃoʊ/ verb, noun
● *verb* (showed, shown /ʃoʊn/ or, rarely, showed)
▸ **MAKE CLEAR 1** [T] to make something clear; to prove something: **~ (that)...** *The figures clearly show that her claims are false.* ◆ **~ sb that...** *Market research has shown us that people want quality, not just low prices.*

B. Look up the definitions of these pairs of words. Write an appropriate sentence using each word. Take turns reading your sentences to a partner.

1. assume / suppose (*v.*)

    _____

    _____

2. age / mature (*v.*)

    _____

    _____

3. response / reply (*n.*)

    _____

    _____

4. order / instruct (*v.*)

    _____

    _____

5. cover / hide (*v.*)

    _____

    _____

SPEAKING

Phrasal verbs are verbs that consist of two words used together. The first word is a verb and the second word is called a *particle*. Particles sometimes look like prepositions, but they have different meanings. The verb and the particle together make a new meaning. For example, *take on* is a phrasal verb. When you put the words *take* and *on* together, they mean "to accept."

☐   She **took on** a lot of responsibilities.

There are two kinds of phrasal verbs: *transitive* and *intransitive*.

Transitive Phrasal Verbs

A transitive phrasal verb requires a direct object.

She **picked up** her brother from school.
verb participle object

 **for Success**

In the dictionary, phrasal verbs are usually located with the definition(s) of the verb in the phrasal verb. Many dictionaries also have example sentences that follow the definitions. Example sentences are an easy way to see if a phrasal verb is *transitive* or *intransitive* and *separable* or *inseparable*.

Most transitive phrasal verbs are *separable*. This means the direct object can also go between the verb and the particle.

She **picked** her brother **up** from school.
verb object participle

When the direct object is a pronoun, it must go between the verb and the particle.

✓ She **picked** <u>him</u> up from school.
✗ She **picked up** <u>him</u> from school.

Some transitive phrasal verbs are inseparable. This means the direct object cannot go between the verb and the particle.

✓ My mother is busy today, so I'll **look after** the baby.
✗ My mother is busy today, so I'll **look** the baby **after**.

Intransitive Phrasal Verbs

Intransitive phrasal verbs don't take a direct object at all. They are never separable.

☐   In some situations, children **grow up** faster than in others.

It can be difficult to understand the meaning of a phrasal verb by looking at the words that make it up. Also, some phrasal verbs have more than one meaning. When you learn a new phrasal verb's meaning, you must also learn if it is transitive or intransitive and whether it is separable or inseparable.

CD 1
Track 31

A. Listen to the sentences with phrasal verbs. Write the particles you hear.

1. count ___on___

2. show ___up___

3. run ___away___ from

4. talked my son ___into___

5. look it ___up___

6. drop ___in___

B. Read the sentences. Underline each phrasal verb. Write *T* (transitive) or *I* (intransitive).

___T___ 1. I don't know what to do about this problem, but we need to work it out.

___T___ 2. I waved goodbye to my parents and got on a plane.

___I___ 3. It's a negotiation that continues to go on throughout childhood.

___T___ 4. Parentified children may feel they are giving up their childhoods.

___T___ 5. The child has to take care of the sick parent.

___T___ 6. An ill mother may need help from her child because she is too ill to get out of bed.

Pronunciation | **Sentence stress** | web

Words in a sentence are not pronounced with equal stress. Words that contain important information, called content words, are said with more stress. They are longer, louder, higher pitched, and clearer. Words that serve a grammatical purpose are called function words. They are usually unstressed.

Stressing words focuses the listener's attention on the most important ideas in sentences. Using sentence stress correctly makes it easier to communicate your ideas.

Content words: usually stressed		Function words: usually unstressed	
Nouns	father, birthday, etc.	Articles	a, an, the
Main verbs	come, walks, etc.	Auxiliary verbs	be, have, can, etc.
Adjectives	beautiful, red, etc.	Prepositions	in, at, etc.
Adverbs	quickly, very, etc.	Personal pronouns	I, you, me, etc.
Negatives	not, can't, etc.	Possessive pronouns	my, your, his, etc.
Question words	where, how, etc.	Relative pronouns	that, which, who, etc.
Demonstrative pronouns	this, that, etc.	Short connector words	and, so, when, then, etc.

CD 1
Track 32

For example, listen to the following sentence. The underlined words are stressed.

I <u>became</u> an <u>adult</u> when I got <u>married</u> and <u>started</u> a <u>family</u>.

CD 1
Track 33

A. Listen to the sentences. Underline the stressed words you hear. Then practice saying the sentences with a partner.

1. When you <u>become employed</u>, you can <u>call yourself</u> an <u>adult</u>.

2. I <u>think</u> it's <u>how much</u> you can <u>provide</u> for <u>yourself</u>.

3. I <u>think</u> it's when you <u>get married</u>.

4. I <u>think</u> you <u>become</u> an <u>adult</u> at <u>16</u>.

5. The <u>day that</u> I'm an <u>adult</u> is the day that <u>I</u> can do <u>whatever</u> I want to do.

6. The <u>age</u> at which you <u>become</u> an <u>adult varies</u>.

B. Underline the important content words in the conversation. Then work with a partner to read the conversation. Stress the content words.

Speaker A: Happy Birthday!

Speaker B: Thanks! I can't believe that I'm already 18 years old.

Speaker A: Yeah. You're an adult now!

Speaker B: But I don't feel like an adult. I still feel like a kid.

Speaker A: Really? Well, I have been taking care of my younger siblings for years now, so I feel pretty grown up.

Speaker B: I still live at home. I still rely on my parents a lot.

Speaker A: Well, maybe that will change now that you are 18!

Speaking Skill | Giving a presentation web+

When you give a presentation, it is important to look and feel confident. People will be more interested in your ideas if they see that you believe in yourself and your ideas. Here are some steps to follow.

Before you give your presentation

1. Make sure you can clearly pronounce all the key words in your speech. Concentrate on proper word stress.

2. Make sure your notes are well organized. Memorize the main points of your speech so that you won't need to read your presentation. You want to look at your audience, not down at your notes.

3. Practice your presentation several times. Practice in front of a mirror and in front of a friend or family member.

When you begin your presentation

1. Introduce yourself clearly and confidently.

2. Remember to smile.

During your presentation

1. Make eye contact with members of the audience. You want them to feel you want to communicate with each of them.

2. Think about your hand gestures and posture as you speak. You want to appear relaxed and in control. If you move too much, or too little, you will appear nervous. Use gestures for emphasis and to make your points clearer.

A. Listen to a presentation about becoming an adult. Then list five suggestions you would give the speaker. Compare your suggestions with a partner.

Suggestions:

1. _____
   _____

2. _____
   _____

3. _____
   _____

4. _____
   _____

5. _____
   _____

B. Create a brief presentation to tell about one important event in your life. Practice the presentation once and then present it to a partner. Take note of the suggestions your partner gives you. Take turns presenting and giving suggestions.

Unit Assignment | Give a presentation to a group

 In this section, you will give a short presentation. As you prepare your presentation, think about the Unit Question, "When does a child become an adult?" and refer to the Self-Assessment checklist on page 62.

For alternative unit assignments, see the *Q: Skills for Success Teacher's Handbook*.

CONSIDER THE IDEAS

 CD 1
Track 35

A. Listen to one person's story about the point when she became an adult. Take notes as you listen.

1. What important event became a turning point in the speaker's life?	
2. What dream did the speaker give up?	
3. How did she realize she was growing up?	

B. Work with a partner. Compare your notes and discuss the speaker's main points.

PREPARE AND SPEAK

 **for Success**

When you are brainstorming, no idea is a bad idea. Write down any ideas you have.

A. GATHER IDEAS Brainstorm about important events in your life that made you feel more like an adult. Make notes in the spider map.

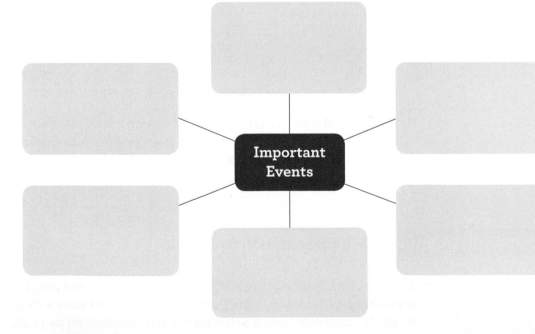

Important Events

B. **ORGANIZE IDEAS** **Complete the activities.**

1. Choose one event to use for your presentation.

2. Use the chart to organize your ideas. It is not necessary to write full sentences. Just make notes. Try to include some phrasal verbs in your presentation.

Introduction (main idea)	
Important ideas and details	
Conclusion	

3. Work with a partner to practice your presentation until you can answer *yes* to the following questions.
   a. Did you introduce yourself clearly?
   b. Did you pronounce all the key words correctly?
   c. Did you use stress correctly?
   d. Did you use your notes to tell your ideas rather than read them?
   e. Did you make eye contact?
   f. Did you use relaxed gestures?
   g. Did you smile?

C. **SPEAK** Present your personal story. Follow these steps. Refer to the Self-Assessment checklist below before you begin.

1. Work in a group. Take turns presenting your personal stories.

2. Pay attention to how your classmates make their presentations. Try to make predictions about what they will say. Offer suggestions to group members when they complete their presentations.

CHECK AND REFLECT

A. **CHECK** Think about the Unit Assignment as you complete the Self-Assessment checklist.

Yes	No	SELF-ASSESSMENT
☐	☐	I was able to speak easily about the topic.
☐	☐	My partner, group, class understood me.
☐	☐	I made predictions about the presentations.
☐	☐	I used vocabulary from the unit.
☐	☐	I gave a presentation.
☐	☐	I used sentence stress correctly.

B. **REFLECT** Discuss these questions with a partner.

What is something new you learned in this unit?

 Look back at the Unit Question. Is your answer different now than when you started this unit? If yes, how is it different? Why?

Track Your Success

Circle the words you learned in this unit.

Nouns
barrier 🔑
burden
confusion 🔑
contradiction AWL
contributor AWL
frustration
guidance
initiation AWL
isolation AWL
marker
milestone
satisfaction 🔑
sibling
transition 🔑 AWL

Adjectives
capable 🔑 AWL
carefree
entitled

Verbs
assume 🔑 AWL
pinpoint
resent
reverse 🔑 AWL
run 🔑

Adverb
morally 🔑

Phrase
in charge of 🔑

🔑 Oxford 3000™ words
AWL Academic Word List

Check (✓) the skills you learned. If you need more work on a skill, refer to the page(s) in parentheses.

LISTENING	●	I can make predictions. (p. 48)
VOCABULARY	●	I can use the dictionary. (p. 53)
GRAMMAR	●	I can use phrasal verbs. (p. 55)
PRONUNCIATION	●	I can use sentence stress. (p. 56)
SPEAKING	●	I can give a presentation. (p. 58)
LEARNING OUTCOME	●	I can present a personal story describing an important event in my life that made me feel like an adult.

LISTENING • listening for reasons
VOCABULARY • collocations with verbs and nouns
GRAMMAR • past unreal conditionals
PRONUNCIATION • *can* and *can't*
SPEAKING • asking open-ended and follow-up questions

LEARNING OUTCOME ●

Participate in an interview about the advantages and disadvantages of medical tourism.

Unit QUESTION

How is health care changing?

PREVIEW THE UNIT

Ⓐ **Discuss these questions with your classmates.**

If you need a new doctor, how will you find one? Where would you look to find information about possible choices of doctors?

Would you go to a hospital very far away because it is less expensive than one close to where you live?

Look at the photo. Would you want to receive health care in your home? Why or why not?

Ⓑ **Discuss the Unit Question above with your classmates.**

🔊 Listen to *The Q Classroom*, Track 2 on CD 2, to hear other answers.

C What characteristics do you want your doctor to have? Rate these characteristics from most important (1) to least important (6). Then compare your answers with a partner.

_2_ friendly

_6_ inexpensive

_1_ experienced

_5_ located near your home

_3_ recommended by a friend

_4_ attended a well-known medical school

D The map shows countries that many people are traveling to for certain medical treatments. Look at the map and discuss the questions.

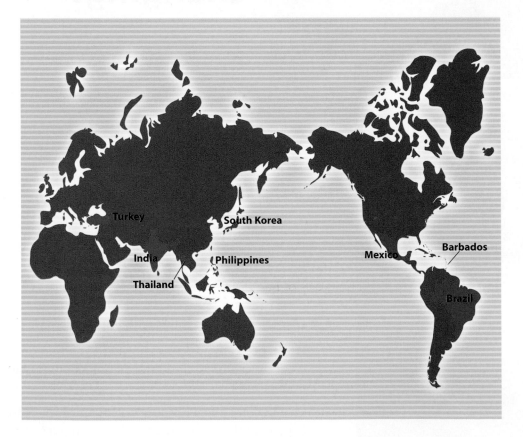

1. If you needed a medical treatment that you couldn't get where you live, would you travel to another country in order to get it? Why or why not?

2. Which country would you be most likely to choose? Give reasons for your answer.

LISTENING 1 | Vacation, Adventure, and Surgery?

VOCABULARY

Here are some words from Listening 1. Read the definitions. Then complete each sentence with the correct word.

> **access** (*n.*) the chance or right to use or have something
>
> **deteriorate** (*v.*) to become worse
>
> **environment** (*n.*) the conditions in a place that you live or stay
>
> **export** (*v.*) to send goods to another country
>
> **image** (*n.*) a mental picture of something
>
> **luxurious** (*adj.*) very comfortable; containing expensive and enjoyable things
>
> **practice** (*v.*) to work as a doctor, lawyer, etc.
>
> **procedure** (*n.*) a medical operation
>
> **standard** (*adj.*) average or normal
>
> **state-of-the-art** (*adj.*) the most modern or advanced techniques or methods

1. The man needed a hip replacement, which is a very difficult medical
   _____procedure_____.

2. Every patient must fill out this form. It is a _____standard_____ form
   at our hospital.

3. When he thought about Thailand, he had a clear _____image_____
   of the busy city of Bangkok.

4. Most modern hospitals around the world are now using
   _____state-of-the-art_____ equipment and computers.

5. I believe people everywhere should have _____access_____ to
   affordable health care.

6. China _____export_____ medical equipment to nations all over the
   world. Much of our hospital's equipment was made there.

7. Dr. Saleem wanted to _____practice_____ medicine in India, so he
   returned home after finishing medical school in the United States.

8. When he travels, he stays in the most expensive and ___luxurious___ hotels wherever he goes.

9. The man's health started to ___deteriorate___ after his surgery. Soon he was back in the hospital.

10. The ___environment___ at the hospital was very pleasant and comfortable. It was a nice place to stay.

PREVIEW LISTENING 1

| Vacation, Adventure, and Surgery?

You are going to listen to a news report on medical tourism. It investigates the reasons patients are traveling to other countries for medical treatment.

What do you think are the main reasons that people leave their countries to get medical care? Check (✓) your answers.

☐ to be treated by the best doctors
☐ to find more affordable medical care
☐ to go to hospitals with state-of-the-art equipment
☐ to get treatment not available in their own country
☐ to combine their treatment with a vacation

LISTEN FOR MAIN IDEAS

**CD 2
Track 3**

Listen to the news report. Circle the answer that best completes each statement.

1. This report focuses on hospitals that provide treatment for patients ___.
   a. who have little money
   b. from other countries
   c. who want a vacation

2. The main reason patients travel long distances to these hospitals is because the treatment they need is ___.
   a. too expensive in their own country
   b. too dangerous in their own country
   c. uncommon in their own country

3. Many of the doctors at these hospitals ____.
   a. have practiced medicine in the United States
   b. have not completed medical school
   c. provide treatment for free

4. The hospitals discussed in the report are in ____.
   a. Indonesia and Thailand
   b. Malaysia and India
   c. Thailand and India

LISTEN FOR DETAILS

CD 2
Track 4

Read the statements. Then listen again. Write *T* (true) or *F* (false).

_F_ 1. Bumrungrad Hospital is in Chennai, India.

_F_ 2. The first patient interviewed, Byron Bonnewell, found out about Bumrungrad Hospital online.

_F_ 3. Byron Bonnewell needed surgery to treat his cancer.

_T_ 4. The rooms at Bumrungrad Hospital are designed to look like hotel rooms.

_F_ 5. Every doctor at Bumrungrad was trained in the United States.

_F_ 6. Medical travel in India is usually more expensive than in Thailand.

_T_ 7. India wants to be the world destination for health care.

_T_ 8. Sometimes patients have procedures that are not approved in their home countries.

Q WHAT DO YOU THINK?

Discuss the questions in a group.

1. The report presented several positive aspects of being a medical tourist. What are some possible negative aspects?

2. Should hospitals try to attract patients from other countries? Why or why not?

When someone speaks about an action, condition, or event, it is important to listen for any reasons that explain why it happened. Speakers often use words or phrases to make it clear that they are giving reasons. Listen to the following examples.

CD 2
Track 5

> Harrison is flying to Brazil **because** his mother is sick and he wants to see her.
> I decided to delay the surgery. **Here's why . . .**

In many cases, speakers do not use words and phrases to signal their reasons. Instead they give reasons by supplying more details.

CD 2
Track 5

> Harrison is flying to Brazil. **His mother is sick and he wants to see her.**
> I decided to delay the surgery. **It's too expensive.** Plus **I want to find a better doctor.**

Pay attention to the details that follow a statement about an action, condition, or event. Those details may provide the reasons.

CD 2
Track 6

A. Listen to excerpts from Listening 1. Complete the chart with the reasons given for each action.

Action	Reason(s)
1. At first, Byron Bonnewell decided not to have surgery.	Its very expensive
2. Mr. Bonnewell later decided to have surgery in Thailand.	Its cheaper and a good doctor
3. Bumrungrad Hospital is able to offer medical care at low costs.	everything cheaper in Thailand
4. Bumrungrad Hospital was designed not to look like a hospital.	Nobody wants to go to a hospital and suites every taste and nationality
5. Stephanie Sedlmayr decided to have surgery performed at the Apollo Hospital in Chennai, India.	Couldn't get the surgery at home

Tip Critical Thinking

Activity B asks you to use words and phrases to give reasons. When you **use what you have learned** in new situations, you will remember it better.

B. Work with a partner. Read the situations below. Take turns giving possible reasons for each situation. Use words and phrases that indicate your reasons.

1. You are going out of town to see a friend.

2. A relative has to go to the hospital.

3. You are not sure if you want to go on a trip.

4. You are taking a few days off from work or school.

LISTENING 2 | Medical Travel Can Create Problems

VOCABULARY

Here are some words from Listening 2. Read the definitions. Then complete each sentence with the correct word.

> **benefit** (v.) to have a good or useful effect
>
> **facility** (n.) a building where a service is provided
>
> **focus** (v.) to give all your attention to something
>
> **found** (v.) to start a business or organization
>
> **obligation** (n.) something that you must do because it is your duty
>
> **private sector** (n.) the part of an economy that is not under the control of the government
>
> **resident** (n.) a person who lives in a particular place
>
> **resign** (v.) to leave your job
>
> **rural** (adj.) connected with the countryside
>
> **shortage** (n.) a situation where there is not enough of something
>
> **skilled** (adj.) having the ability to do something well
>
> **typical** (adj.) having the usual qualities of something

1. Every doctor has an ___obligation___ to provide patients with the best possible care.

2. The hospital hires doctors that are ___skilled___ and experienced. It has the best medical staff in the country.

3. Bumrungrad Hospital tries to ___focus___ on attracting and treating medical travelers from overseas. They are its main source of business.

4. Bumrungrad is a state-of-the-art ___facility___ that provides medical care at very low prices.

5. After Ricardo worked for the government for several years, he went to work for a company in the ___private sector___ instead.

6. My last job was too stressful. I decided to ___resign___ and find a new job.

7. Because of the water ___shortage___ this summer, everyone needs to use less water so we will all have enough.

8. For Dr. Chittarong, a ___typical___ workday begins with a staff meeting. Then he usually visits patients at the hospital.

9. Some of the doctors want to ___found___ their own hospital to help people with low incomes.

10. I grew up in a small ___rural___ community where most of the people were farmers.

11. I'm sure it will ___benefit___ you to take that test-preparation class. You'll get much better grades on your exams.

12. My cousin has been a ___resident___ of New York for a long time. He moved there when he was a young boy.

New York City

PREVIEW LISTENING 2

| Medical Travel Can Create Problems

You are going to listen to a report about the challenges Thailand and India face as they try to meet everyone's medical needs.

Discuss this question with a partner. What problems do you think medical tourism could cause in these countries?

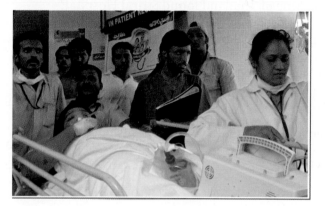

LISTEN FOR MAIN IDEAS

CD 2
Track 7

Read the statements. Then listen to the radio report. Write *T* (true) or *F* (false) for each sentence.

___T__ 1. Some people are worried about the effect of medical tourism on the residents of the host countries.

___T__ 2. Most of the money spent on health care in India is spent in the public sector.

___T__ 3. Rural health care facilities in India sometimes don't have enough medicine or doctors.

___F__ 4. Medical tourism in Thailand is attracting doctors to the public hospitals.

___F__ 5. Doctors at public hospitals receive the same amount of money as doctors at private hospitals.

___T__ 6. Medical tourism is causing some doctors in India to leave public hospitals.

___T__ 7. Medical tourism requires more specialists than primary-care doctors.

___T__ 8. Medical tourism usually involves surgery.

LISTEN FOR DETAILS

Read the questions. Then listen again. Answer the questions.

1. What percentage of the money India spent on health care in 2003 was in the private sector?

   _____ 75% _____

2. Why did the king of Thailand found Siriraj Hospital?

   He wanted to have a hospital that would serve the basic medical needs of people and provide training for doctors.

3. What are two main reasons doctors leave public hospitals?

   To practice in private sector hospitals. make more money in private sector

4. What kind of doctors do medical tourists usually need?

   Surgeons and specialists

5. What is the main difference between Siriraj Hospital and Bumrungrad Hospital?

   Private   Public
   Surgeons and specialists   General
   Travel patients   citizens/residents

6. What do Maria Torres and Dr. Chittarong think will be the solution in countries like Thailand and India?

   Use the training and experience in public and private hospitals.

 ## WHAT DO YOU THINK?

A. Discuss the questions in a group.

1. Should all residents of Thailand have access to treatment at private hospitals like Bumrungrad? Give reasons for your answer.

2. If you were a doctor in Thailand or India, would you work at a public hospital? Why or why not?

B. Think about both Listening 1 and Listening 2 as you discuss the questions.

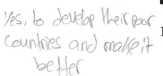
Yes, to develop their poor countries and make it better

1. After hearing both reports, has your opinion of medical tourism changed? Do you think hospitals in places like Thailand and India should try to attract medical tourists? Why or why not?

2. Some people believe that doctors and hospitals have an obligation to provide service to the poor. In your opinion, what other professions and facilities have an obligation to serve the poor? Why?

   Banks, because poor people don't have money

Part of using a word correctly is knowing which words are often used with it. Words that are often used together are called **collocations**. Some nouns are commonly used with certain verbs, but not with other verbs. As you learn to use new nouns, pay attention to collocations that are often used with them.

For example, the noun *surgery* is often used with the verb *perform*, but it isn't used with *work* or *make*.

✓ Dr. Chittarong will **perform** the **surgery**.
✗ Dr. Chittarong will **work** the **surgery**.
✗ Dr. Chittarong will **make** the **surgery**.

The noun *choice* is often used with the verb *make*, but not with some other verbs, such as *do* or *choose*.

✓ I had to **make** a difficult **choice**.
✗ I had to **do** a difficult **choice**.
✗ I had to **choose** a difficult **choice**.

Learning collocations will help you speak more fluently, and it will make it easier to understand what you read and hear.

A. Read the collocations. Then complete each sentence with the correct verb.

have a baby	make an appointment	take a trip
have a procedure	make time	take medicine

1. A year and a half ago, he _____had_____ a procedure to fix a problem in his knee.

2. I went on the Internet to _____make_____ an appointment to see my doctor.

3. My sister just _____had_____ a baby last week. I want to go see the baby soon.

4. I need to _____make_____ time to work out. My doctor says I need more exercise.

5. Next month I'm going to _____take_____ a trip to Thailand. I'm going to see a doctor there.

6. I've been very sick recently. I have to _____take_____ medicine several times a day.

B. **Listen to the sentences. Complete each collocation with the verb you hear.**

1. This new trend is ___creating___ several <u>problems</u>.

2. Every winter, the Reyes family ___takes___ a <u>trip</u> to South America.

3. If I ___do___ enough <u>research</u>, I can find the best doctor.

4. Remember that you have to ___see___ the <u>doctor</u> on Monday.

5. Mrs. Blake can walk much more easily ever since she ___had___ hip <u>surgery</u>.

6. Although the problem was complicated, we ___found___ a <u>solution</u>.

7. We're not sure if we should go, but we have to ___make___ a <u>decision</u> soon.

8. The man went to the hospital to ___have___ some <u>tests</u> done.

C. **Choose five collocations from Activities A and B. Write a sentence using each. Then take turns reading your sentences to a partner. Listen for the collocations your partner uses.**

1. ___I had a procedure to do my tasks___

2. ___My relative will a have a baby soon___

3. ___Every person should make time for himself___

4. ___My brother need to make an appointment quickly___

5. ___We should take medicine on time.___

Grammar   Past unreal conditionals

Past unreal conditional sentences are used to talk about imaginary situations that were actually not true in the past.

It is made of two clauses: the *if* clause and the main clause.

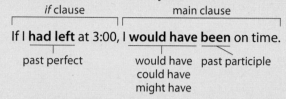

| *if* clause | main clause |

If I **had left** at 3:00, I **would have been** on time.

past perfect

would have   past participle
could have
might have

Here are some examples.

If he **had practiced** medicine in India, he **could have seen** his family.
(He didn't practice medicine in India, and, as a result, he didn't see his family.)
If he **had had** surgery on his knee, he **might have been** able to walk better.
(He didn't have surgery on his knee, and, as a result, he couldn't walk better.)

Use *not* after *would*, *could*, or *might* to make the conditional negative.

If I had left at 3:00, I **would not (wouldn't) have been** so late.
(She didn't leave at 3:00, and, as a result, she was late.)

Conditionals with no *if* clause

A speaker may not say the *if* clause when the information is understood from the context.

Byron Bonnewell lives in Shreveport, Louisiana. A year and a half ago, he had a heart attack, and his doctor told him he really needed bypass surgery. <u>He would have paid over $100,000 for the operation he needed</u>, a complicated quintuple bypass.

It is understood from the context that Mr. Bonnewell would have paid over $100,000 for the operation *if he had had the operation in the United States.*

A. Read the conditional statements. Then answer the questions. Write *Y* (yes) or *N* (no).

If I had known about the trip, I would have saved more money.

_N_ 1. Did the speaker know about the trip?

_N_ 2. Did the speaker save enough money?

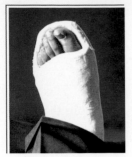

Sharon would have gone to work if she hadn't hurt her foot.

_N_ 3. Did Sharon go to work?

_Y_ 4. Did she hurt her foot?

If he hadn't been late, he could have had dinner with us.

_Y_ 5. Was he late?

_N_ 6. Did he have dinner with them?

If I had seen the news report, I might have gone to a hospital in India.

_N_ 7. Did the speaker see the news report?

_N_ 8. Did the speaker go to a hospital in India?

B. **Change each pair of sentences into a single conditional sentence. Then practice the sentences with a partner.**

1. Melanie didn't study. As a result, she failed the exam.

   If Melanie had studied, she would have passed the exam.

2. Paulo did not have surgery. As a result, his knee still hurts.

   If Paulo had had surgery, his knee would not still hurt

3. We didn't know James was sick. As a result, we didn't take him to the doctor.

   If we had known James was sick, we would have taken him to the doctor

4. I didn't bring a map. As a result, I couldn't find the hotel.

   If I had brought a map, I would have found the hotel

5. You missed your last appointment. As a result, you didn't get a blood test.

   If you hadn't missed your last appointment, you would have gotten a blood test

6. Cristina fell down. As a result, she hurt her leg.

   If Cristina hadn't fallen down, she wouldn't have hurt her leg

7. Stephanie Sedlmayr didn't have surgery in the U.S. In the U.S. it would have cost her over $10,000.

   If Stephanie Sedlmayr had had surgery in the US, it would have cost her over $10,000.

The words *can* and *can't* sometimes sound very similar in conversation. The context will often help someone understand if you said *can* or *can't*, but not always. Here is an example.

> **You say to a friend:** Can you go to the concert on Saturday?
> **Your friend may say:** I can go. OR I can't go.

There is no context to help you understand which word your friend said. To help someone understand the word, make sure that you pronounce *can* and *can't* with different vowel sounds.

Pronounce *can't* with a clear /æ/ sound, like the vowel in *pant* and *rant*.

> can't   /kænt/

When you use can in a sentence, use a schwa (/ə/) sound. This is the same sound as the second vowel in *taken*.

> can   /kən/

CD 2
Track 10

Listen to these two sentences. Notice the difference between the vowels in *can* and *can't*.

> I can go.
> I can't go.

CD 2
Track 11

A. Listen to each sentence. Circle the word you hear. Then listen again and repeat.

1. The nurses (can / can't) speak Thai and English.

2. Patients (can / can't) stay as long as they want.

3. You (can / can't) make an appointment online.

4. His doctor (can / can't) see him today.

5. Patients (can / can't) usually spend time at a beach resort.

6. I (can / can't) return for a checkup this month.

7. I (can / can't) find the address of the doctor's office.

8. Most patients (can / can't) get the care they need.

9. Patients (can / can't) visit the hospital before they have surgery.

10. Sometimes a patient (can / can't) choose which doctor to have.

B. Complete the conversations. Match the statements in column A with the responses in column B. Then practice the conversations with a partner.

A   B

1. You can come with me.   Why not?
   You can't come with me.   Thanks.

2. She can speak French.   Neither can I.
   She can't speak French.   So can I.

3. Dr. Lee can see you now.   I'll come back later.
   Dr. Lee can't see you now.   I'll be right in.

4. I can be there at 3:00.   Great. I'll see you then.
   I can't be there at 3:00.   Then we'll have to reschedule.

5. Grace said she can swim.   Great! Let's go swimming.
   Grace said she can't swim.   I'll teach her.

6. James can afford a vacation.   That's too bad. He needs the time off.
   James can't afford a vacation.   Good. He needs the time off.

Speaking Skill | Asking open-ended questions [web+]

In a conversation, when you are asking questions in order to get information, avoid asking only *yes/no* questions. *Wh–* questions are **open-ended questions**. Open-ended questions encourage the speaker to give more information than *yes/no* questions do.

Yes/No question

☐ Do you think medical tourism is a good idea?

Open-ended questions

What do you think are the pros and cons of medical tourism?
How do you feel about medical tourism?
Which countries do you think are good to go to for medical tourism?

Open-ended questions allow you to ask follow-up questions.

Open-ended question

☐ When was the last time you went to the hospital?

Possible follow-up questions

Why did you go there?
Can you tell me about your experience?
Would you go there for medical treatment again?

A. Read the *yes/no* questions. Change the questions to open-ended questions. Then practice asking and answering the new questions with a partner.

1. Were you experiencing a lot of pain before you had surgery?

   How did you feel before you had surgery?

2. Have you ever had to stay in the hospital?

   When was the last time you stayed at a hospital?

3. Is medical travel causing any problems for the people of India?

   What sort of problems do medical travel cause for the people of India?

4. Can people get cheaper health care in other places?

   Where can people get cheaper health care?

5. Do you think your doctor is a good physician?

   How good is your doctor?

6. Have you been to a hospital in this city?

   Which hospital have you been to in this city?

CD 2
Track 12

B. Listen to the excerpts from Listening 1. For each one, write one or more follow-up questions that would help the interviewer get more information.

1. **Reporter:** "What's wrong with . . . I mean, this is a hospital. What's wrong with looking like a hospital?"

   Schroeder: "Because nobody really wants to go to a hospital."

   Reporter: _Why doesn't anyone want to be in a hospital?_

2. **Reporter:** "This place where we're sitting right now is the number one international hospital in the world?"

   Schroeder: "I haven't heard anybody yet who's told us that they take more than 350,000 international patients a year."

   Reporter: _when did it become the number one hospital?_

3. **Reporter:** "Why is it important to get foreign patients here?"

   Bissell: "It makes sense to establish India as sort of like the world destination for health care."

   Reporter: _What sort of things do they offer?_

In this assignment, you are going to conduct a brief interview about health-care choices. As you prepare your interview, think about the Unit Question, "How is health care changing?" and refer to the Self-Assessment checklist on page 84.

For alternative unit assignments, see the *Q: Skills for Success Teacher's Handbook*.

CONSIDER THE IDEAS

Work in a group. Imagine that a close friend has an illness that will be expensive to treat. Would you recommend medical tourism to your friend? Why or why not? List your reasons below.

_____

_____

_____

_____

_____

_____

_____

PREPARE AND SPEAK

A. **GATHER IDEAS** Read the statements below. Are they statements for or against medical tourism? Write *F* (for) or *A* (against).

____ Medical procedures can be much less expensive in other countries.

____ Doctors can make more money working in private hospitals.

____ Patients often have to travel far from home for long periods of time.

____ Public hospitals in some countries are crowded and have fewer doctors.

_____ Doctors often must choose between helping the poor and making a good salary.

_____ Patients in some countries have long waits at hospitals.

_____ Public hospitals have a hard time keeping doctors in rural areas.

_____ Some procedures that are not available in the U.S. are available in other countries.

B. ORGANIZE IDEAS Consider medical tourism from the perspective of both patients and the medical professionals. Think about the statements in Activity A. Then complete the chart. Give at least two examples for each question.

What are the advantages to patients?	What are the disadvantages for patients?
What are the advantages to medical professionals?	**What are the disadvantages for medical professionals?**

C. **SPEAK** Work in a group of three students. Create a short interview about the advantages and disadvantages of medical tourism. Refer to the Self-Assessment checklist below before you begin.

1. One person will play the role of the interviewer. One person will play the role of someone who supports medical tourism. The third person will play the role of someone who is against medical tourism.

2. Create questions for the interviewer to ask based on your ideas in Activity B. Then create answers for each of the people being interviewed. Each answer should be less than two minutes in length.

3. Conduct the interview for the class.

CHECK AND REFLECT

A. **CHECK** Think about the Unit Assignment as you complete the Self-Assessment checklist.

SELF-ASSESSMENT		
Yes	**No**	
☐	☐	I was able to speak easily about the topic.
☐	☐	My partner, group, class understood me.
☐	☐	I used collocations with nouns and verbs.
☐	☐	I used vocabulary from the unit.
☐	☐	I asked open-ended and follow-up questions.
☐	☐	I used *can* and *can't*.

B. **REFLECT** Discuss these questions with a partner.

What is something new you learned in this unit?

 Look back at the Unit Question. Is your answer different now than when you started this unit? If yes, how is it different? Why?

Track Your Success

Circle the words you learned in this unit.

Nouns	Verbs	Adjectives
access 🔑 AWL	benefit 🔑 AWL	luxurious
environment 🔑 AWL	deteriorate	rural 🔑
facility 🔑 AWL	export 🔑 AWL	skilled 🔑
image 🔑 AWL	focus 🔑 AWL	standard 🔑
obligation	found 🔑 AWL	state-of-the-art
private sector	practice 🔑	typical 🔑
procedure 🔑 AWL	resign	
resident 🔑 AWL		
shortage		

🔑 Oxford 3000™ words

AWL Academic Word List

Check (✓) the skills you learned. If you need more work on a skill, refer to the page(s) in parentheses.

LISTENING ●	I can listen for reasons. (p. 70)
VOCABULARY ●	I can use collocations with verbs and nouns. (p. 75)
GRAMMAR ●	I can use past unreal conditionals. (p. 77)
PRONUNCIATION ●	I can use *can* and *can't*. (p. 79)
SPEAKING ●	I can ask open-ended and follow-up questions. (p. 80)
LEARNING OUTCOME ●	I can participate in an interview about the advantages and disadvantages of medical tourism.

LISTENING	●	making inferences
VOCABULARY	●	word forms
GRAMMAR	●	present perfect and present perfect continuous
PRONUNCIATION	●	basic intonation patterns
SPEAKING	●	avoiding answering questions

Role-play a conversation expressing personal opinions about what makes art popular.

Unit QUESTION

What makes a work of art popular?

PREVIEW THE UNIT

A Discuss these questions with your classmates.

What do you first think of when you hear the word *art*?

Do you have a favorite movie, book, or song? What do you enjoy most about it?

Look at the photo. What is the artist doing?

B Discuss the Unit Question above with your classmates.

 Listen to *The Q Classroom*, Track 13 on CD 2, to hear other answers.

C Complete the survey. Which of the choices do you consider forms of art?

What Is Art?

☐ a painting	☐ a comic book/graphic novel
☐ a video game	☐ a poem
☐ a building	☐ a horror movie
☐ classical music	☐ a cartoon movie
☐ an unusual haircut	☐ a TV commercial
☐ pop music	☐ a novel
☐ a plate of delicious food	☐ a designer dress

D Work in a group. Think about your answers in Activity C. Then discuss these questions.

1. What makes something art?

2. Does everyone have to agree that something is art for it to be art? Why or why not?

3. What is one form of art you especially like? Why?

LISTENING

LISTENING 1 | Manga's New Popularity

VOCABULARY

Here are some words from Listening 1. Read the definitions. Then complete each sentence with the correct word.

> **appreciation** (*n.*) the feeling of being thankful for something
> **breed** (*n.*) a particular type of something
> **circulation** (*n.*) the passing of something from one person to another
> **convention** (*n.*) a large meeting or conference
> **development** (*n.*) change or growth experienced by someone
> **encounter** (*n.*) an unexpected meeting
> **expand** (*v.*) to make bigger in size
> **generation** (*n.*) all of the people born at about the same time
> **panel** (*n.*) a group of people who are chosen to discuss or answer questions about something
> **recall** (*v.*) to remember something
> **series** (*n.*) a number of books telling stories about the same characters
> **take note of** (*idm.*) to pay close attention to something

1. Dr. Nakayama is on the _____ that will be discussing modern Japanese culture.

2. It's been a long time since I read that book. It's hard for me to _____ some of the details.

3. Next week I'm going to a comic book _____ in New York. About 5,000 people are expected to attend.

4. Before you buy an old piece of art, _____ its condition. It affects the value.

5. I bought you this gift to show my _____ for your kindness.

6. Andrea liked the first superhero book so much she decided to read all of the books in the _____.

7. It takes a special _____ of writer to understand what an audience wants and how to give it to them.

8. Teresa didn't expect to run into her mean neighbor at the library. The brief _____ with him made her upset.

9. The book tells the story of a hero's _____ from a normal teenager into a fearless superhero.

10. The library never seems to have the book I want. It's always in _____. Everybody else wants to read it, too!

11. The store decided to _____ its video game section. It's now twice as big.

12. My grandfather's _____ did not grow up with TVs in their homes. People of his age often had radios.

PREVIEW LISTENING 1

Manga's New Popularity

You are going to listen to a radio report describing why manga is popular. Manga is a style of comic book created in Japan.

Manga and other kinds of comic books are popular in many countries. Why do you think people like them? Check (✓) possible reasons.

☐ People can buy comic books for low prices.
☐ Readers identify with the characters.
☐ The stories are exciting.
☐ People enjoy looking at the illustrations.
☐ Comic books are easy to read.

LISTEN FOR MAIN IDEAS

CD 2
Track 14

Listen to the report. Circle the correct answer.

1. How is manga different from typical American comic books?
   a. Manga is usually about superheroes.
   b. Manga has many different types of stories.

2. How are the readers of manga different from the readers of American comics?
   a. More girls read manga.
   b. Fewer young people read manga.

3. Why do the big bookstore chains like the interest in manga?
   a. Manga has all sorts of storylines.
   b. Readers will often buy a whole series.

4. Why do libraries and librarians like manga?
   a. They feel that manga is better than other types of comic books.
   b. Manga encourages young people to read.

LISTEN FOR DETAILS

CD 2
Track 15

Read the statements. Then listen again. Write *T* (true) or *F* (false).

_____ 1. Manga started to become popular in the U.S. in the 1950s.

_____ 2. John Abrams says manga attracts readers because of the variety of storylines.

_____ 3. Tina likes *shoju* because it is about girls who are superheroes.

_____ 4. Tokyopop was started in Tokyo in 1997.

_____ 5. Manga have more character development than American comics.

_____ 6. Margaret Brown thinks manga helps young people develop an appreciation for other kinds of literature.

Q WHAT DO YOU THINK?

Discuss the questions in a group.

1. Why do people enjoy reading manga? Give reasons based on your own experience or on what you heard in Listening 1.

2. Do you think schools should use manga in reading or literature classes? Why or why not?

3. According to the librarian in the report, "On any given day . . . at least three-quarters of our manga titles are in circulation, so we plan to expand that section of the library." What are some possible negative effects of libraries deciding to expand manga sections?

Listening Skill | **Making inferences**

We often understand ideas that the speaker has not actually stated. **Making inferences** involves "reading between the lines," or figuring out more than is actually said to understand the full meaning. Listen carefully to make inferences based on the information available to you.

In the excerpt below, the speaker, Tina, tells us about an experience at a convention.

**CD 2
Track 16**

> At Planet Comic last year, I saw Rumiko Takahashi. I couldn't believe it! She writes *Inu Yasha*, a really good story about a girl who goes back in time. These conventions are really cool because sometimes you get to meet the artists.

Based on this information, we can infer that Tina has been to other conventions and that she thinks meeting a manga artist is a very exciting experience.

Often, speakers communicate how they feel about the ideas they are presenting. To fully understand someone, listen closely to infer attitudes and emotions. Pay attention to the following.

Speed and pitch: If a speaker is talking quickly, and his or her pitch goes up and down, this may indicate that the speaker is excited or passionate about the topic.
Tone: Does the speaker laugh or sound serious?
Descriptive Words: Listen for words that express feelings and opinions, like *love, hate, terrible, wonderful, terrific,* and so on.

CD 2
Track 17

A. Listen to the excerpts from Listening 1. Circle the correct answer.

1. Based on these statements, what can you infer?
   a. Brown thinks it's better for children to read than watch TV.
   b. Brown prefers playing video games to reading.

2. Based on this statement, what can you infer?
   a. Bookstores believe they can sell a lot of manga.
   b. Bookstores want to support manga, even if manga doesn't sell well.

3. Based on these statements, what can you infer?
   a. Shorter stories are usually about heroes.
   b. Manga attracts younger readers with different interests.

CD 2
Track 18

B. Listen to the excerpts from Listening 1. Circle the correct answers.

Excerpt 1

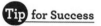

Tip for Success

Many tests require students to answer several inference questions. Learning to make inferences based on what you hear or read is an important part of preparing for tests.

1. You can infer that the speaker is _____ .
   a. bored by the convention
   b. excited about manga

2. Circle all the clues that helped you make this inference.
   a. her speed and pitch
   b. her tone or laughter
   c. her descriptive words

Excerpt 2

3. You can infer that the speaker is _____.
   a. excited by Stuart Levy's books
   b. disappointed in Stuart Levy's decisions

4. Circle all the clues that helped you make this inference.
   a. his speed and pitch
   b. his tone or laughter
   c. his descriptive words

LISTENING 2 | Thomas Kinkade

VOCABULARY

Here are some words from Listening 2. Read the sentences. Then write each bold word next to the correct definition.

1. I enjoyed the movie because I could **identify with** the main character. Her experiences were so similar to mine.

2. Our company spends a lot of money on advertising because we know that **marketing** is a key to success.

3. I wish I could afford an original painting by Salvador Dalí. This one is just a **reproduction**.

4. Vero's music is **unique**. You'll never hear other songs like his.

5. I wish I could **clone** myself so that I could get all my work done. One of me is not enough to do it all.

6. Mrs. Chen's business is a growing **operation**. She just hired twenty more employees.

7. Andrew's paintings are in a show at the new **gallery** downtown that features local artists.

8. I've always wanted to move **overseas** and live in a foreign country for a while.

9. Mehmet is still an **amateur**, but he hopes to develop the skills he needs to be a professional author someday.

10. I **regard** Mike as the most intelligent person I know.

a. _____ (v. + prep.) to feel that you understand and share the feelings of somebody else

b. _____ (v.) to produce an exact copy of something

c. _____ (v.) to think of somebody or something in a particular way

d. _____ (n.) a copy of a piece of art

e. _____ (n.) the act of presenting, advertising, and selling a product

f. _____ (n.) a room or building for showing works of art, especially to the public

g. _____ (*n.*) a person who does an activity for enjoyment, not as a job

h. _____ (*adj.*) being the only one of its kind

i. _____ (*n.*) a business or company

j. _____ (*adv.*) in or to another country

PREVIEW LISTENING 2

| Thomas Kinkade

You are going to listen to a report about the artist Thomas Kinkade. He is a popular artist who produces and sells many paintings every year.

Twilight Cottage by Thomas Kinkade

What makes someone like a painting? Check (✓) the reasons you agree with.

☐ The painting is beautiful.
☐ The painting is inexpensive.
☐ The subject is familiar.
☐ The artist is famous.

LISTEN FOR MAIN IDEAS

CD 2
Track 19   **Read the statements. Then listen to the report. Write *T* (true) or *F* (false).**

____ 1. Thomas Kinkade has sold more paintings than anyone else in history.

____ 2. Thomas Kinkade says people cannot identify with his art.

____ 3. The paintings are produced in a small operation.

____ 4. All of the reproductions are personally painted by Thomas Kinkade.

LISTEN FOR DETAILS

CD 2
Track 20

Read the sentences. Then listen again. Circle the answer that best completes each statement.

1. The reporter compares Thomas Kinkade to ____.
   a. Van Gogh
   b. Craig Fleming
   c. Henry Ford

2. Thomas Kinkade's fans come to see his home in ____.
   a. California
   b. New York
   c. Paris

3. Thomas Kinkade's paintings are cloned by ____.
   a. hundreds of workers
   b. Thomas Kinkade himself
   c. many of his galleries

4. According to Craig Fleming, Thomas Kinkade ____.
   a. wants to be the greatest painter in the world
   b. wants his paintings to hang in every home
   c. wants to be more like Picasso

 ## WHAT DO YOU THINK?

A. Discuss the questions in a group.

1. What do you think is the main reason Thomas Kinkade creates paintings?

2. Why do you think it is Thomas Kinkade's goal to "populate every single wall in every single home" with reproductions of his paintings?

B. Think about both Listening 1 and Listening 2 as you discuss the questions.

Many people enjoy manga, and many people enjoy the paintings of Thomas Kinkade. Still, some people might say that these are not examples of "good" art. Why do you think people might say this? Do you agree? Why or why not?

Many words have several forms. For instance, a verb may have a noun form, an adjective form, and an adverb form. Notice all the forms of the verb *appreciate*.

Verb: I **appreciate** all the help you have given us.
Noun: We applauded to show our **appreciation**.
Adjective: It feels great to perform for an **appreciative** audience.
Adverb: The children responded **appreciatively** when they received the gifts.

In some cases, different parts of speech of a word have the same form.

Noun: John knew that he would never forget that **encounter** with the boss.
Verb: When we arrive, I expect to **encounter** some problems.

When you look up a word in the dictionary, take note of other forms of the word. This will help you build your vocabulary. Each word form will be marked with its part of speech. Common abbreviations for *verb, noun, adjective,* and *adverb* are *v., n., adj.,* and *adv.*

Tip Critical Thinking

In Activity A, you have to **distinguish** between words that are related to a verb and words that are not. When you distinguish between things, you show you understand how things are different.

A. Look at verbs. Circle the word that is not a form of the verb. Use a dictionary to help you.

1. **produce** (*v.*)
   productive   (prodigy)   productivity

2. **inspire** (*v.*)
   inspiration   inspirational   perspire

3. **develop** (*v.*)
   deviate   development   developer

4. **operate** (*v.*)
   opera   operation   operator

5. **identify** (*v.*)
   identification   ideally   identifiable

6. **market** (*v.*)
   marker   marketing   marketable

B. Complete the sentences with the correct form of the word in parentheses. Use a dictionary to help you.

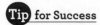 **for Success**

When a word takes a different form, the stress pattern of the word often changes. When looking up a new form of a word in the dictionary, use the pronunciation guide to see the proper stress pattern for that form.

1. Thomas Kinkade is a very _____productive_____ artist. He sells thousands of pictures each year. (produce, *adj.*)

2. He gets his _____ from scenes with which he is very familiar. (inspire, *n.*)

3. The _____ of the artist's style took many years of hard work. (develop, *n.*)

4. Thomas Kinkade's _____ employs hundreds of people. (operate, *n.*)

5. The reproductions of the paintings are _____ because the brush marks are different. (identify, *adj.*)

6. The paintings are very _____ because so many people can relate to the subjects. (market, *adj.*)

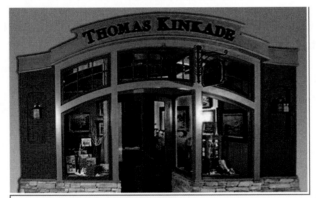

a Thomas Kinkade gallery

SPEAKING

| Grammar | Present perfect and present perfect continuous | |

Present Perfect

The **present perfect** can describe actions that happened at an unspecified time in the past. The present perfect construction is *has/have* + past participle.

Thomas Kinkade **has finished** another painting.
(He finished the painting in the past, but we don't know when.)

The present perfect also describes actions that started in the past and continue in the present time. The words *for* and *since* are used to describe actions that started at a definite time in the past

She **has collected** art **for** twenty years.
(She started collecting twenty years ago. She still collects now.)
He **has painted** pictures **since** 1995.
(He started painting in 1995. He still paints now.)

The present perfect is often used to talk about past actions that happened more than once.

We**'ve seen** a lot of Thomas Kinkade paintings lately.
(We saw paintings several times in the recent past.)

Present Perfect Continuous

The **present perfect continuous** describes actions that started in the past, but were not finished. The present perfect continuous construction is *has/have* + *been* + present participle.

Jane **has been thinking** about studying art in Paris.
(She started thinking about it in the past and is still thinking about it.)
Yong-hwa **has been studying** there **since** last year.
(He started studying there last year. He is still there.)
Ahmad and his family **have been** in New York **since** 2010.
(The family moved there in 2010. They are still there.)

A. Rewrite the sentences. Use the present perfect.

Tip for Success

When using present perfect and present perfect continuous verbs, speakers often contract *have* and *has* so they sound like *'ve* and *'s*. Listen for these contractions to help you understand a speaker's meaning.

1. Alonzo started the project.

   Alonzo has started the project.

2. I thought a lot about going to art school.

   _____

3. Ellen took several painting classes at the school.

   _____

4. Min-ju gave several paintings to her mother.

   _____

5. There were several very good artists at my school.

   _____

B. Complete the conversation. Circle the correct verb form. Then practice the conversation with a partner.

Jamal: Sarah and I (have gone /~~have been going~~) to the Museum of Modern
   Art on Saturdays. We (have seen / have been seeing) so much during
   each visit.

Ryan: I (haven't gone / haven't been going) since last winter even though
   it's very close to my apartment. I walk past the museum to get to work,
   but I (haven't gone / haven't been going) in. I should stop in.

Jamal: Yes, you should. It's a great place. I (have taken / have been taking)
   several friends there recently.

Ryan: So, what did you see there?

Jamal: Well, lately I (have read / have been reading) a lot about a painting
   style called *photorealism*.

Ryan: What is photorealism, exactly? I (have heard / have been hearing)
   of it before, but I'm not sure what it is.

Jamal: Basically, they're paintings that look almost like actual photographs.

Ryan: Wow, I ('ve never seen / 've never been seeing) a painting like that, but
   I'd like to!

Intonation Pattern

When speaking, the pitch of your voice goes up and down. This change in pitch is called an **intonation pattern**. Intonation patterns carry a lot of information. For instance, your intonation will let your listener know if you are asking a question or making a statement. It's important to use the correct intonation pattern to effectively communicate your meaning.

Rising/Falling

One of the most common intonation patterns in English is the *rising/falling* pattern, where the pitch rises and falls on the last word. This pattern is common in simple declarative sentences, direct commands, and *wh*-questions.

I enjoyed it very much.

Hand me that brush, please.

What have you seen?

Rising

For *yes/no* questions, use a *rising* pattern.

Are you concerned?

 CD 2
Track 21

A. Listen to each sentence. Write *R* (rising intonation pattern) or *RF* (rising/falling pattern). Then repeat each sentence.

____ 1. How much do these paintings cost?

____ 2. Is the library open?

____ 3. We're looking for Broadway.

____ 4. Walk north for two blocks.

____ 5. Are you sure?

____ 6. Please sign on the dotted line.

____ 7. Call me tomorrow at six.

____ 8. Have you read her new book?

B. Listen to the conversation. Draw arrows to show the intonation patterns. Listen again and repeat. Then practice the conversation with a partner.

Alex: Did you watch *Gravity* yet?

Lee: Yeah, Jae and I watched it last weekend.

Alex: What did you think of it?

Lee: The special effects were great.

Alex: That's it? Come on. Tell me what you thought.

Lee: Well, the plot was ridiculous. I mean, it was hard to believe.

Alex: It's science fiction. It's not supposed to be realistic.

Lee: I know. I guess sci-fi isn't me. Jae thought it was pretty good. Did you like it?

Speaking Skill Avoiding answering questions web

There are times when you prefer not to answer a question that someone has asked you. Here are several ways that you can avoid answering questions without being impolite.

Refuse politely.

> **A:** Who did you vote for?
> **B:** Actually, I'd prefer not to say.

Ask another question.

> **A:** Did you see the movie *Gravity*?
> **B:** Did you see it?

Answer a different question. You can provide related information without addressing the real question.

> **A:** Are you looking for a new job?
> **B:** I like this job very much.

Use vague phrases. Phrases like *you might say* or *one could conclude* avoid stating your own opinion directly.

> **A:** What do you think about the new law?
> **B:** You might say it's good for some people.

Refusing politely is the simplest and most direct way to avoid answering a question. Using vague phrases is the least direct way. These strategies can be used in all types of situations.

A. Listen to the conversations. Write the strategy that each speaker uses. Then practice the conversations with a partner.

1. **A:** How old are you?

   B: I'd rather not say.

   Strategy: _____

2. **A:** What did you think of that book?

   B: What did you think of it?

   Strategy: _____

3. **A:** Hello. Is Nico there?

   B: Who's calling?

   Strategy: _____

4. **A:** Is Joseph doing a good job?

   B: Joseph is a very hard worker.

   Strategy: _____

5. **A:** Can I have your address, please?

   B: I'm sorry, but I don't give out that information.

   Strategy: _____

6. **A:** Where were you on Friday?

   B: Why do you need to know?

   Strategy: _____

7. **A:** Where do you want to have dinner?

   B: Where would you like to go?

   Strategy: _____

8. **A:** How much did you pay for that car?

   B: It was affordable, and we're very happy with it.

   Strategy: _____

B. Read the questions. Write responses that avoid answering the questions directly. Then practice with a partner.

1. **A:** Why did you decide to leave that job?

   B: _____

2. **A:** What do you think of this picture?

   B: _____

3. **A:** Which painting do you prefer?

   B: _____

4. **A:** What is your email address?

   B: _____

Unit Assignment	Role-play a conversation about popular art

 In this assignment, you are going to role-play a conversation that gives opinions about some kinds of art. As you prepare your conversation, think about the Unit Question, "What makes a work of art popular?" and refer to the Self-Assessment checklist on page 106.

For alternative unit assignments, see the *Q: Skills for Success Teacher's Handbook.*

CONSIDER THE IDEAS

Look at the painting below. In a group, discuss these questions.

1. What do you think the artist wanted to communicate in this piece?

2. Why do you think this piece is famous?

3. Is this piece "good" art? Why or why not?

Stepping Out by Roy Fox Lichtenstein

PREPARE AND SPEAK

A. **GATHER IDEAS** Read the statements. Check (✓) the ones you agree with.

☐ A work of art is only good if many people agree it is good.

☐ People should appreciate all kinds of art.

☐ Manga and other kinds of modern art aren't as good as classic paintings.

☐ Good art is worth a lot of money.

☐ A piece of great art has to be unique. There can't be many pieces like it.

☐ Art becomes popular when everyone can identify with it.

☐ Popularity and fame are needed to be a great artist.

☐ It is a personal opinion whether a piece of art is good or bad.

☐ All art has to communicate an important message.

B. **ORGANIZE IDEAS** Work with a partner. Choose two statements from Activity A you agree with and two you disagree with.

1. Write notes to explain why you agree or disagree.

_____

_____

_____

_____

_____

_____

_____

2. Then write questions asking for your partner's opinion about the statements he or she chose from Activity A.

_____

_____

_____

_____

_____

3. Take turns asking and answering the questions. Use a strategy to avoid answering one of the questions.

C. **SPEAK** Present your conversation to the class. Ask and answer each other's questions about what makes art popular. You can refer to your written notes from Activity B, but do not read exactly what you wrote. Refer to the Self-Assessment checklist on page 106 before you begin.

CHECK AND REFLECT

A. **CHECK** Think about the Unit Assignment as you complete the Self-Assessment checklist.

SELF-ASSESSMENT		
Yes	**No**	
☐	☐	I was able to speak easily about the topic.
☐	☐	My partner, group, class understood me.
☐	☐	I used present perfect and present perfect continuous.
☐	☐	I used vocabulary from the unit.
☐	☐	I used strategies to avoid answering questions.
☐	☐	I used correct intonation patterns.

B. **REFLECT** Discuss these questions with a partner.

What is something new you learned in this unit?

 Look back at the Unit Question. Is your answer different now than when you started this unit? If yes, how is it different? Why?

Track Your Success

Circle the words you learned in this unit.

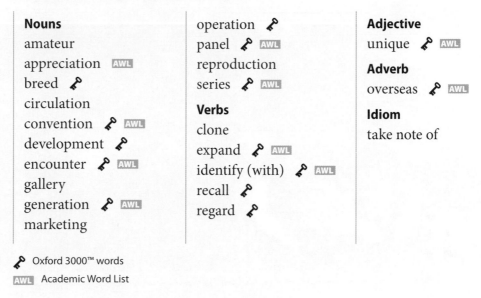

Nouns
amateur
appreciation AWL
breed 🔑
circulation
convention 🔑 AWL
development 🔑
encounter 🔑 AWL
gallery
generation 🔑 AWL
marketing

operation 🔑
panel 🔑 AWL
reproduction
series 🔑 AWL

Verbs
clone
expand 🔑 AWL
identify (with) 🔑 AWL
recall 🔑
regard 🔑

Adjective
unique 🔑 AWL

Adverb
overseas 🔑 AWL

Idiom
take note of

🔑 Oxford 3000™ words
AWL Academic Word List

Check (✓) the skills you learned. If you need more work on a skill, refer to the page(s) in parentheses.

LISTENING	○	I can make inferences. (p. 92)
VOCABULARY	○	I can use word forms. (p. 97)
GRAMMAR	○	I can use present perfect and present perfect continuous. (p. 99)
PRONUNCIATION	○	I can use basic intonation patterns. (p. 101)
SPEAKING	○	I can avoid answering questions. (p. 102)
LEARNING OUTCOME	○	I can role-play a conversation expressing personal opinions about what makes art popular.

LISTENING	●	understanding bias in a presentation
VOCABULARY	●	prefixes and suffixes
GRAMMAR	●	comparative forms of adjectives and adverbs
PRONUNCIATION	●	common intonation patterns
SPEAKING	●	expressing interest during a conversation

LEARNING OUTCOME ●

Participate in a debate on food science, stating and supporting your opinions about food modification.

Unit QUESTION

How has science changed the food we eat?

PREVIEW THE UNIT

Ⓐ Discuss these questions with your classmates.

Which is more important in the food you choose: flavor, cost, or nutrition? Why?

Scientists have developed ways to genetically modify plants. What do you know about genetically modified food?

Look at the photo. How have the tomatoes been modified? Would you want to try them?

Ⓑ Discuss the Unit Question with your classmates.

🔊 Listen to *The Q Classroom*, Track 24 on CD 2, to hear other answers.

C Think about the food that you usually eat. Then look at the list. Check (✓) the foods that you buy and eat frequently.

What Foods Do You Buy Frequently?

☐ bread   ☐ breakfast cereal   ☐ canned soup

☐ milk   ☐ chicken   ☐ ice cream

☐ soda   ☐ fresh fruit   ☐ beans

☐ meat   ☐ vegetables   ☐ fast food

☐ rice   ☐ potato chips   ☐ energy drinks

☐ pizza   ☐ chocolate   ☐ other: _____

☐ fish   ☐ frozen meals   ☐ other: _____

D Work in a group. Discuss the selections you made in Activity C. Do you know how those foods are created? Are any of them all natural? Which foods do you think have added chemicals or are genetically modified? Explain. Give reasons for your answers.

LISTENING 1 | Food Additives Linked to Hyperactivity in Kids

VOCABULARY

Here are some words from Listening 1. Read the definitions. Then write each bold word next to the correct definition.

1. The plan to build a big road though the neighborhood caused a lot of **controversy**. Many residents disagreed with it.

2. I don't have time to take care of real plants, so I have **artificial** plants in my home. I don't have to worry about watering or feeding them.

3. The results of the study were **significant**, so the scientists wrote about them in a scientific journal.

4. It rained for three days. The **adverse** weather conditions made it impossible for us to enjoy our vacation.

5. My friend's sons are **identical** twins. The boys look so similar that I often mistake one for the other.

6. Teenage boys often **consume** a lot of food because they are growing quickly.

7. The additional information was **superfluous** because I had already made up my mind. I didn't need to hear more about the topic.

8. Researchers have found a **substantial** link between high-cholesterol diets and heart disease. Their research shows the importance of healthy eating.

9. A vegetarian diet may **consist of** mostly vegetables, fruit, grains, and beans. Meat is not part of a vegetarian's diet.

10. Warm, sunny weather is **optimal** for spending a day at the beach.

a. ___adverse___ (*adj.*) making something difficult

b. ___artificial___ (*adj.*) not natural; made by people

c. ___consist of___ (*v. + prep.*) to be made up of

d. ___consume___ (*v.*) to eat or drink something

e. ___identical___ (*adj.*) exactly the same as something else

f. ___optimal___ (*adj.*) the best possible

g. ___Controversy___ (*n.*) public discussion and disagreement

h. ___Significant___ (*adj.*) great or important

i. ___Substantial___ (*adj.*) very large or important amount

j. ___Superfluous___ (*adj.*) more than what you need or want

PREVIEW LISTENING 1

Food Additives Linked to Hyperactivity in Kids

You are going to listen to a radio report about food chemicals and their effects on children's behavior.

Work with a partner. Why might chemicals in food affect a child's behavior? Give reasons for your answer.

LISTEN FOR MAIN IDEAS

 CD 2 Track 25

Listen to the radio report. Check (✓) the main ideas mentioned in the report.

☑ Artificial additives can make young children hyperactive.

☐ Some of the fruit juice had more food coloring than the rest.

☑ Food coloring significantly affects the behavior of some children.

☐ Preservatives have an important function in food.

☐ Dr. Feingold has written several books.

☑ The study is a source of controversy because some other studies do not have the same results.

☑ Feeding children heavily processed food is not optimal for health.

☐ The study is well designed and important.

LISTEN FOR DETAILS

 CD 2
Track 26

Listen again. Write two examples for each statement. Compare your ideas with a partner.

1. Colorings and preservatives have adverse effects on some children.

   Adverse effects are seen in general Population

   Causes hyperactivity

   Differences in behavior

   _____

   _____

2. The effect of artificial chemicals on children's behavior has been a controversy for decades.

   Children reacted poorly toward the mixtures

   May cause hyperactive disorder

   One that a child can avoid

   _____

   _____

 WHAT DO YOU THINK?

Discuss the questions in a group.

1. How concerned are you about the additives in your food? Do you avoid food that contains additives? _Not much concerned_ _Trying to but not much_

2. Preservatives are added to food to keep it fresh for a longer period of time. Do you think the advantages outweigh the disadvantages? Explain.
   No, because there are still chemicals added to the food

3. Should there be stricter rules about the food additives in foods children commonly consume? Why or why not?
   Yes, to maintain children health

Bias is a strong feeling for or against something. Understanding the bias in a presentation is important. Speakers may express biases even when they're trying to sound objective. In Listening 1, the speaker presents research both for and against a link between food additives and hyperactivity, but the speaker's bias appears to be against food additives.

There are several clues to help you understand the bias of a presentation.

Title: Listening 1 is "Food Additives Linked to Hyperactivity in Kids." This is a negative idea, and it sounds very definite. This probably means the speaker agrees with the research in the report. A different title, such as "Some Researchers Believe Food Additives May Affect Hyperactivity" does not show such a strong bias.

Introduction: Pay attention to how a speaker introduces a topic. For example, if a speaker starts with, *I'm going to talk about the negative effects of food additives on children's behavior*, that statement alone tells you the speaker's bias.

Imbalance: Reports with a bias usually report on both sides of the issue, but the information is not balanced well. In Listening 1, most of the report is about the research results that show a link between additives and hyperactivity, and only a small part of the report is about research that doesn't show any link.

Information source: Consider who is providing the information. For example, suppose a company that sells chocolate presents research that shows eating chocolate is good for you. Knowing the company sells chocolate can help you decide how much to trust the information.

CD 2
Track 27

A. Listen to the short report. Then answer the questions.

1. Check (✓) the clues you hear that tell you the bias.

   ☐ Title
   ☑ Introduction
   ☐ Imbalance
   ☐ Information source

2. Is the speaker against organic food or in favor of organic food?

   against organic food

CD 2
Track 28

B. Listen to excerpts from four news reports. What bias is being shown in each report? Circle the correct answer.

Excerpt 1

a. Some scientists believe there are many causes of obesity.

(b.) Some scientists believe fast food is the main cause of obesity.

Excerpt 2

a. Drinking soda may cause heart disease.

b. Drinking soda is part of a healthy lifestyle.

Excerpt 3

a. Drinking too much tea can be harmful.

b. Drinking tea is an old tradition.

Excerpt 4

a. Food labels can help us make good choices.

b. Food labels can be difficult to believe.

LISTENING 2 | The "Flavr Savr" Tomato

VOCABULARY

Here are some words from Listening 2. Read the definitions. Then complete each sentence with the correct word.

---

alter (*v.*) to make something different

commodity (*n.*) something that you buy or sell

compound (*v.*) to make something worse

consumer (*n.*) a person who buys things or uses services

debate (*n.*) a general discussion or disagreement about something

disturbing (*adj.*) making someone worried or upset

ethics (*n.*) moral beliefs about what is right and wrong

hurdle (*n.*) a problem that you must overcome

modification (*n.*) a small change made to something

reaction (*n.*) something you do or say because of something that has happened

trait (*n.*) characteristic

ultimate (*adj.*) the greatest, best, or worst

---

1. I don't eat enough vegetables. To _____compound_____ the problem, my grocery store does not have much fresh produce.

2. Getting people to eat newly created foods is a _____hurdle_____ that many companies must deal with. They work hard to make their products marketable.

3. I find it very ___disturbing___ that people eat so much processed food. How can they eat that stuff instead of fruits and vegetables?

4. Advertisers try to catch the interest of any ___consumer___ who will want to buy their products.

5. When they said the newly created carrots were bright red, my first ___reaction___ was to say I didn't believe it.

6. We need to ___alter___ our diet. I want to reduce the amount of processed food we eat.

7. Some people wanted the new factory in their town and some didn't. The ___debate___ over building the new factory went on for years.

8. This plant has an important ___trait___ that makes it able to survive in a dry area.

9. Milk is a valuable ___commodity___. When cows can't produce enough, the price of milk goes up quickly.

10. I think a bowl of ice cream with hot fudge sauce is the ___ultimate___ dessert. Nothing could be better than that!

11. I question the ___ethics___ of creating "super foods." I'm not sure I agree that genetic engineering is always good.

12. This corn is very similar to normal corn, but scientists made a small ___modification___ to its genes that makes it resist disease.

a corn field

PREVIEW LISTENING 2

The "Flavr Savr" Tomato

You are going to listen to a news report about a genetically engineered, or altered, tomato called the "*Flavr Savr*" *tomato*. Scientists have changed this tomato to give it different traits.

Do you think altering the genes of plants is a good thing? Why or why not? Discuss with a partner.

LISTEN FOR MAIN IDEAS

CD 2
Track 29

Listen to the news report. Circle the correct answer.

1. In general, the consumers in the news report ____.
   a. didn't like the idea of biotechnology
   b. didn't have strong feelings about biotechnology
   c. didn't understand biotechnology

2. According to the news report ____.
   a. consumers will not buy genetically altered food
   b. consumers are very excited about genetically altered food
   c. consumers are not sure if genetically altered food is safe or not

3. According to the report, genetically modified foods will probably ____.
   a. cost less than naturally grown foods
   b. become popular as people get used to them
   c. be banned by governments

4. In general, the report was ____.
   a. in favor of genetically modified foods
   b. against genetically modified foods
   c. not biased about genetically modified foods

LISTEN FOR DETAILS

CD 2
Track 30

Read the statements. Then listen again. Write *T* (true) or *F* (false).

_T_ 1. The "Flavr Savr" tomato is supposed to stay riper longer than an ordinary tomato.

_F_ 2. Science has influenced farming for a long time.

_F_ 3. Genetic modification is only used for food.

_T_ 4. Many people like watermelon with no seeds. This shows people are willing to eat some genetically altered food.

_F_ 5. The biggest hurdle to getting people to buy genetically modified food may be the cost.

Q WHAT DO YOU THINK?

A. Discuss the questions in a group.

1. Some genetically altered plants need less water to grow, are resistant to insects, or are more nutritious. Farmers may be able to feed more people by growing genetically modified crops. Do the benefits of growing genetically modified crops outweigh possible risks? Give reasons for your answer. _No, because the plants aren't natural so they might have side effects on consumers._

2. In some countries, genetically altered foods must have a label explaining that they are altered. Is this law a good idea? Why or why not? _Yes, because it helps people know what is in their food._

B. Think about both Listening 1 and Listening 2 as you discuss the questions.

Do you know if any foods you eat have been genetically modified? _Yes, banana._ Do you know which foods contain additives? _No_ How can you find out? _Ask about it._ How will this information affect what you buy? _I will be more informed about it._

Vocabulary Skill   Prefixes and suffixes

Prefixes

Adding a **prefix** to the beginning of a word changes the meaning of the word. Understanding a prefix can help you identify the meaning of a word. Here are some prefixes you heard in this unit.

Prefix	Meaning	Example
dis-	opposite of	disorders
under-	less than enough	underdeveloped
re-	again	rebound
un-	not	uneasy

Suffixes

Adding a **suffix** to the end of a word often changes the part of speech. For example, adding -*ly* to the adjective *wide* changes the word to the adverb *widely*. Here are some examples of common suffixes used in Listening 2.

Suffix	Meaning	Example
-al, -ic	(*adj.*) about, connected with	chemical, genetic
-(at)ion	(*n.*) a state or process	reaction
-ist	(*n.*) a person who does	scientist
-less	(*adj.*) not having something	seedless
-(al)ly	(*adv.*) in a particular way	genetically
-ness	(*n.*) a quality	freshness

A. Write the meaning of each word. Look at the prefixes in the chart on page 118 to help you.

1. disapprove _opposite of approving (not approving)_

2. redo _doing something again_

3. unfair _not fair_

4. underfeed _not ___ feeding_

5. untie _not being_

6. dislike _not liking something_

B. Look at the words and phrases below. Write the correct form of the word. Use the suffixes in the chart above to help you.

Tip for Success

Many words drop letters before a suffix is added. Look in the dictionary to see if there are spelling changes when adding suffixes to a word.

1. science (*n.* person) _scientist_

2. origin (*adv.*) _originally_

3. unique (*n.* quality) _uniqueness_

4. no weight (*adj.*) _weightless_

5. about a topic (*adj.*) _topical_

6. relate (*n.*) _relation_

C. Choose five words from Activities A and B. Write a sentence for each word. Then take turns reading your sentences to a partner.

| Grammar | Comparative forms of adjectives and adverbs | |

Comparative forms of *adjectives* and *adverbs* compare two things or actions. The rules for making comparatives are similar for both adjectives and adverbs.

Condition	Rule	Example
one-syllable adjectives	add -*er*	older
one-syllable adverbs		faster
one-syllable adjectives ending in -*e*	add -*r*	nicer
two-syllable adjectives ending in -*y*	change the *y* to *i* and add -*er*	healthier
most other adjectives	use *more* or *less* before the word	more interesting
all other adverbs		less naturally

Some adjectives take either –*er* or *more*.

    narrow   →   narrower, more narrow
    simple   →   simpler, more simple
    quiet   →   quieter, more quiet
    gentle   →   gentler, more gentle
    handsome   →   handsomer, more handsome

Some adjectives and adverbs are irregular. This means the comparative adjective and adverb forms are not based on the base forms.

    good   →   better   badly   →   worse
    well   →   better   far   →   farther / further
    bad   →   worse   little   →   less

To compare things or actions, use the word *than* after the comparative adjective or adverb.

    Vegetables are healthier **than** junk food.
    Many people are concerned about eating more healthfully **than** they were
       in the past.

A. Write the comparative forms of the adjectives and adverbs. Then work with a partner. Take turns saying sentences using these comparative forms.

1. flavorful _____ more flavorful
2. uneasy _____ more uneasy
3. high _____ higher
4. tasty _____ tastier
5. widely _____ more widely
6. unnatural _____ more unnatural
7. acceptable _____ more acceptable
8. bad _____ worse
9. loyal _____ more loyal
10. expensive _____ more expensive

B. Work with a partner. Take turns asking and answering comparative questions.

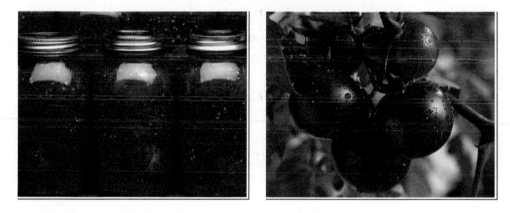

Example:

tomato / flavorful / canned / fresh

> A: *Which kind of tomato do you think is more flavorful, canned or fresh?*
> B: *I think fresh tomatoes are more flavorful than canned tomatoes.*

1. juice / sweet / pineapple / orange

2. ice cream / tasty / chocolate / strawberry

3. TV show / disturbing / the news / reality TV

4. drink / widely enjoyed / tea / coffee

5. food / expensive / organic / genetically engineered

Intonation is an important part of communicating your ideas. There are common intonation patterns for specific conversational actions. Make sure you are using the correct pattern to help express your meaning.

To ask for clarification, use a rising intonation.

CD 2
Track 31

> This tomato is genetically altered?
> **Meaning:** I am not sure I heard you, or I am not sure I understand you.

To express surprise, use a rising intonation.

> You eat five hamburgers a day!
> **Meaning:** I am surprised by this information.

To list items, use a rising intonation for each item on the list. For the last item, use a rising/falling intonation.

> I ate eggs, bacon, and cereal.
> **Meaning:** I ate three things.

For *yes/no* questions, use a rising intonation.

> Would you like coffee?
> **Meaning:** You can say *yes* or *no* to my question.

To offer a choice between two things, use a rising/falling intonation.

> Would you like coffee or iced tea?
> **Meaning:** Which would you prefer?

CD 2
Track 32

A. Listen to the sentences. Draw intonation arrows over each one. Then practice saying the sentences with a partner.

1. What? You've never eaten a tomato?

2. Do you prefer water or juice?

3. My favorite foods are rice, yams, and pizza.

4. What did you say? You don't like ice cream?

5. Are you hungry? Do you want some bread and cheese?

B. Work with a partner. Take turns asking and answering the questions. Ask follow-up questions if needed. Focus on using the correct intonation.

1. What are your favorite foods?

2. What is the strangest food you have ever eaten?

3. What are three foods you would never try?

4. Who usually cooks at your house?

Speaking Skill   Expressing interest during a conversation   web

Expressing interest during a conversation shows the speaker you are paying attention. There are several ways to express interest in the speaker's ideas. In addition to leaning forward and making eye contact, you can use special words and phrases to show you are interested.

Encouraging words: Yeah. / Wow! / Mm-hmm. / Cool!
Comments: How interesting! / That's amazing!
Emphasis questions: Really?
Repeating words: Speaker: I went to Paris. You: Oh, Paris!

It is not necessary to wait until the speaker has finished talking to use these words and phrases. You can use them throughout the conversation, whenever the speaker completes a thought.

CD 2
Track 33

A. Listen to the conversation between two students who are eating lunch. Fill in the blanks with the words in the box. Then practice the conversation with a partner.

| mm-hmm | that's interesting | wow |
| really | every day | yeah |

Noriko: Hey, Marc. Is this seat free? Do you mind if I sit here?

Marc: Not at all. How are you doing?

Noriko: I'm absolutely starving!

Marc: _Really_? Why?

Noriko: I went to the gym this morning before school, and by 11:00, my

stomach was growling in class.

Marc: _Wow_, that had to be embarrassing.

Noriko: Definitely. So, what did you get for lunch?

Marc: Well, they're serving French onion soup today, so I got some of that. It's not bad, but not like home!

Noriko: _Yeah_____! French food is famous around the world, but I've never had it.

Marc: Well, I am from Provence, in the south of France. People take food very seriously there.

Noriko: _mm-hmm_____.

Marc: People buy fresh fruit and vegetables from the market every day.

Noriko: _Every day_____!

Marc: Yeah, and the cheese is amazing! It tastes nothing like what we buy in the grocery stores here.

Noriko: _That's interesting_ I feel that way about Japanese food here, too. It's not quite the same.

B. **Work in a group to answer the questions. As you listen, use different ways to express interest and show you are paying attention.**

1. What food or drink would you recommend to someone who has a cold? Are there any traditional remedies you use in your family?

2. Which meal is the most important of the day to you? Why?

3. Can you cook? If so, what is a dish that you make particularly well? How do you make it?

4. Do you watch any cooking shows on TV? What do you watch and why do you like it?

| Unit Assignment | Express your opinion on an issue |

 In this assignment, you are going to pick a side on the topic of food science and present your opinions in a debate. As you prepare your opinions, think about the Unit Question, "How has science changed the food we eat?" and refer to the Self-Assessment checklist on page 126.

For alternative unit assignments, see the *Q: Skills for Success Teacher's Handbook.*

CONSIDER THE IDEAS

Tip Critical Thinking

In the Consider the Ideas discussion, you have to give reasons to **support** your opinion. When you support your opinion, you put ideas together from different sources. This allows you to use information in new ways.

Work in a group. Discuss the photos below. What do you think the advantages and disadvantages of each of these modifications are? Give reasons that support your opinion.

Strawberries preserved by radiation, a type of energy that can cause illness in large amounts.

Strawberries that have not been preserved by radiation.

A chicken that eats non-chemically treated food.

A chicken that eats food that has been treated with artificial chemicals to make it grow much larger than normal.

PREPARE AND SPEAK

A. **GATHER IDEAS** Think about the opinions you shared in the Consider the Ideas activity. Which ideas did you find most convincing? Make a short list of the three most convincing opinions on this issue.

_____

_____

_____

_____

B. ORGANIZE YOUR IDEAS Put the reasons from your list into the chart. Add details and examples to support the reasons.

Reasons	Details and examples
1.	
2.	
3.	

C. SPEAK Work with a partner who has different opinions on this issue. Take turns presenting your opinions and the reasons that support them. Show interest in your partner's opinions and ask questions to get more information. Refer to the Self-Assessment checklist below before you begin.

CHECK AND REFLECT

A. CHECK Think about the Unit Assignment as you complete the Self-Assessment checklist.

SELF-ASSESSMENT		
Yes	No	
☐	☐	I was able to speak easily about the topic.
☐	☐	My partner, group, class understood me.
☐	☐	I used comparative forms of adjectives and adverbs.
☐	☐	I used vocabulary from the unit.
☐	☐	I expressed interest during the conversation.
☐	☐	I used special intonation patterns.

B. REFLECT Discuss these questions with a partner.

What is something new you learned in this unit?

 Look back at the Unit Question. Is your answer different now than when you started this unit? If yes, how is it different? Why?

Track Your Success

Circle the words you learned in this unit.

Nouns
commodity `AWL`
consumer 🔑 `AWL`
controversy `AWL`
debate 🔑 `AWL`
ethics 🔑 `AWL`
hurdle
modification `AWL`
reaction 🔑 `AWL`
trait

Verbs
alter 🔑 `AWL`
compound `AWL`
consist (of) 🔑 `AWL`
consume `AWL`

Adjectives
adverse
artificial 🔑
disturbing 🔑
identical `AWL`
optimal
significant 🔑 `AWL`
substantial 🔑
superfluous
ultimate 🔑 `AWL`

🔑 Oxford 3000™ words
`AWL` Academic Word List

Check (✓) the skills you learned. If you need more work on a skill, refer to the page(s) in parentheses.

LISTENING	●	I can understand bias in a presentation. (p. 114)
VOCABULARY	●	I can recognize and use prefixes and suffixes. (pp. 118–119)
GRAMMAR	●	I can use comparative forms of adjectives and adverbs. (p. 120)
PRONUNCIATION	●	I can use common intonation patterns. (p. 122)
SPEAKING	●	I can express interest during a conversation. (p. 123)
LEARNING OUTCOME	●	I can participate in a debate on food science, stating and supporting my opinions about food modification.

UNIT **7**

From School to Work

LISTENING ●	listen for contrasting ideas
VOCABULARY ●	synonyms for formality
GRAMMAR ●	simple, compound, and complex sentences
PRONUNCIATION ●	highlighted words
SPEAKING ●	changing the topic

LEARNING OUTCOME ●

Participate in a group
discussion about people's
job qualifications and arrive
at a hiring decision.

Unit QUESTION

Is one road to success better than another?

PREVIEW THE UNIT

A **Discuss these questions with your classmates.**

What does being successful mean to you?

In your life, have you taken a traditional path or a non-traditional path to reach your educational and career goals? What are the advantages and disadvantages of each path?

Look at the photo. What do you think the person dressed as a chicken is doing? Could this kind of job eventually lead to success?

B **Read and discuss the Unit Question above with your classmates.**

🔊 Listen to *The Q Classroom*, Track 2 on CD 3, to hear other answers.

C Imagine you are meeting with a career counselor to decide what career you want to have. What kind of skills and experiences would help you get the job you desire? Complete the form below.

Career Questionnaire

Career Questionnaire

Name: _Hamad Al Hebsi_   Age: _19_

Answer these questions.
What is one skill or talent you wish you had?

leadership

What are some ways you could learn that skill or talent?

practicing
working in group

In what kinds of jobs or careers can you use that skill?

Most companies

Here are some ways to learn more about yourself and develop your skills. Check (✔) the ones that interest you.

- ☑ volunteer work
- ☐ teaching
- ☐ taking classes
- ☑ international travel
- ☑ working with animals
- ☐ reading how-to books

D Discuss these questions in a group.

1. What are some possible benefits of taking a year off from school or work to do something else? What might the disadvantages be? _You will have to catch up you will have progress but and succeed_

2. If you took a year off from school, what kinds of experiences would you seek? Why? _Work and get a job to see how things work (leadership)_

LISTENING 1 | Changing Ways to Climb the Ladder

VOCABULARY

Here are some words from Listening 1. Read the definitions. Then complete each sentence with the correct word.

> **advancement** (*n.*) a move forward
>
> **attitude** (*n.*) the way you think, feel, or behave toward someone or something
>
> **career path** (*n.*) the progression someone makes through his or her profession
>
> **climb the ladder** (*phr.*) to make progress in a career, much like using a ladder (climbing device) to move upward
>
> **count on** (*phr. v.*) to rely on someone or something
>
> **currently** (*adv.*) at the present time
>
> **devote** (*v.*) to give a lot of time or energy to something
>
> **loyal** (*adj.*) not changing your friendship or beliefs
>
> **model** (*n.*) a simple description of a system
>
> **radically** (*adv.*) very great (used about change)
>
> **stable** (*adj.*) not likely to move, change, or end
>
> **structure** (*n.*) the way the parts of something are put together or organized

1. This company is very ____stable____. They have a strong business plan, and they won't go out of business any time soon.

2. I'd like to help you, but I don't have any free time to ____devote____ to anything else right now. I spend all my time working on this project.

3. She has a very negative ____attitude____ toward her job. She never has anything good to say about it.

4. After she cut her hair, she looked ____radically____ different. It was such a big change that we didn't even recognize her when we saw her.

5. We have to work really hard to finish this project. Our boss is ____counting on____ us to finish it before Friday.

6. We are going to examine two different educational systems. Each _____model_____ has advantages and disadvantages.

7. I used to live in New York, but I moved. I _____currently_____ live in London, where I plan to stay for a couple of years.

8. I am thinking about accepting a new job, but I need to find out about the opportunities for _____advancement_____ first. I hope to be promoted soon.

9. Adán is very _____loyal_____ to our company. He has been offered jobs at other companies, but he always stays here.

10. Our department's _____structure_____ is very simple. I report to my boss, and he reports to the company president.

11. In this company, the usual _____career path_____ is to go from a salesperson to a senior manager in a few years.

12. It took me many years to _____climb the ladder_____ at this company. I started in the mailroom and I finally became a vice president last year.

PREVIEW LISTENING 1

Changing Ways to Climb the Ladder

You are going to hear an excerpt from a college lecture. In the lecture, a professor compares types of career paths.

Is it better to work for one company for many years or to change companies often to move up the ladder? Discuss with a partner. Give reasons for your opinion.

LISTEN FOR MAIN IDEAS

CD 3
Track 3

Read the statements. Then listen to the lecture. Write *T* (true) or *F* (false).

__T__ 1. Workers today are most likely to follow the new model in their careers.

__F__ 2. The typical career path has not changed much in the last few decades.

__F__ 3. The workers are more loyal to their company in the new model.

__T__ 4. The new model gives workers more choices about their personal lives.

__T__ 5. Some people choose to slow down their career advancement.

LISTEN FOR DETAILS

Listen again. Check (✓) the correct model for each statement.

Detail	Traditional model	New model
1. This model was more common in the 1950s in North America.	✓	☐
2. This model is currently more common in the United States.	☐	✓
3. Workers start at small companies to get experience.	☐	✓
4. Workers start at the bottom level of a big company.	✓	☐
5. Workers are loyal to one company and expect the company to take care of them.	✓	☐
6. Workers are not very loyal to the companies they work for.	☐	✓
7. Workers are like family in a company.	✓	☐
8. Workers get to the top of the ladder about four years faster.	☐	✓
9. This model is more flexible.	☐	✓
10. Companies don't often take care of workers when they retire.	☐	✓

 # WHAT DO YOU THINK?

Discuss the questions in a group.

1. Which model of climbing the ladder best matches your personality? *New model* Do you think this method would work well in your current or future career? *Yes*

2. What are some careers that would work well in each model? Give specific reasons for your choices. *CEO because its long way to get to*

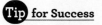

When speakers **contrast** things or ideas, they use special words and phrases to point out different characteristics of the things being discussed.

The simplest way to show a contrast is to use a comparative adjective + *than*.

> In fact, jumping up a few steps at a time . . . is actually quite common in this model, and now business leaders are getting to the top an average of four years **faster than** in the days of the traditional model.

Speakers also contrast things and ideas by using phrases such as *in contrast to, instead of, however, on the other hand, but, rather than,* and *whereas*. In Listening 1, the speaker contrasts the traditional model with the new model.

> **In contrast to** the single ladder model . . .
> **On the other hand**, often the worker is able to move to a position . . .
> In the new model, workers are starting their careers at smaller companies **rather than** bigger ones.

Tip for Success

To understand a speaker's meaning, it's important to analyze the words and phrases they use. The way a speaker organizes and presents information is usually an important clue about what the speaker wants you to know.

 CD 3 Track 5

A. Listen to a discussion about two candidates for a job. Fill in the blanks with the contrasting words and phrases you hear.

Mr. Doshi: Bob Quintero and Susan Miyamoto are the final candidates for the marketing position at our company. Bob has a degree from Harvard University in the U.S.A., _____whereas_____ Susan has a degree from Keio Business School in Japan.

Ms. Stanz: Bob and Susan both have good work experience. Bob has worked for five years at a small marketing company, _____but_____ Susan has worked for eight years at our company.

Mr. Doshi: Susan speaks more languages. Bob speaks Arabic and Spanish. _____However_____ Susan speaks French, Spanish, and Japanese.

Ms. Stanz: Bob has a lot of sales experience. _____On the other hand_____ Susan has a lot of experience at our company.

Mr Doshi: Hmmm. This is going to be a tough decision!

CD 3
Track 6

B. Listen to Listening 1 again. As you listen, complete the chart. Circle *Yes* or *No*.

	Traditional model	New model
Are employees loyal?	Yes / No	Yes / No
Is the model like a family?	Yes / No	Yes / No
Is it a single-ladder model?	Yes / No	Yes / No
Can workers advance quickly?	Yes / No	Yes / No
Is the model more common today?	Yes / No	Yes / No

LISTENING 2 | Life Experience Before College

VOCABULARY

Here are some words from Listening 2. Read the sentences. Then write each bold word next to the correct definition.

1. Taking time off before going to college is a new **concept** for most students in the United States. Many students have never thought about it before.

2. I am too afraid to leave my family, so I wouldn't **dare** travel alone in another country.

3. Many teenagers buy the clothes their friends buy. It's important to them to look like their **peers**.

4. I am not sure what time it is, but the sun is high in the sky, so I **figure** it must be around 12:00 p.m.

5. The **point** of the class was to prepare the students for the exam.

6. I am interested in that **particular** English class because I've heard that teacher is very good.

7. My new math class is much more **rigorous** than the last one. There are a lot more tests and the homework assignments are much harder.

8. My father has to **commute** two hours a day. It takes about an hour to drive between his home and his office.

9. You need to **log** the hours you worked on this sheet. Accurate records help us know how much time the job is taking.

| Listening and Speaking   135

10. Because so many people applied for the job my sister wanted, she had to **face** the possibility that she might not get hired.

11. My brother studied hard. He hoped it would **serve him well** by making it easier to get a good job after graduation.

12. The new student knew she would **stand out** because she didn't have a school uniform yet. She looked completely different from the other students.

a. ___figure___ (*v.*) to think or guess

b. ___serve him well___ (*phr.*) be an advantage to someone

c. ___particular___ (*adj.*) one specific person, place, thing, or time

d. ___peers___ (*n.*) people who are of the same age or social status

e. ___log___ (*v.*) to keep a written record of something

f. ___commute___ (*v.*) to travel from home to work every day by car, bus, or train

g. ___stand out___ (*phr. v.*) to be easily seen or noticed

h. ___dare___ (*v.*) to be brave enough to do something

i. ___face___ (*v.*) to deal with something unpleasant

j. ___rigorous___ (*adj.*) strict or demanding

k. ___concept___ (*n.*) an idea or basic principle

l. ___point___ (*n.*) the purpose of something

PREVIEW LISTENING 2

| Life Experience Before College

Some students go backpacking during their gap year.

You are going to listen to a radio program about students who take a "gap year," a year off between high school and college.

What are two reasons a student might want to take a year off from school? Discuss with a partner.

LISTEN FOR MAIN IDEAS

Read the statements. Then listen to the report. Write _T_ (true) or _F_ (false).

_F_ 1. Taking a gap year is a familiar concept in the United States.

_T_ 2. Gap years give students a chance to do something that really interests them.

_T_ 3. Taking a gap year requires a lot of planning.

_F_ 4. A gap year can hurt your resume.

_T_ 5. A gap year gives students an experience that many of their classmates in college don't have.

LISTEN FOR DETAILS

Read the questions. Then listen again. Circle the correct answer.

1. In which country is taking a gap year the least common?
   a. The United States
   b. Australia
   c. Great Britain

2. How did Antonia House become interested in traveling?
   a. She studied international relations in high school.
   b. She graduated from high school in Berlin.
   c. She spent a summer in France.

3. How does taking a year off school affect most students' grades?
   a. Their grades get worse.
   b. Their grades improve.
   c. There is no change in their grades.

4. Why does the speaker say that you need a lesson plan for a gap year?
   a. Because students should learn a lot from the experience.
   b. Because schools require it.
   c. Because students need to make arrangements ahead of time.

5. What advice does Trudee Goodman have for people interested in taking a gap year?
   a. Live with family members because it will save you money.
   b. Learn as much as possible through your experiences.
   c. Write about the experience on your resume so you can get a job.

Q WHAT DO YOU THINK?

A. Discuss the questions in a group.

1. If you could go anywhere in the world for a year, where would you go? Why?

   Europe to discover it and look around

2. If a close friend were considering taking off a year between high school and college, what advice would you give your friend?

   Do whatever you wanted to do.

3. What types of gap year activities could help prepare someone for a career in education? In banking?

   observation   Internship

B. Think about both Listening 1 and Listening 2 as you discuss the questions.

1. Think about your education or career. Which have you chosen more often: a traditional or non-traditional path? Why?

   Because it is better to stay with one family and learn a lot.

2. Has there ever been a time when you wanted to follow a non-traditional path but you didn't? Why didn't you?

   Yes, because it is risky to find another job.

| Vocabulary Skill | Using the dictionary | web+ |

English doesn't have strong rules of formality like some languages do. However, in some situations, it may be more appropriate to use certain words than others. In other more casual situations, it may be more appropriate to use less formal vocabulary, such as *phrasal verbs* and *idioms*. It is helpful to know when to use certain words and phrases.

A dictionary can guide you on which word to use. It will tell you if a word is informal or slang. If a definition doesn't say this, you can usually assume it is more formal or neutral.

Here are some examples.

PHR V ,hang a'round (…) (*informal*) to wait or stay near a place, not doing very much: *You hang around here in case he comes, and I'll go on ahead.* ,hang a'round with sb (*informal*) to spend a lot of time with someone ,hang 'back to remain

so·cial·ize /'souʃəˌlaɪz/ *verb* **1** [I] ~ (with sb) to meet and spend time with people in a friendly way, in order to enjoy yourself **SYN** MIX: *I enjoy socializing with the other students.* ◆ *Maybe you should socialize more.* **2** [T, often passive] ~ sb

---

those old photos—they may be valuable. ,hang 'out (*informal*) to spend a lot of time in a place: *The local kids hang out at the mall.* ⊃ related noun HANGOUT ,hang 'out with sb (*informal*)

The dictionary categorizes *hang around* and *hang out* as informal, but *socialize* has no description like this.

Here are some examples of appropriate use.

To your friends: I'll be <u>hanging around</u> all day.
To your family: I'm going to <u>hang out</u> with my friends today.
In a presentation: Most teenagers enjoy <u>socializing</u> with friends.

All dictionary entries are from the *Oxford Advanced American Dictionary for learners of English* © Oxford University Press 2011.

A. Read the pairs of sentences. Check (✓)the sentence that sounds more formal.

1. ☐ a. I can always **count on** you to help me out.
   ☑ b. I always **trust** that you'll assist me.

2. ☑ a. My brother must **select** a new suit for his interview.
   ☐ b. My brother has to **pick out** a new suit for his interview.

3. ☑ a. Lately I've been **enthusiastic about** volunteering.
   ☐ b. These days I'm really **into** the idea of volunteering.

4. ☐ a. I have to **cut back** on my work hours this semester.
   ☑ b. I have to **reduce** the number of hours I work this semester.

B. Read the sentences. Circle the answer that means almost the same as the bold word in each sentence.

1. I don't think we need to **hang around** here until he returns.
   a. wait
   b. climb
   c. joke

2. He was hoping to **get** a promotion at work.
   a. find
   b. receive
   c. give

3. You don't need to **put up with** a job that is so boring! Get a new one.
   a. tolerate
   b. look for
   c. create

4. Have you **looked into** other companies to work for? There must be many others like that one.
   a. answered
   b. counted
   c. researched

5. **Jumping up** a few steps at a time is almost impossible in a traditional career path.
   a. bouncing
   b. advancing
   c. returning

6. I've been working so hard at school. I'm **worn out**. I need to rest!
   a. prepared
   b. tired
   c. worried

C. Circle the appropriate synonym to complete each sentence. Then work with a partner to read the conversations.

Interviewee: Good morning. I'm here to (have a word / speak) with Mr. Simon.

Receptionist: Please (wait / hang around) here. I'll tell Mr. Simon you're here.

Mr. Simon: Good morning. So let's (get going / begin). Can you tell me why you'd like to work for this company?

Interviewee: Well, I'm really (interested in / into) your products.

SPEAKING

Using a variety of sentence types will allow you to express a range of ideas in your speeches and presentations.

There are **three basic kinds** of **sentences: simple**, **compound**, and **complex**.

A **simple sentence** is one independent clause (one subject + verb combination) that makes sense by itself.

> I want to do research.
> subject verb

A **compound sentence** is made of at least two independent clauses joined together with a conjunction, such as *for, and, nor, but, or, yet, so,* or *as.*

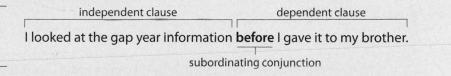

> independent clause   independent clause
> The worker went to a new company, and she moved up the ladder faster.
> conjunction

A **complex sentence** is made of at least one independent clause and one dependent clause. A dependent clause is not a complete idea by itself. The dependent clause begins with a subordinating conjunction, such as *because, since, after, although, if,* or *when.*

> independent clause   dependent clause
> I looked at the gap year information **before** I gave it to my brother.
> subordinating conjunction

If the dependent clause comes before the independent clause, then a comma separates the two clauses.

> Although it is less stable, many workers prefer the new career model.

A. Read each sentence. Is the sentence simple, compound, or complex? Circle the correct answer. Then compare answers with a partner.

1. This model is similar to the business cultures in other countries.
   simple / compound / complex

2. The right training is important, but what other steps do you need to take to reach your career goal?
   simple / compound / complex

3. Because he moved in and out of companies as positions opened, he could move faster toward his career goal.

simple / compound / (complex)

4. Many countries in Asia follow this business model.

(simple) / compound / complex

5. After she worked for a year, she was ready to return to school.

simple / compound / (complex)

B. Read the conversation. Rewrite it in your notebook. Combine the simple sentences using the words in parentheses. Then practice the conversation.

When Sam was walking down the street, He saw his friend Inez. **(when)**

Inez: Hey, Sam! How did your job interview go?

Sam: Hi! It went really well, ~~and~~ I might get the job! (and)

Inez: That's great! When will you know for sure?

Sam: They'll make the decision this afternoon; ~~after that,~~ They'll call me. (after)

Inez: Good luck! By the way, did you hear about Angela?

Sam: No. I sent her an email last week, ~~but~~ She hasn't answered it. (but)

Inez: Well, she's taking a year off to study penguins. She's going to Antarctica, ~~because~~ (because)

Sam: Wow! That sounds amazing.

Inez: Yeah. It seems like an incredible opportunity, ~~although~~ I can't imagine living in Antarctica. (although)

Sam: What about you? How are you going to spend the summer?

Inez: I applied to two programs. I might volunteer for a group that builds houses for poor people, ~~or~~ I might work in a program for street kids. (or)

Sam: Those both sound like good causes! ~~and~~ They'll look good on your college application. (and)

Inez: Yeah. I need to do something big, ~~if~~ I want to get into a good school! (if)

Sam: Well, I should get home, ~~so~~ I can wait for the call about the job. (so)

Inez: See you later!

CD 3
Track 9

Speakers typically use a higher pitch and longer vowel sounds to emphasize or highlight content words.

For example, a speaker might stress the words in the following sentence normally.

<u>Colleges</u> say a <u>gap year</u> doesn't <u>have</u> to be <u>costly</u>.

Sometimes a speaker will shift the stress from this regular stress pattern to emphasize an idea. **Highlighted words** often present a contrast or a correction. A speaker who wants to emphasize that taking a gap year can be inexpensive might place a heavier stress on *have*.

<u>Colleges</u> say a <u>gap year</u> doesn't **<u>have</u>** to be <u>costly</u>.

Or, if the speaker wants to communicate that this idea is supported by colleges but not by students, a heavier stress might be shifted to *Colleges*.

<u>Colleges</u> say that a <u>gap year</u> doesn't <u>have</u> to be <u>costly</u>.

CD 3
Track 10

A. Listen to each sentence. Underline the highlighted words you hear. Then practice saying the sentences with a partner.

1. I would <u>love</u> to take a gap year to work in India.

2. If I had to pick just <u>one place</u> to go, it would be Turkey.

3. When <u>Carlos was there</u>, they didn't have the volunteer program.

4. Chris and Ilona are going too? Hassan told me <u>they're</u> not going.

5. You'll learn <u>a lot</u> while you're there, and you'll have <u>so much</u> fun!

CD 3
Track 11

B. Listen to each sentence. What is the speaker's meaning? Circle the correct answer.

1. I would like to get a job in Africa taking care of wild animals.
   a. I am interested in Africa.
   b. I hope I can get the job.
   c. My main interest is wild animals.

2. I change jobs often. My father's career path was more traditional.
   a. My career path is different from my father's career path.
   b. I like to change jobs to help my career.
   c. I prefer traditional career paths.

3. I think I can build skills for this career if I take a year off to study.
    a. I'm not sure I can build my skills.
    b. I can only build skills by taking time off.
    c. If I take a year off, I have to study the whole time.

4. The best reason to take a gap year is the chance to learn about yourself.
    a. This reason is very important.
    b. Learning is very important.
    c. You are very important.

5. No one ever told me that the group would leave before school is over.
    a. I thought the group was staying at the school.
    b. I thought the group would leave after school is over.
    c. They told other people, but they forgot to tell me.

volunteering at a summer camp

C. Work with a partner. Practice the conversation. Stress the bold words.

A: Have you heard about Laura's **latest** plan?

B: No. What does she want to do **now**?

A: She says she **finally** decided to volunteer at a summer camp.

B: She wants to **volunteer**? I thought she wanted a paying job.

A: Well, it seems she changed her mind **again**.

B: Hmm. She **would** be good at it. She's a natural leader.

A: She's good at **lots** of things, so I'm sure she'll think of more ideas.

B: Yeah. She probably won't figure out where to go until **right** before she leaves!

| Speaking Skill | Changing the topic | web+ |

In the middle of a conversation you may want to **change the topic** a little. However, you don't want to sound like you are uninterested in what someone else is saying. To let someone know you want to add something related to the topic, you can use *transition phrases*. Here are some examples.

By the way . . .
Speaking of (previous topic) . . .
That reminds me . . .

For example, if your friend is talking about a movie he saw yesterday, you can say, "Oh, speaking of movies, did you hear about that new action movie?"

Sometimes you remember something in the middle of a conversation that is not at all related to the current topic. It is important to let others know you are about to switch to an unrelated topic. Here are some expressions you can use.

Hold that thought.
Oh, before I forget . . .
Oh, I wanted to tell / ask you . . .

For example, you and two friends are talking about a concert. You suddenly remember you wanted to ask them about an important class project. You wait for a short pause in the conversation and then say, "Oh, before I forget, I wanted to ask you if you want to go over the project notes today."

To return to the previous topic, you can then use phrases like these.

But you were saying . . .
Back to (the topic) . . .
Anyway . . .

CD 3
Track 12

A. Complete the conversation with the words you hear. Then practice the conversation with a partner.

A: I've had a very long day. I just came from my job.

B: ___That reminds me___. I need to get your resume. My company is hiring, and you would be perfect for the position.

A: Really? That's great! You make your job sound fun.

B: It is, most of the time. We all get along well at work.

A: Oh, ___I wanted to ask you___ if you have time to help me with my homework.

B: Sure I can. We'll do it after class.

A: ___Anyway___, I'd love to give you my resume. I've been looking for a new job.

B: I know. ___Speaking of which___, my boss says she's interviewing people next week. Are you free in the morning?

A: I'll make sure I'm available if she calls me.

B: ___Hold that thought,___ I have to get to my next class. We'll talk about this later.

A: See you.

B. Work in a group. Discuss the questions. Practice changing and returning to topics.

1. What does it mean to be successful? How do you define it for yourself?

2. What are the characteristics of a dream job? What steps should someone take, traditional and non-traditional, to get their dream job?

3. What type of person is most likely to achieve his or her dream job?

Unit Assignment   Reach a group decision

In this assignment, you are going to have a discussion in order to reach a group decision. As you prepare for your discussion, think about the Unit Question, "Is one road to success better than another?" and refer to the Self-Assessment checklist on page 148.

For alternative unit assignments, see the *Q: Skills for Success Teacher's Handbook.*

CONSIDER THE IDEAS

Complete the activities.

1. Read the following advertisement for a job opening.

GapStaff needs you!

GapStaff is looking for a consultant to join our exciting and energetic team. Consultants are responsible for working with clients to organize their gap year opportunities. Candidates for the job should be well organized, interested in working with students, and passionate about traveling, learning, and volunteering.

The minimum requirements for the position are an undergraduate degree and five years of related work experience.
Travel experience and the ability to speak another language are a plus.

Call 1-888-555-5210

---

2. Read the information about four people who applied for the GapStaff consultant job. Then listen to their personal statements. Take notes in the chart.

Personal information	Notes

Susan Jones (age 59)
Education:
  A.A. in Journalism from Central Texas College
  B.A. in English from the University of Chicago
Work Experience:
  English teacher in Poland (3 years)
  English teacher in Thailand (2 years)
  English teacher in Peru (6 years)	

Doug Orman (age 43)
Education:
  B.A. in History from the University of Maryland
  M.A. in History from the University of Maryland
Work Experience:
  Teaching Assistant at the University of Maryland (3 years)
  Lecturer at the University of Maryland (16 years)	

Narayan Tej (age 24)
Education:
  B.A. Tourism from Columbia Southern University
Work Experience:
  Part-time work at the tourism desk of the Hilton Hotel	

Teresa Lopez (age 35)
Education:
  B.S. in Business Administration from National
    American University
Work Experience:
  Guide at local art museum (3 years)
  Receptionist for travel agent (2 years)
  Receptionist for gym (5 years)
  Salesperson at a clothing store (2 years)	

PREPARE AND SPEAK

A. GATHER IDEAS Imagine you are part of a GapStaff group choosing the best candidate for the position. Consider the four job applicants. Who do you think is most qualified? Who is least qualified? Rank the applicants from 1 (your first choice) to 4 (your last choice) based on your notes in the chart above.

_____ Susan Jones   _____ Narayan Tej

_____ Doug Orman   _____ Teresa Lopez

Activity B asks you to **rank** the candidates. When you rank things, you make a judgment about different characteristics. This is an important higher-level thinking skill.

B. **ORGANIZE YOUR IDEAS** Why did you rank the candidates in this order? Complete the chart with brief notes.

Candidate name	Reasons for ranking
1.	
2.	
3.	
4.	

C. **SPEAK** Work in a group. Discuss who should be hired for the position. Share your reasons with the group. Work to reach a group decision on the best person to hire. Refer to the Self-Assessment checklist below before you begin.

CHECK AND REFLECT

A. **CHECK** Think about the Unit Assignment as you complete the Self-Assessment checklist.

SELF-ASSESSMENT		
Yes	No	
☐	☐	I was able to speak easily about the topic.
☐	☐	My partner, group, class understood me.
☐	☐	I listened for contrasting ideas.
☐	☐	I used vocabulary from the unit.
☐	☐	I changed the topic in the discussion.
☐	☐	I highlighted words to emphasize ideas as I spoke.

B. **REFLECT** Discuss these questions with a partner.

What is something new you learned in this unit?

 Look back at the Unit Question. Is your answer different now than when you started this unit? If yes, how is it different? Why?

Track Your Success

Circle the words you learned in this unit.

Nouns
advancement
attitude 🔑 AWL
career path
concept 🔑 AWL
model 🔑
peer
point 🔑
structure 🔑 AWL

Verbs
commute
dare 🔑
devote 🔑 AWL
face 🔑
figure 🔑
log

Phrasal verbs
count on
stand out

Adjectives
loyal 🔑
particular 🔑
rigorous
stable 🔑 AWL

Adverbs
currently 🔑
radically

Phrases/Idioms
climb the ladder
serve one well

🔑 Oxford 3000™ words
AWL Academic Word List

Check (✓) the skills you learned. If you need more work on a skill, refer to the page(s) in parentheses.

LISTENING	●	I can listen for contrasting Ideas. (p. 134)
VOCABULARY	●	I can use synonym for formality. (p. 138)
GRAMMAR	●	I can use simple, compound, and complex sentences. (p. 141)
PRONUNCIATION	●	I can highlight words to emphasize ideas. (p. 143)
SPEAKING	●	I can change the topic. (p. 144)
LEARNING OUTCOME	●	I can participate in a group discussion about people's job qualifications and arrive at a hiring decision.

UNIT 8

Discovery

LISTENING ● listening for signal words and phrases
VOCABULARY ● collocations with prepositions
GRAMMAR ● indirect speech
PRONUNCIATION ● linked words with vowels
SPEAKING ● using questions to maintain listener interest

Q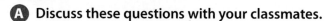

Unit QUESTION

How can chance discoveries affect our lives?

PREVIEW THE UNIT

A Discuss these questions with your classmates.

The journalist Franklin Adams once wrote, "I find that a great part of the information I have was acquired by looking up something and finding something else on the way." What do you think he meant?

Have you ever discovered something important by accident? If so, what was it? How did the discovery affect you?

Look at the photo. What is this man doing? What has he found?

B Discuss the Unit Question above with your classmates.

Listen to *The Q Classroom*, Track 14 on CD 3, to hear other answers.

C The products below were all discovered or invented by accident. Check (✓) the three products you think have had the greatest effect on the world. Compare your choices with a partner. Discuss reasons for your choices.

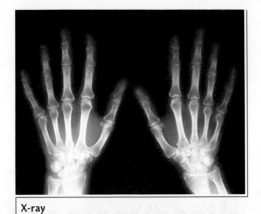
X-ray

potato chips

dynamite

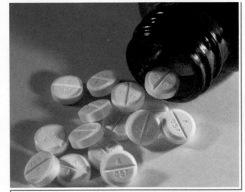
penicillin

microwave oven

plastic

D If you discover something by accident, how do you know if the discovery is important? Discuss with a partner.

LISTENING 1 | The Power of Serendipity

VOCABULARY

Here are some words from Listening 1. Read the sentences. Circle the answer that best matches the meaning of each bold word.

1. Please keep **flammable** objects away from the stove. It isn't safe while we're cooking. *Gasoline is highly flammable.*
    a. easily breaks
    b. easily burns

2. My car is **unreliable**. I often have to take the bus to work because my car won't start. *Some people are unreliable on arriving on time.*
    a. cannot be depended on
    b. cannot be understood

3. Nick made an **inadvertent** discovery as he drove to the airport. He took the wrong exit, turned left, and was at the airport. Now he's happy he knows a faster route.
    a. not done on purpose
    b. not important to remember

4. Solar energy is a great source of power but not enough people use it. We must learn to **exploit** it more fully.
    a. to use something for benefit
    b. to save something

5. After the hurricane, the citizens worked hard to repair the damage and make their city beautiful again. They turned the disaster into a **triumph**.
    a. success
    b. misfortune

6. There is an **obvious** connection between getting overtired and getting sick. *There is an obvious difference between a car and a plane.*
    a. hard to understand
    b. easy to see

7. We need a strong **adhesive** to hang the poster on the wall. Otherwise, the poster will just fall off.
    a. glue
    b. surface

8. Not long ago, there was no wireless communication. But now, living without it is **inconceivable** for many people.
   a. hard to find
   b. hard to imagine

9. Josh and I have **vastly** different taste in clothes.
   a. hardly
   b. very greatly

10. Many people like to use websites to **interact** with people with similar interests.
    a. find people's contact information
    b. talk with other people

    Teachers interact with students using blackboard.

11. Attendance at our monthly meetings is **mandatory**. Everyone must attend.
    a. exciting
    b. required

    Attending classes is mandatory for all students.

12. According to my auto mechanic, **synthetic** oil is better for my car than regular oil. He says man-made oil lasts longer.
    a. not natural
    b. not expensive

a scientific experiment

PREVIEW LISTENING 1

The Power of Serendipity

You are going to listen to a report about how accidents and chance events led to some important scientific developments.

Scientists work hard to keep control of their work and make sure mistakes do not happen. How often do you think chance plays a role in scientific discoveries? Discuss with a partner.

LISTEN FOR MAIN IDEAS

Read the statements. Then listen to the report. Write *T* (true) or *F* (false).

_T_ 1. Serendipity is looking for one thing and finding something more valuable by accident.

_F_ 2. Food serendipity has little to do with animals.

_F_ 3. Most products we purchase today aren't the result of serendipity.

_T_ 4. Serendipity is a major source of innovation.

_F_ 5. Serendipity is a luxury that is nice but not necessary.

LISTEN FOR DETAILS

Listen again. Then match each scientific breakthrough with the accident or chance event that led to it.

Scientific Breakthrough

a. The effects of coffee were discovered.

b. Rubber became a useful product.

c. Cheese was made for the first time.

d. Dynamite was discovered.

e. Silly Putty® was invented.

f. Post-It Notes® were invented.

Accident or Chance Event

_D_ 1. Alfred Nobel put flammable medicine on a cut.

_B_ 2. A sticky substance was mixed with sulfur and dropped on a hot stove.

_A_ 3. An Ethiopian goat herder watched his goats eating.

_C_ 4. Nomads traveled on camels carrying milk in stomach bags.

_F_ 5. A scientist tried to invent a new form of adhesive, but it was very weak.

_E_ 6. Scientists tried to create synthetic rubber but failed.

Q WHAT DO YOU THINK?

Discuss these questions in a group.

1. Several of the products mentioned in the report were invented by scientists who were working hard to invent something else. What do you think this tells us about serendipity? Is serendipity simply a matter of chance, or are there other reasons?

2. Some of the research and experiments mentioned in the report are paid for by businesses. Do you think this is a wise investment for the businesses? Why or why not?

3. One speaker in the report says serendipity is mandatory. Do you agree with this? Give reasons to support your answer.

Listening Skill	Listening for signal words and phrases	web

When you are listening to a speaker and hear a word you don't recognize, continue listening for a definition. Sometimes, speakers will give the meaning of a word they just used. Good speakers use **signal words and phrases** to clarify what they mean. Here are some examples.

> This refers to . . .
> This means . . .
> A(n) ___ is . . .
> What I mean by ___ is . . .
> What is ___? It's . . .
> ___, or ___, . . .

Sometimes speakers say the same idea in a different way to make the meaning clear. Here are some ways that speakers signal they are about to provide an explanation.

> What I mean is . . .
> In other words . . .
> Here's what this means . . .
> In simpler terms, this means . . .

Listening for signals like these will help you to understand important words and concepts that speakers introduce.

A. Read and listen to the lecture. Fill in the blanks with the signal words and phrases you hear.

Professor: Many people use a microwave oven every day. How many of you know that the microwave oven was the result of an accident?

During World War II, scientists invented the magnetron, _____which is_____ a kind of electronic tube that produces microwaves. We're all familiar with microwave ovens, but _____what is_____ a microwave? Well, it's a very short electromagnetic wave.

a magnetron

Anyway, in 1946, an engineer named Dr. Percy Spencer was standing close to a magnetron he was testing. He suddenly noticed something unusual. He felt something warm in his shirt pocket. He reached in and discovered that the candy bar in his pocket was a hot, chocolaty mess. _____In other words_____, the candy bar had melted. Dr. Spencer was so excited because he realized that microwaves could raise the internal temperature of food. _____In other words_____, microwaves were able to cook food from the inside out! And do it very quickly.

Dr. Spencer saw the possibilities here. His next step was to build a metal box into which he fed microwave power that couldn't escape. He put various foods inside the metal box and tested cooking them. In time, he invented something that would revolutionize cooking—the ubiquitous microwave oven. By that _____I mean_____ that we see microwave ovens just about everywhere.

B. Read the sentences. Complete each sentence with a signal word or phrase from the Listening Skill box. Then practice reading the sentences with a partner.

1. It was all by chance. _____This means_____ the invention was the result of serendipity.

2. There were endless possibilities. _____In other words_____ the new discovery could be used for many different things.

A light bulb went off.

3. Then a light bulb went off. ___Which means___ I realized what I had to do to make it work correctly.

4. It was a stupendous success. ___This means___ it worked better than anyone had hoped.

5. Soon it will be commonplace. ___In other words,___ everyone will own one and love it!

LISTENING 2 | Against All Odds, Twin Girls Reunited

VOCABULARY

Here are some words from Listening 2. Read the definitions. Then complete each sentence with the correct word.

> **ache** (*v.*) to feel a dull, continuous pain   *I had a headache this morning.*
> **adopt** (*v.*) to become the legal parent of a child who is not your own
> **alert** (*adj.*) quick to notice things; aware   *We got alerted about snowfall.*
> **biological** (*adj.*) connected by direct genetic relationship
> **deprived** (*adj.*) without enough food, money, or other basic things
> **face to face** (*phr.*) close together and looking at each other
> **in all probability** (*phr.*) very likely to happen
> **miracle** (*n.*) a lucky event that you did not expect or think was possible
> **odds** (*n.*) the chance of something happening
> **reunion** (*n.*) a social event for a group of people who have not seen each other for a long time

1. Amy and Ed have one son. Next year they want to ___adopt___ another baby boy. Then they will have two sons.

2. I'm looking forward to our class ___reunion___. I haven't seen my classmates in so many years!

3. Derek is usually late to class. ___In all probability___, he'll be late today as well.

4. My brother may be adopted, but I feel like he's my ___biological___ brother.

5. Ever since Lisa was a baby, she has been very ____alert____. She seems to notice everything that happens around her.

6. Eric was in a serious car accident, but the ____odels____ that he will recover completely are very good.

7. I think I'm getting old. Every morning my knees ____ache____, and my back hurts, too.

8. Although we have texted and emailed each other many times, Janet and I have never met ____face to face____. I hope I get to meet her someday.

9. I hardly ever see my brother because we're both so busy. We considered it a ____miracle____ when we were finally able to visit our parents at the same time.

10. Lucas was born in a very poor city and was ____deprived____ of many things. He rarely had a home to sleep in.

PREVIEW LISTENING 2

Against All Odds, Twin Girls Reunited

You are going to listen to a report about how twins were reunited by chance.

If two siblings were separated as babies and then met many years later, do you think they would still feel an emotional connection? Check (✓) *yes* or *no*. Discuss your answer with a partner.

☑ yes
☐ no

LISTEN FOR MAIN IDEAS

CD 3
Track 18

Listen to the report. Then answer the questions.

1. How did Eileen Surrey and Andrea Ettingoff first get to know each other?

   They exchanged emails with pictures

2. Why was Annie's mother, Andrea, shocked when she saw the photograph of Renee?

   Because they looked the same.

3. How did Renee and Annie get along when they saw each other for the second time at a reunion?

They were best friends

4. Why did the parents decide to have a DNA test performed?

To check if they're really biological sisters

5. What did the DNA test results show?

They are twins

6. How did Renee react to the test results?

They were very happy.

LISTEN FOR DETAILS

CD 3
Track 19

Listen again. Then answer the questions.

1. Where were Renee and Annie born?
   a. They were born in Florida.
   b. They were born in China.

2. How did Renee behave when she first went to live with her adoptive parents?
   a. She cried a lot.
   b. She slept a lot.

3. At first, what did Eileen Surrey believe was the cause of Renee's behavior?
   a. She believed Renee was ill.
   b. She believed Renee was scared.

4. How did Annie behave when she went to live with her new parents?
   a. She ate a lot.
   b. She cried a lot.

5. What advice did Eileen Surrey give Andrea about dealing with Annie's eating problem?
   a. She suggested that they share a plate in the middle of the table.
   b. She suggested that they let Annie eat as much as she wanted.

6. Why did Eileen and Andrea exchange photographs of their daughters?
   a. They noticed that their daughters shared the same birthday.
   b. They noticed that their daughters were from the same orphanage.

7. What reason do Renee and Annie give for why they would like to live next door to each other?
   a. They want to go to the same school.
   b. They want to play together.

8. According to Eileen Surrey, why did Renee never want to be alone?
   a. She was scared of her new parents.
   b. She had never been alone, even before she was born.

WHAT DO YOU THINK?

A. Discuss the questions in a group.

1. Do you think it is a good idea to encourage the relationship between the two sisters? If so, do you think these families are doing enough to help the sisters?

2. According to the mothers, the girls seemed to "remember" each other and have a natural bond. How would you explain the girls' immediate relationship?

B. Think about both Listening 1 and Listening 2 as you discuss the questions.

1. In Listening 1 you heard about some scientific discoveries that resulted from accidents. In Listening 2 you heard about a personal discovery that was made when two strangers made contact online. Do you think all these discoveries were really the result of chance? What other factors may have helped lead to these discoveries?

2. Can you think of any ways in which chance discoveries may have a negative effect on our lives? Discuss any examples you can think of. Consider both scientific discoveries and personal discoveries.

Collocations are combinations of words that are used together frequently. For example, some adjectives and verbs are commonly used with particular prepositions. Part of learning to use these adjectives and verbs correctly involves knowing which prepositions are often used with them.

Here are a few **adjective + preposition** collocations.

embarrassed about	happy about	ready for
fond of	proud of	upset about

Here are a few **verb + preposition** collocations.

complain about	believe in	decide on
arrive at	trip over	approve of

Some collocations are *separable*. A direct object can come between the verb and the preposition.

bring the twins **together**   **combine** the rubber **with** sulfur

Paying attention to collocations will help you develop your fluency because you will know which words to use together.

CD 3
Track 20   **A. Listen to these sentences. Circle the prepositions that you hear.**

1. She was looking around, and she was very aware _____ what was going on.
   a. for
   b. over
   c. of

2. Since it's important _____ Annie, I think it's important to all of us.
   a. at
   b. for
   c. to

3. Because we hardly ever fight, and we agree _____ a lot of things.
   a. about
   b. on
   c. in

Look up verbs
and adjectives
in a collocations
dictionary to find out
which prepositions
they are commonly
used with.

4. My daughter has not asked me a single question about her birth family or

searching _____ them since she's got Annie in her life.

a. with

b. about

c. for

B. Read the sentences. Complete each sentence with a collocation from the box.

afraid of	stumbling over
filled ___ with	thank for
mix ___ with	

1. The idea is to have them interact in open play-like environments, to encourage

them not to be ____afraid of____ failure, and to build together.

2. Serendipity refers to looking for one thing and ____stumbling over____

something else.

3. Rubber was an unreliable, smelly mess until Charles Goodyear

____mixed____ it ____with____ sulfur.

4. We have Horace Walpole, an eighteenth-century English writer and

politician, to ____thank for____ the word *serendipity*.

5. Nomads ____filled____ them ____with____ milk and hung

them from their saddles as they rode live camels.

SPEAKING

Grammar | **Indirect speech** | web+

Direct speech reports what someone said using the speaker's exact words.

⌐ The teacher said, "You will have a test on Friday."

Indirect speech also reports what someone said, but without using the speaker's exact words.

⌐ The teacher said we would have a test on Monday.

When using indirect speech to report what a speaker said in the past, the verb the speaker used must be changed to a past form.

> **Direct speech:** Moss said, "The whole idea **is** to bring together people with vastly different backgrounds."
> **Indirect speech:** Moss said the whole idea **was** to bring together people with vastly different backgrounds.

When using indirect speech to report a *yes/no* question, use *if* or *whether*.

> **Direct speech:** Annie asked her mother, "Is Renee from China?"
> **Indirect speech:** Annie asked her mother **if** Renee was from China.

When using indirect speech to report a *wh-* question, use the same *wh-* word as the speaker.

> **Direct speech:** He asked the professor, "**When** was the microwave oven developed?"
> **Indirect speech:** He asked the professor **when** the microwave oven was developed.

When using indirect speech to report someone's belief, it is not necessary to shift the verb to a past form.

> **Direct speech:** Annie said, "**It's** fun being with Renee."
> **Indirect speech:** Annie said that **it's** fun being with Renee.

 CD 3 Track 21

A. Listen to each sentence. Is it direct or indirect speech? Circle the correct answer.

1. a. direct   (b.) indirect

2. (a.) direct   b. indirect

3. (a.) direct   b. indirect

4. a. direct   (b.) indirect

164   **UNIT 8** | How can chance discoveries affect our lives?

5. a. direct   b. indirect

6. a. direct   b. indirect

7. a. direct   b. indirect

8. a. direct   b. indirect

B. **Read these sentences. Rewrite each sentence changing the direct speech to indirect speech. Then work with a partner to practice saying both versions of each sentence.**

1. Martha Teichner said, "The list of serendipity stories is as long as the history of discovery."

   Martha Teichner said that the list of serendipity stories was as long as the history of discovery

2. The professor said, "Many people use a microwave oven every day."

   The professor said that many people used a microwave oven everyday

3. The professor said, "He invented something that would revolutionize cooking."

   The professor said that he invented something that would revolutionize cooking.

4. The professor said, "We see microwave ovens just about everywhere."

   The professor said that they see microwave ovens just about everywhere.

5. Andrea said, "I was shocked."

   Andrea said that she was shocked.

6. Renee said, "The hole in my heart is getting smaller."

   Renee said that the hole in her heart is getting smaller.

7. Renee said, "I am Annie," and Annie said, "I am Renee."

   Renee said that she's Annie and Annie said that she's Renee.

8. In her message, Eileen said, "I don't know if my baby knows Andrea's baby."

   In her message Eilee said that she didn't know if her baby knows Andrea's baby

Pronunciation	Linked words with vowels	web

Speakers often link words together so that the last sound in one word connects to the first sound in the next word. Sometimes it's difficult to tell where one word ends and another word begins.

When words ending with the vowel sounds *-ee*, *-ey*, *-ah*, and *-oh* are followed by a word beginning with a vowel, the vowels in the two words link together with the /y/ sound. Because the words are pronounced with no pause in between them, it may sound like the second word begins with /y/.

CD 3
Track 22

Listen to these sentences and notice how the bold words link with a /y/ sound.

> She always wants to say it.
>
> Tell me why it's important to be early.

When words ending with the vowel sounds *-oo*, *-oh*, and *-ah* are followed by a word beginning with a vowel, the vowels link together with the /w/ sound. Because the words are pronounced with no pause in between them, it may sound like the second word begins with /w/.

CD 3
Track 22

Listen to these sentences and notice how the bold words link with a /w/ sound.

> Can she go out with us?
>
> Please show us your new invention.

Linking words is an important part of fluent pronunciation. Practicing this skill will help to make your speech sound more natural.

CD 3
Track 23

A. Listen to these pairs of words. Then repeat the words.

1. early age
2. very alert
3. stay awake
4. fly out
5. you opened
6. know about
7. go over
8. how interesting

CD 3
Track 24

B. Listen to these sentences. Draw a line to show where the vowels link together. Write *y* or *w* between the words to show the linking sound. Then practice saying the sentences with a partner.

1. Annie also seemed very deprived, because they noticed she ate as if she'd never eat again.

2. After the fact, serendipity always seems so obvious.

3. Because we hardly ever fight, we agree on a lot of things.

4. Eventually somebody else at the company thought maybe it would keep bookmarks from falling out of his hymnal at church.

5. Try and spot the next big thing.

6. So after you opened the file, can you recall how it felt?

Using questions to maintain listener interest web+

When giving a presentation or telling a story, you can keep listeners interested by asking them questions. At the beginning of a presentation, a question can spark interest in your topic. During a presentation, a question can help maintain interest. At the end of your presentation, a question encourages your listeners to keep thinking about your topic after you are done speaking.

There are two main types of questions that speakers ask an audience.

Rhetorical questions are questions that do not require an answer from the audience. Use them to get your listeners to think about what you are about to say.

> What was the most important invention of the twentieth century?
> We all might not agree, but today I'd like to talk to you about one
> very important invention . . .

Interactive questions are questions for which you expect an answer. Use them to interact with your listeners and encourage them to respond to what you are saying.

> **Presenter:** Does anyone know who discovered the law of gravity?
> **Audience member:** I think it was Isaac Newton.
> **Presenter:** That's right. And the story behind that discovery is an
> interesting one . . .

Using questions when you present is an effective way to keep the audience paying attention and to help them remember your most important points.

 CD 3 Track 25

A. Listen to the excerpts from lectures. Which questions are rhetorical and which are interactive? Circle the correct answer.

1. (rhetorical)   interactive

2. (rhetorical)   interactive

3. rhetorical   (interactive)

4. rhetorical   (interactive)

CD 3
Track 26

B. Listen to this short story about another accidental invention. Then answer the questions.

The Popsicle™

The Popsicle™ is a popular summertime treat in the United States. Kids have been enjoying them for decades. But most people don't know that the Popsicle™ was invented by an 11-year-old.

In 1905, Frank Epperson filled a cup with water and fruit-flavored "soda powder," a mix that was used to make a popular drink. Frank left his drink outside on his porch with a stir stick in it. He forgot all about it and went to bed. That night, the temperature dropped to below freezing in San Francisco, where Frank lived. When he woke up the next morning, he discovered that his fruit drink had frozen to the stir stick. He pulled the frozen mixture out of the cup by the stick, creating a fruit-flavored ice treat.

In 1923, Frank Epperson began making and selling his ice treats in different flavors. By 1928, Frank had sold over 60 million Popsicles™, and his business had made him very wealthy. Nowadays, over three million Popsicles™ are sold each year.

Popsicles™ aren't the only invention made by accident. But they might be the tastiest.

Tip for Success

When asking interactive questions, make sure to give your listeners enough time to answer.

1. Which of these would be the most appropriate rhetorical question to start a presentation about this story?
   a. What is one of the tastiest treats ever invented?
   b. What year did Frank Epperson sell his first Popsicle™?
   c. What is the number of Popsicles™ sold every year?

2. Which of these would be the most appropriate interactive question to ask about how Frank Epperson discovered his frozen treat?
   a. What was Frank's favorite flavor of soda water?
   b. What city did Frank live in?
   c. What do you think Frank found the next morning when he went outside?

3. Which of these would be the most appropriate question to ask at the conclusion of your presentation?
   a. Why did Frank choose the name Popsicle™?
   b. Doesn't a Popsicle™ sound tasty right now?
   c. Which is the most popular flavor?

C. In a group, practice telling the story in Activity B in your own words. Use questions to keep your listeners' interest.

In this section, you are going to tell a story about a personal discovery you made by accident. As you prepare your story, think about the Unit Question, "How can chance discoveries affect our lives?" and refer to the Self-Assessment checklist on page 170.

For alternative unit assignments, see the *Q: Skills for Success Teacher's Handbook*.

CONSIDER THE IDEAS

Look at the list of ideas about discovery. Choose the four ideas you think are the most important factors in making any kind of discovery. Then discuss your answers and reasons with a partner.

desire to succeed	making difficult choices	taking chances
fortunate accidents	previous experience	time
intelligence	self-confidence	tools and resources
luck or chance	supportive people	trying new things

PREPARE TO SPEAK

A. GATHER IDEAS Think about your discussion in the Consider the Ideas activity. Write down some brief notes on what you discussed. Include reasons that support your ideas.

Important Ideas about Chance Discoveries

_____

_____

_____

_____

_____

Tip Critical Thinking

In Activity B, you have to **combine** your ideas from Activity A with the specifics of your experience. Putting ideas together in a new way shows you understand material and can think creatively.

B. ORGANIZE IDEAS Think of a personal discovery in your life. For example, think about a time when you discovered you had a talent for a sport or a subject in school. If you can't think of a personal discovery, borrow one from someone else's life experience.

1. How do the ideas in your notes from Activity A apply to this discovery?

2. Make notes about the major events involved in the discovery. List them in the order they happened. Say how this discovery affected you.

Personal discovery:	
Event	**Detail**
Effect:	

C. SPEAK Use your notes to present your story. Remember to explain the steps in how the discovery occurred, and how it affected you. As you tell your story, use one or more questions to maintain the interest of your listeners. Refer to the Self-Assessment checklist below before you begin.

CHECK AND REFLECT

A. CHECK Think about the Unit Assignment as you complete the Self-Assessment checklist.

SELF-ASSESSMENT		
Yes	**No**	
☐	☐	I was able to speak easily about the topic.
☐	☐	My partner, group, class understood me.
☐	☐	I used signal words.
☐	☐	I used vocabulary from the unit.
☐	☐	I used questions to maintain listeners' interest.
☐	☐	I linked words with vowels.

B. REFLECT Discuss these questions with a partner.

What is something new you learned in this unit?

 Look back at the Unit Question. Is your answer different now than when you started this unit? If yes, how is it different? Why?

Track Your Success

Circle the words you learned in this unit.

Nouns
adhesive
breakthrough
innovation AWL
miracle
odds AWL
reunion
sponsor
triumph

Verbs
ache
adopt 🔑
exploit AWL
interact AWL

Adjectives
alert
biological
deprived
flammable
inadvertent

inconceivable AWL
mandatory
obvious 🔑 AWL
synthetic
unreliable AWL

Adverb
vastly

Phrases
face to face
in all probability

🔑 Oxford 3000™ words
AWL Academic Word List

Check (✓) the skills you learned. If you need more work on a skill, refer to the page(s) in parentheses.

LISTENING ●	I can listen for signal words and phrases. (p. 156)
VOCABULARY ●	I can use collocations with prepositions. (p. 162)
GRAMMAR ●	I can use direct and indirect speech. (p. 164)
PRONUNCIATION ●	I can link words with vowels. (p. 166)
SPEAKING ●	I can use questions to maintain listener interest. (p. 167)
LEARNING OUTCOME ●	I can recount the events involved in a personal discovery I made accidentally and tell how it affected me.

LISTENING ● listening carefully to an introduction

VOCABULARY ● word forms

GRAMMAR ● relative clauses

PRONUNCIATION ● reduced forms

SPEAKING ● using persuasive language

LEARNING OUTCOME

Role-play a meeting in which you present and defend an opinion in order to persuade others.

Unit QUESTION

How can we maintain a balance with nature?

PREVIEW THE UNIT

A Discuss these questions with your classmates.

What kinds of things do you or other people you know do to protect the environment?

What should we do to protect animals that are endangered?

Look at the photo. Why do people enjoy watching animals play?

B Discuss the Unit Question above with your classmates.

Listen to *The Q Classroom*, Track 2 on CD 4, to hear other answers.

C Rank these issues. 1 = not a problem, 2 = a mild concern, 3 = a serious problem. Compare your answers with a partner. Explain the reasons for your choices.

____ air and water pollution

____ deforestation (cutting down trees)

____ climate change

____ loss of homes for animals

____ limited drinking water

____ limited natural resources, such as oil

____ the need for places to live

____ the need for public parks and outdoor recreation facilities

D There are many ways people work to protect nature. Read the list below and check (✓) your answers. Then work with a partner to compare answers.

How Can People Protect Nature?

	I do this or I would do this.	I might do this.	I probably wouldn't do this.
donate money to an environmental group	☐	☐	☐
recycle electronics	☐	☐	☐
protest the cutting down of trees in a forest	☐	☐	☐
volunteer to pick up trash in a public place	☐	☐	☐
buy products that do not harm the environment	☐	☐	☐
read newspapers or magazines online instead of buying paper copies	☐	☐	☐
only buy natural and organic foods	☐	☐	☐

LISTENING 1 | Polar Bears at Risk

VOCABULARY

Here are some words from Listening 1. Read the sentences. Then write each bold word next to the correct definition.

1. I had to **grip** the glass tightly so I wouldn't drop it.

2. Frogs and toads are very **fragile** animals. Even small changes in the environment can harm them.

3. The 1990s saw more record high temperatures than any other **decade**.

4. Scientists are very worried because some species of fish are disappearing at an **alarming** rate. Soon there may not be any more of them.

5. Studies indicate that the amount of polar ice will **decrease** in the future. There will be less and less every year.

6. Some banks failed and companies closed because they had no money. The economy was in a terrible **crisis**.

7. The earthquake had a **devastating** effect on the town. Most of the buildings were ruined.

8. The new manager made many changes at the company, and it was difficult for some employees to **adapt** to the changes.

9. He could barely pay rent with his **meager** salary, so he asked for a raise at work.

10. As Earth becomes hotter, the rain forests may **retreat** and the desert areas may become larger.

11. That car is too old to be on the road. It could break down and **potentially** cause an accident.

12. The lion population was shrinking, so the government put them into a **refuge** where hunters could not harm them.

a. _____ (*adj.*) too small in amount

b. _____ (*n.*) a place that is safe

c. _____ (*v.*) to become smaller in size, number, or amount

d. _____ (*n.*) a period of ten years

| Listening and Speaking   175

e. _____ (adj.) easy to hurt or damage

f. _____ (n.) a time of great danger or difficulty

g. _____ (adv.) possibly or probably

h. _____ (v.) to change your behavior to meet challenges

i. _____ (v.) to hold tightly

j. _____ (v.) to move away or pull back

k. _____ (adj.) frightening or worrying

l. _____ (adj.) very harmful or damaging

PREVIEW LISTENING 1

| Polar Bears at Risk

You are going to listen to a report about polar bears and their changing environment. The ice near Wrangel Island, a Russian island in the Artic Ocean, is home to many polar bears. The ice has been melting due to climate change.

Polar bears depend on sea ice to hunt and survive. What do you think would happen if the bears lost their home on the ice? Discuss your answer with a partner.

LISTEN FOR MAIN IDEAS

 CD 4
Track 3

Read the questions. Then listen to the report. Answer the questions.

Tip for Success

Write down unfamiliar words you hear. The context will often give you a general idea of the meaning. You can look up the words later to find the exact meaning.

1. Why are scientists at Wrangel Island?

   _____

2. What are two changes scientists have observed?

   _____

3. How is climate change affecting the ice?

   _____

4. How do the polar bears hunt for food?

   _____

5. How do changes in the ice affect the bears' ability to hunt?

_____

6. What is one way that people can help the polar bear in the short term?

_____

LISTEN FOR DETAILS

CD 4
Track 4

Read the questions. Then listen again. Circle the correct answer.

1. What is the polar bear's main source of food?
   a. ice
   b. fish
   c. seals

2. When do the polar bears hunt?
   a. mostly early summer
   b. late summer and early fall
   c. winter and early spring

3. How far can a well-fed bear swim?
   a. At least 5 miles.
   b. At least 15 miles.
   c. At least 50 miles.

4. What is a change scientists have noticed in polar bears?
   a. Their weights and skull sizes have decreased.
   b. The number of cubs and size of cubs has increased.
   c. Their diets and sleeping habits have changed.

5. What does the report say scientists need to conduct more research on?
   a. what polar bears need to survive
   b. the role humans are playing in climate change
   c. why polar bears stay on the ice to hunt

Q WHAT DO YOU THINK?

Discuss the questions in a group.

1. The scientists present an idea for helping the polar bears. What else could help polar bears survive climate change?

2. Some governments have taken steps to protect endangered animals. For example, China has laws protecting pandas. Why do you think governments do this?

| Listening Skill | Listening carefully to an introduction | web |

Introductions often contain important information about the organization and focus of a presentation. Listen actively as soon as the speaker starts to say the key words and ideas.

Speakers often begin with organizational phrases, like number phrases, that explain the content or structure of the presentation.

> Today, we'll look at **three reasons why** . . .
> We're going to discuss **four ways to** . . .
> In the **first part** of the lecture we will talk about . . .

Listen for repeated ideas, words and phrases, and synonyms.

> Here on Wrangel Island, a team of scientists watches three polar bears that grip the edge of the ice. To these scientists, the polar bears' fragile hold on the ice is a symbol of their slipping hold on a disappearing world.

The word *ice* is repeated to show it is an important part of the polar bears' survival. The phrases *grip*, *fragile hold*, and *slipping hold* are used to emphasize that the bears are losing their home.

Listen for rhetorical questions.

A professor might begin a lecture by asking,

> "What are scientists doing to solve the problems the polar bear faces?"

This question tells you the lecture will probably be about solutions to the problem.

A. Listen to the introduction of a lecture on honeybees and the environment. Read along and underline repeated words, synonyms, and any rhetorical questions. Circle the organizational words and phrases.

PROFESSOR: Hello! Um, today, I want to continue our discussion about the impact of human behavior, specifically pollution, on the environment. I want to draw your attention to the effect humans are having on one of the smaller animals with which we share the planet: honeybees. You might be thinking, "Why should we care about honeybees?" Well, in the first part of this lecture, I'll explain the important role honeybees play in our daily lives. You might be surprised to find out just how vital their health is to you!

In the second half of the lecture, I'll review some recent research on how pollution in the environment is causing flowers to lose their smell. I'll also talk about how the bees are confused by this lack of smell. Finally, we'll finish up today with my predictions for the future for bees and, consequently, for humans. OK, let's get started . . .

B. Answer these questions about the lecture introduction.

1. What is the general topic of the lecture?

   _____

2. What is the specific focus of the lecture?

   _____

3. What will the professor explain about flowers?

   _____

4. What will the two main parts of the lecture be about?

   _____

VOCABULARY

Here are some words from Listening 2. Read the sentences. Circle the answer that best matches the meaning of each bold word or phrase.

1. No one knew where the key was, but after we asked some questions, the truth started to **emerge**. Thomas had lost it, but he didn't want to tell us.
   a. become hidden
   b. become dangerous
   c. become known

2. We have moved to this country **indefinitely**. We are not sure how long we will be here, but it may be for a long time.
   a. for an unknown period of time
   b. unable to remember something well
   c. for a very short period of time

3. The strong wind **dispersed** the seeds through the air. They covered the whole field.
   a. made more stable
   b. spread over a wide area
   c. gathered together

4. What is that **substance** in the bottle? It looks like a mixture of sand and water.
   a. pattern or design on the surface
   b. solid or liquid material
   c. crack or break in a container

5. There are many **species** of flowers: roses, lilies, tulips, daisies, and many more.
   a. varieties
   b. sellers
   c. colors

6. The directions on the can of paint say not to paint in an **enclosed** space. We need to open some windows or paint this outside.
   a. surrounded by walls or barriers
   b. small and unattractive
   c. with a lot of area inside

7. Don't drink that! It is not juice. It's a **toxic** liquid used for cleaning. It could kill you!
   a. delicious
   b. poisonous
   c. safe

8. If you allow children to play with matches, there will probably be an **injury**. Someone could get burned very badly.
   a. fun experience
   b. harm done to someone
   c. sickness or virus

9. Although you are just an **individual**, you can find other people who share your opinion and form a powerful group.
   a. different person
   b. unmarried person
   c. one person

10. The scientists prepared a report to **present** to the local government. They hoped the leaders would listen to their ideas.
    a. try to sell something
    b. show something to others
    c. work hard to change

11. The economist **tracked** the economic situation closely. He watched for new trends or possible problems.
    a. caused
    b. changed
    c. followed

12. The oldest **inhabitant** of our town is 99 years old. He's been here his whole life.
    a. a person or animal that lives in a place
    b. someone who does things regularly
    c. someone who works hard

PREVIEW LISTENING 2

The Effects of Oil Spills

You are going to listen to a lecture about the effect of an oil spill, which is the release of oil into the environment, usually into a body of water. The lecture focuses on the *Exxon Valdez* oil spill, which occurred in Prince William Sound on March 24, 1989.

Look at the pictures below. How do you think an oil spill affects wild animals in the area? How does it affect the people? Discuss possible effects with a partner.

cleaning an animal after an oil spill

LISTEN FOR MAIN IDEAS

 CD 4
Track 6

Listen to the lecture. Check (✓) the main ideas presented in the lecture.

☐ The Exxon Valdez spill was one of the worst environmental disasters in U.S. history.

☐ When the oil spilled, the weather was dangerous.

☐ Many of the problems were caused by the location of Prince William Sound.

☐ The spill still affects the area many years later.

☐ Some animals died from being too warm.

☐ Many animals suffered and died because of the oil spill.

☐ Washing animals causes them to get oily.

☐ People are working on new ways to deal with oil spills.

LISTEN FOR DETAILS

 CD 4
Track 7

A. Read the statements. Then listen to the report again. Write *T* (true) or *F* (false).

_____ 1. Five hundred million gallons of crude oil spilled out from the *Exxon Valdez*.

_____ 2. The *Exxon Valdez* was the largest oil spill in world history.

_____ 3. Prince William Sound is enclosed, which kept most of the oil in.

_____ 4. Mousse is a mixture of water and sand.

_____ 5. About 1,300 miles of shoreline were affected.

_____ 6. All the fisheries were able to stay open after the oil spill.

_____ 7. About 250,000 seabirds died as a result of the oil spill.

_____ 8. No more oil is trapped in the water or the beaches.

_____ 9. The harbor seals have recovered, but the killer whales haven't.

_____ 10. Chemicals were used to try to clean up the oil spill.

B. Answer the questions. Then compare answers with a partner.

1. Why did scientists decide it was a bad idea to use hot water to clean up the oil?

   _____

2. How long will the clean-up at Prince William Sound last?

   _____

3. How much did it cost?

   _____

 WHAT DO YOU THINK?

A. Discuss the questions in a group.

1. Could any large environmental problems happen where you live? Why or why not?

2. If there were an environmental disaster near you, what types of things would you do to help? Give reasons for your answers.

3. Do you know if your community has an emergency plan in case of a disaster? How could you find out?

 **Critical Thinking**

Activity B asks you to **compare and contrast** two situations. When you compare, you look at similarities; when you contrast, you look at differences. Practicing these skills helps you to understand information better.

B. Think about Listening 1 and Listening 2 as you discuss the questions.

1. Which situation do you think is more serious: the shrinking polar bear habitat or the damage done by the oil spill? Why?

2. Humans are now working to address both of these problems. How are the solutions to the problems similar? How are they different?

Adding a **suffix** to a **base word** can change the form of the word. For example, a word can be a *verb*, *noun*, *adjective*, or *adverb*, depending on which suffix it has. Some words have more than one suffix. Being able to identify the base word and the suffix can help you easily identify the meanings of many unfamiliar words.

In Listening 1, the reporter says, "The information they have gathered so far is alarming." The word *information* is based on the word *inform*. You can tell from the base word and the context of the sentence that *information* is a noun that means "something that informs, like a fact."

Here are some related forms based on the word *inform*.

Verb	Noun	Adjective
inform	information	informational

These are common suffixes that are added to words to change the word form.

To make nouns	To make adjectives
-ation (*imagine → imagination*)	-ic, -atic (*climate → climatic*)
-tion / -sion (*extinct → extinction*)	-ing / -ed (*shock → shocking / shocked*)
-ity (*rare → rarity*)	-able (*accept → acceptable*)
-ment (*develop → development*)	-al / -ial / -eal (*finance → financial*)
To make verbs	**To make adverbs**
-ify (*simple → simplify*)	-ly (*indefinite → indefinitely*)
-ize (*modern → modernize*)	-ally (*scientific → scientifically*)

A. Identify the form of each word. Use the suffixes in the chart above to help you.

_____noun_____	1. progression	_____	6. exclamation
_____	2. commercial	_____	7. rationalize
_____	3. diversify	_____	8. acidic
_____	4. agreeable	_____	9. intentionally
_____	5. argument	_____	10. solidify

B. Complete each sentence with the correct form of the word in parentheses. Then work with a partner to read your sentences.

1. My uncle is a _____. He studies the effects of climate change in Brazil. (biology, *n.*)

2. The _____ government passed some new environmental laws. (nation, *adj.*)

3. The change in the amount of ice was more _____ than it was five years ago. (drama, *adj.*)

4. There has _____ been an increase in the seal population. (definite, *adv.*)

5. There were strong _____ reasons to develop the coastal areas. (commerce, *adj.*)

6. We need to _____ the plants by variety, size, and color. (category, *v.*)

7. The oil spill had a _____ effect on the beaches and animals. (devastate, *adj.*)

8. Environmentally, it may not be smart to build a factory near the river, but _____ it is a good idea. (commerce, *adv.*)

9. The company decided to _____ for creating too much pollution. They proposed ways to reduce the amount of pollution over time. (apology, *v.*)

10. Which _____ of the company do you work in? (divide, *n.*)

Factories add to water pollution.

Grammar | Relative clauses

When speaking, we often must give extra information so the listener knows what we mean. We use **relative clauses** to tell the listener which noun we are talking about in a sentence. All relative clauses have a *subject* and a *verb*, but they cannot stand alone as complete sentences. They must be added to complete sentences.

Restrictive relative clauses

A restrictive relative clause gives important information about the subject of a sentence.

> The knowledge **that they collect** will help the polar bear in the future.

This restrictive relative clause identifies which knowledge will help the polar bear.

> Individuals **who made their living fishing** were hit especially hard.

The restrictive relative clause *who made their living fishing* identifies which individuals were hit especially hard.

Nonrestrictive relative clauses

A nonrestrictive relative clause is used to give extra information about the subject. A speaker usually pauses very briefly before and after a nonrestrictive clause.

> Wrangel Island, **which is located in the Arctic Ocean**, is home to the largest concentration of polar bears.

The clause *which is located in the Arctic Ocean* is extra information. It doesn't identify the island for us.

Relative pronouns

There are certain pronouns that are used with each type of relative clause.

In restrictive clauses: Use *who*, *whom*, *that*, and *whose* for people. Use *which*, *that*, and *whose* for things and animals.

In nonrestrictive clauses: Use *who*, *whom*, and *whose* for people. Use *which* and *whose* for things and animals.

A. Underline the relative clauses Write *R* (restrictive) and *NR* (nonrestrictive). Then practice reading the sentences with a partner.

_R_ 1. The polar bear is facing a crisis <u>which scientists believe is caused by climate change</u>.

____ 2. This frozen ice of late winter and spring provides the bear with the food that it will need to stay alive during the long summer.

____ 3. The tanker hit Bligh Reef, which is in the northeast part of Prince William Sound.

____ 4. Oil, which is toxic to birds, can kill them and cause serious health problems.

____ 5. Feathers and fur, which protect birds and animals from the cold, lose their insulating value when oil gets onto them.

____ 6. Some of the whales that ate oil-covered seals died after the disaster.

____ 7. Some species that live in Prince William Sound are still feeling the effects after more than twenty years.

____ 8. Volunteers use equipment that can skim the oil off the surface of the water.

____ 9. One particularly effective method is the use of bacteria, which basically eat the oil.

____ 10. Researchers have developed a chemical that promotes the growth of the bacteria.

Prince William Sound

B. Complete each sentence with the appropriate relative clause. Then practice reading the sentences with a partner.

that are adapted to the cold	which is part of Russia
that the oil spill affected	which retreats in the summer
which are creatures of the ice	which was a commercial oil tanker
which has been going on for ten years	which were closed right after the oil spill
which is around 25,000 worldwide	who work on Wrangel Island

1. The scientists _____ have been gathering information on polar bears.

2. The research, _____, shows that the population of polar bears is decreasing.

3. Wrangel Island, _____, has a large concentration of polar bears.

4. Polar bears have bodies _____.

5. Scientists are worried about the future of some of the animals

    _____

6. Polar bears, _____, are not fast enough to catch

    seals in open water.

7. These fisheries, _____, still haven't reopened.

8. The *Exxon Valdez*, _____, caused one of the

    worst environmental disasters in U.S. history.

9. The ice, _____, is melting earlier in the spring

    than it used to.

10. The population of polar bears, _____, has

    dropped in recent years.

Pronunciation   Reduced forms   web+

CD 4
Track 8

It is very common to connect words as we speak. One result is that pronouns, such as *he, she, him, her, this,* and *theirs,* and auxiliary verbs, such as *is* and *have,* are often **reduced,** or shortened.

For example, listen to the reporter in Listening 1. Compare what is written with how she pronounces the words in the sentences.

> Most **people have** read that the ice caps are melting because of climate change, but for most of **us this** problem feels very distant.
> Their research shows that climate **change is** having a devastating effect on the polar bear habitat—the ice.

The reporter cuts off the /hæ/ sound at the beginning of *have* and the /ð/ sound at the beginning of the word *this.* She also cuts off the /ɪ/ sound from *is.* Notice how she links the reduced forms with the sounds before them.

CD 4
Track 8

When we speak rapidly, we often reduce auxiliary verbs as well. Compare what is written with how the sentence is pronounced.

> I want to help the animals **because they are** all affected by the oil spill.

As you learn to connect more sounds, you can reduce some of the words, such as pronouns and auxiliary verbs. It may seem like incorrect pronunciation, but it is in fact very natural, fluent speech.

CD 4
Track 9

A. Listen to the conversation. Pay attention to the reduced sounds. Underline the reduced sounds you hear. Then practice the conversation with a partner.

Sasha: People are doing many things that are helping the environment.

Brian: Yeah, I'm trying to do my part. For instance, I started walking more places.

Sasha: Yeah, but I can't worry about everything at once . . . like all the animals that are endangered.

Brian: What do you mean? That's serious.

Sasha: Don't get me wrong. I'm concerned about them. I just mean climate change is big. It's global—bigger than you or me.

Brian: So, what's your solution?

Sasha: Start at home. I've started recycling and turning off the lights when I leave a room. I'm doing what I can to save energy and resources.

Brian: Yeah, Akbar is trying to remember to unplug laptop cords and phone chargers. They use electricity even when he isn't using them.

Sasha: That's a good idea.

Brian: It's something. We have to start somewhere.

B. Continue the conversation above with a partner. Talk about steps you or other people you know are taking to protect the environment. Try to use at least five of the words below. As you speak, pay attention to the reduced sounds.

he	his	him	himself
she	her	hers	herself
they	their	theirs	them
themselves	am / is / are	was / were	have / has / had

There are times when you may want to convince others to accept your point of view about something. There are a variety of strategies you can use.

State your opinion clearly.

> I think (that) . . .
> I have always thought (that) . . .
> In my opinion . . .
> I mean . . .
> It seems that . . .

Acknowledge other people's opinions before you disagree.

> Yes, but . . .
> I see what you're saying, but . . .

Mention expert sources that share your opinion.

> I heard that scientists . . .
> I read that a climate expert . . .

Think of different opinions others might have and address them first.

> Some people might think . . . but . . .
> Some people say . . . but . . .

Appeal to the emotions of the listener.

> Think about . . .
> What about . . . ?

CD 4
Track 10

A. Listen to a conversation between two friends who disagree about their responsibility to protect the environment. Complete the conversation with the words you hear. Then answer the questions.

don't really think	many people believe
I heard	think about
I mean	

Amir: Wait! What are you doing?

Isabel: Huh?

Amir: Are you throwing that can away?

Isabel: Uh, yeah.

Amir: Aren't you worried about the environment?

Isabel: Well, I have to say that I _____ what I do has

that much effect on the world. _____, I'm just

one person.

Amir: Even one person can make a difference.

Isabel: Yes, but _____ that climate change isn't even

real. You know, almost 20,000 scientists signed a petition saying that they

don't believe that climate change is caused by humans.

Amir: You can't believe that!

Isabel: Well, why not? And _____ that climate

change is something recent. But, actually, there has been warming in the

past. So, climate change is nothing new—and nothing to worry about.

Amir: Well, there might be 20,000 scientists that aren't worried about climate

change, but tell that to the polar bears!

Isabel: The polar bears?

Amir: Yeah, _____ the polar bears that can't find

food because the ice at the North Pole is melting so fast.

Isabel: Really? That's terrible.

Amir: Whether climate change is man-made or not, I think you should

recycle that can, just to be safe!

Tip for Success

During a conversation, you don't always have to wait to be asked a question. You can join a conversation by responding to what the other speaker has just said and then sharing your own ideas.

1. What strategy is Isabel using when she talks about the petition?

   _____

2. What belief does Isabel disagree with?

   _____

3. What strategy is Amir using when he mentions the polar bears?

   _____

4. What does Amir mean when he says, "I think you should recycle that can"?

   _____

B. Work with a group. Write a script for a radio advertisement promoting one of the environmentally friendly products below. Use persuasive language. Then present the advertisement to another group.

1. Energy-saving light bulb

2. T-shirt made from organic cotton

3. Shampoo that has not been tested on animals

4. Hybrid car

5. Solar-powered phone or other electronics

6. Your idea: _____

_____

_____

_____

_____

_____

_____

_____

_____

_____

_____

a solar-powered phone

In this section, you are going to present your opinion to persuade a group of people. As you prepare your presentation, think about the Unit Question, "How can we maintain a balance with nature?" and refer to the Self-Assessment checklist on page 196.

For alternative unit assignments, see the *Q: Skills for Success Teacher's Handbook.*

CONSIDER THE IDEAS

A. Listen to a news report about the situation in a small town. Think about the questions as you listen.

1. Why does Spring Hill need to develop the land near the lake?

2. What are the concerns about developing the land?

3. What outcome does the mayor hope the town hall meeting will produce?

PREPARE AND SPEAK

A. GATHER IDEAS Work in a group. Complete the activities.

1. Imagine you are going to attend the town hall meeting in Spring Hill. Each group member should choose a different role from the list below.

   Scientist from Spring Hill Community College
   Owner of a clothing company
   Member of a local environmental group
   Hotel owner
   Mayor of Spring Hill

2. Read the opinion statement below that matches your role. As you read, circle the plan you have for Clear Lake and underline the statements that support your argument.

Scientist from Spring Hill Community College

You are worried about the possible problems that building something near the lake might cause. You believe that the city should leave this delicate area alone. In your opinion, the best use of this area would be to keep people away and turn the lake into a wildlife refuge. It would attract wild animals that scientists could observe and study.

Owner of a clothing company

You own four clothing factories in other parts of the country, and you want to build another one on the shores of Clear Lake. Your factory would bring jobs to the town. You use the latest technology. You are confident the development will not damage the lake environment. A factory would provide jobs and help solve the town's economic problems.

Member of a local environmental group

You love the quiet beauty of the lake. You and many others enjoy swimming there. Every month your group goes out to Clear Lake to pick up trash and clean up the shore. You want to keep this area as it is for everyone to enjoy and use. You would be willing to charge town residents to use the lake in order to bring some income to the town.

Hotel owner

You have built more than 100 hotels, and you want to build one at Clear Lake. The area is beautiful and would be perfect for a large hotel. Your hotel would attract customers from all over the world and create jobs for the residents of Spring Hill. In your opinion, the best use of this area would be development that is quiet, clean, and beautiful.

Mayor

Clear Lake is small, and there is only enough space for one solution. You need to listen to the ideas at the town hall meeting and make a decision about the best way to use the area to increase the income of the town.

B. **ORGANIZE IDEAS** Meet with other students in the class who have taken the same role as you. Discuss how you will answer the questions below. Take notes.

1. What are the main reasons that support your opinion?

_____

_____

_____

2. What other reasons could you give?

_____

_____

_____

3. What might your opponents say that disagrees with your opinion?

_____

_____

_____

4. How will you respond?

_____

_____

_____

C. **SPEAK** Role-play the town hall meeting. Follow these steps. Refer to the Self-Assessment checklist on page 196 before you begin.

1. Return to your group. Imagine that you are at the town hall meeting. The mayor should introduce each speaker and consider his or her ideas.

2. Take turns presenting your ideas. Your goal is to convince the mayor that your suggestion is the best choice for the town of Spring Hill. Use persuasive language to strengthen your argument. Use relative clauses to add details.

3. The mayor will listen to everyone and decide how to solve the problem. The mayor will then tell the group what the final decision is.

CHECK AND REFLECT

A. CHECK Think about the Unit Assignment as you complete the Self-Assessment checklist.

Yes	No	SELF-ASSESSMENT
☐	☐	I was able to speak easily about the topic.
☐	☐	My partner, group, class understood me.
☐	☐	I used relative clauses.
☐	☐	I used vocabulary from the unit.
☐	☐	I used persuasive language.
☐	☐	I used reduced forms of words.

B. REFLECT Discuss these questions with a partner.

What is something new you learned in this unit?

 Look back at the Unit Question. Is your answer different now than when you started this unit? If yes, how is it different? Why?

Track Your Success

Circle the words you learned in this unit.

Nouns	Verbs	Adjectives
crisis 🔑	adapt 🔑 AWL	alarming 🔑
decade 🔑 AWL	decrease 🔑	devastating
individual 🔑 AWL	disperse	enclosed
inhabitant	emerge 🔑 AWL	fragile
injury 🔑 AWL	grip	meager
refuge	present 🔑	toxic
species 🔑	retreat	
substance 🔑	track	**Adverbs**
		indefinitely AWL
		potentially 🔑 AWL

🔑 Oxford 3000™ words

AWL Academic Word List

Check (✓) the skills you learned. If you need more work on a skill, refer to the page(s) in parentheses.

LISTENING	●	I can listen carefully to and understand an introduction. (p. 178)
VOCABULARY	●	I can use word forms. (p. 184)
GRAMMAR	●	I can use relative clauses. (p. 186)
PRONUNCIATION	●	I can use reduced forms. (p. 188)
SPEAKING	●	I can use persuasive language. (p. 190)
LEARNING OUTCOME	●	I can role-play a meeting in which I present and defend an opinion in order to persuade others.

UNIT **10**

Child's Play

LISTENING ●	listening for causes and effects
VOCABULARY ●	idioms
GRAMMAR ●	uses of real conditionals
PRONUNCIATION ●	thought groups
SPEAKING ●	adding to another speaker's comment

LEARNING OUTCOME ●

Participate in a group discussion about how to encourage children to exhibit good sportsmanship.

Unit QUESTION

Is athletic competition good for children?

PREVIEW THE UNIT

Ⓐ Discuss these questions with your classmates.

Did you play sports or games as a child? If so, what were they? Did you enjoy them? Why or why not?

If a child hopes to be a professional athlete, what are the most important things that the child and his or her parents must do to achieve that goal?

Look at the photo. What can a child learn from winning or from losing?

Ⓑ Discuss the Unit Question above with your classmates.

🔊 Listen to *The Q Classroom*, Track 12 on CD 4, to hear other answers.

C Many young children participate in organized sports. Check (✓) whether each outcome is a benefit, a disadvantage, or neither.

How Do Organized Sports Affect Children?	Benefit	Disadvantage	Neither
getting exercise	☐	☐	☐
the risk of injury	☐	☐	☐
needing to practice	☐	☐	☐
making new friends	☐	☐	☐
time away from school work	☐	☐	☐
building confidence	☐	☐	☐
learning new skills	☐	☐	☐

D Put a check (✓) next to the sport you think is best for young children to participate in. Then work with a partner to compare answers. Give reasons for your answer.

☐ gymnastics
☐ soccer
☐ basketball
☐ martial arts
☐ swimming
☐ another sport: _____

LISTENING 1 | Training Chinese Athletes

VOCABULARY

Here are some words from Listening 1. Read the sentences. Then write each bold word next to the correct definition.

1. Our school's basketball team started to **dominate** the game last Friday in the first few minutes. The other team was able to score very few points.

2. The artist was very **modest**. She didn't like to talk about how famous she had become.

3. Runners sometimes become exhausted and **collapse** before they reach the finish line.

4. The talented ice skater reached the **apex** of her career at age 18. She never won a competition after that.

5. The competition was **brutal**, and some of the athletes had a hard time dealing with the stress and sore muscles.

6. Very good athletes usually have a high level of **intensity** when they compete. They focus all their energy on the sport.

7. The team needed more **funding** to pay for new uniforms.

8. Although you're a talented athlete, you should also **invest** your energy in getting a good education.

9. Eating well is an **integral** part of any fitness program. It's one of my main strategies to stay in shape.

10. After speaking with my advisor, I **concluded** that law school wasn't the right choice for me.

11. I've been the **beneficiary** of my father's hard work. For one thing, he paid for me to go to college.

12. My grandparents grew up in an **era** before the Internet.

a. _____ (*n.*) a defined period of time in history

b. _____ (*adj.*) being an important, basic part of something

c. _____ (*n.*) the highest or best part of something

d. _____ (*adj.*) extremely difficult and painful

e. _____ (v.) to fall down suddenly

f. _____ (v.) to have more power or skill and to control someone or something with it

g. _____ (n.) a quality of great strength or seriousness

h. _____ (n.) a person or group who gains (usually money) as a result of something

i. _____ (n.) money given to support an event, program, or organization

j. _____ (v.) to put money, effort, time, etc., into something good or useful

k. _____ (v.) to reach a belief or opinion as a result of thought or study

l. _____ (adj.) not talking much about one's own abilities or possessions

PREVIEW LISTENING 1

| Training Chinese Athletes

You are going to listen to an interview about young athletes in China. It explains how children are selected and trained to be future gymnastics champions.

What do you think are important qualities for a champion athlete? Check (✓) the qualities that you agree with. Then discuss your answers with a partner.

☐ physical strength
☐ intelligence
☐ commitment
☐ youth
☐ speed

LISTEN FOR MAIN IDEAS

CD 4
Track 13

Listen to the interview. Circle the answer that best completes each statement.

1. Jacinta Muñoz wanted to learn more about the Chinese system for training athletes because of ____.
   a. the age of the athletes
   b. their recent rise in dominance
   c. the time she spent in China

2. According to the report, funding to support the sports system in China comes from ____.
   a. the athletes
   b the parents
   c. the government

3. Jacinta Muñoz thinks Chinese children are different from American children mainly because Chinese children ____.
   a. are taught to share, not to stand out
   b. want to train harder for sports
   c. train to go to the Olympics

4. Young Chinese athletes are beneficiaries of the Chinese training system because they ____.
   a. receive housing, food, and training
   b. make many sacrifices
   c. learn to share

5. China is also a beneficiary of this training system because ____.
   a. there are Chinese athletes in many sports
   b. it can provide travel to rural children
   c. it has begun a new era of Chinese sports

LISTEN FOR DETAILS

CD 4
Track 14

Read the statements. Then listen again. Write *T* (true) or *F* (false).

____ 1. Jacinta Muñoz quit gymnastics because of the brutal training.

____ 2. Young athletes in China don't see their parents often.

____ 3. Young athletes in the United States usually get funding from their parents or businesses.

____ 4. Chinese athletes get free health care and sports training.

____ 5. Susan Brownell was a gymnastics coach in China and in the United States.

____ 6. According to the interview, Chinese children are selected based on how good they are in a sport.

WHAT DO YOU THINK?

Tip **Critical Thinking**

This activity asks you to **appraise** different approaches in the United States and in China. When you make an appraisal or judgment, you evaluate the information from many angles. This demonstrates a deeper understanding of the material.

Discuss the questions in a group.

1. In the United States, parents often spend a lot of money to help their children become better athletes. In China, parents send their children away to school and often don't see them for a long time. Why do you think parents make these kinds of sacrifices?

2. Jacinta Muñoz talks about Susan Brownell's idea that in the United States parents raise their children to succeed and train them to share, but in China they raise their children to share and train them to succeed. Do you think one approach produces better results than the other? Why or why not?

Listening Skill	Listening for causes and effects	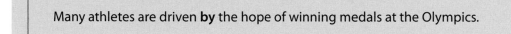

A speaker may talk about what **causes** something to happen or what **happens because of** some other action or event. Speakers usually use **signal words** that connect two events or ideas.

These are some of the **signal words** that speakers use to show a **cause**.

because (of)	as a result of	due to	since	by

 CD 4 Track 15

Many athletes are driven **by** the hope of winning medals at the Olympics.

The athlete won two gold medals **as a result of** years of hard work.

Due to bad weather, the baseball tournament was canceled.

These are some of the signal words that speakers use to show a **result**.

because of this / that	as a result	therefore	so	the result is

CD 4 Track 15

The kids live far from home and practice very hard.
Therefore, they only see their parents every few months.

Some kids start playing some sports too young.
The result is they often get injured before they even reach high school.

Knowing these words and phrases will help you to understand how the information is organized and predict what a speaker will say next.

A. Listen to the sentences. Circle the word or phrase you hear in each sentence.

1. a. as a result of
   b. the result is

2. a. therefore
   b. because of this

3. a. because of
   b. due to

4. a. as a result
   b. the result is

5. a. therefore
   b. because

6. a. since
   b. now that

B. Read each sentence. Is the underlined section the *cause* or the *effect*? Write C (cause) or E (effect).

Tip for Success

When listening to a presentation that mentions causes and effects, mark each cause or effect in your notes. Label them with a C or an E. This will help you make important connections when you review your notes.

_____ 1. <u>Our team won the game</u> because of our hard work and practice.

_____ 2. Due to <u>a knee injury</u>, Stephanie will not be at the track meet this weekend.

_____ 3. Kwan was late to our last competition, so <u>our coach made him sit out this one, too</u>.

_____ 4. Susan is a better kicker than I am. Therefore, <u>she will start in the soccer game tomorrow</u>.

_____ 5. I will have to miss my brother's baseball game as a result of <u>my busy class schedule</u>.

_____ 6. Since <u>Eduardo couldn't make it today</u>, I will take his place on the team.

LISTENING 2 | *Until It Hurts* Discusses Youth Sports Obsession

VOCABULARY

Here are some words from Listening 2. Read the definitions. Then complete each sentence with the correct word.

> **ambition** (*n.*) a strong desire to achieve a goal
>
> **burnout** (*n.*) a state of being very tired or sick because you have worked too hard
>
> **escalate** (*v.*) to become or make something greater, worse, or more serious
>
> **former** (*adj.*) of an earlier time
>
> **fundamental** (*adj.*) important or basic
>
> **journalist** (*n.*) a person whose career is to collect information and write news stories
>
> **obsession** (*n.*) the state of being able to only think of one thing
>
> **reasonable** (*adj.*) fair, practical, or sensible
>
> **regret** (*v.*) to feel sorry or sad about something; to wish that you had not done something
>
> **spectator** (*n.*) a person who watches a sport
>
> **ultimately** (*adv.*) in the end
>
> **vulnerable** (*adj.*) easy to hurt; open to danger

1. Mark's first job as a _____ was writing for an online magazine.

2. History has become an _____ for Lindsey. It's all she talks about.

3. After Oscar developed the _____ skills he needed to become a swimmer, his trainer started working on more advanced skills.

4. When we are tired and overworked, we are especially _____ to sicknesses like the flu.

5. After weeks of working long hours and getting little sleep, Song Min was suffering from _____, and he couldn't continue.

6. Thomas was not always a lawyer. In a _____ career, he was a professional football player.

7. Anita's highest _____ is to be a gold medalist at the Olympics, and she believes that she can do it.

8. I considered many universities, but _____ this one proved to be the right school for me.

9. A _____ at the game jumped up and cheered loudly as her team won the game.

10. It didn't seem _____ for the coach to expect the team to practice four hours every day.

11. Quitting the team was a big mistake. It has been many years, and I still _____ it.

12. The players' slight disagreement quickly began to _____ into a big fight.

PREVIEW LISTENING 2

Until It Hurts Discusses Youth Sports Obsession

You are going to listen to a sports journalist and his views on youth sports today. He discusses a recent book by Mark Hyman called *Until It Hurts*.

Do you think sports should be a major focus in a child's life? Why or why not? Discuss with a partner.

LISTEN FOR MAIN IDEAS

CD 4
Track 17

A. Listen to the interview. Make a chart like the one below in your notebook and take notes while you listen. Then compare your notes with a partner.

Major changes in youth sports	Negative effects of these changes
1.	1.
2.	2.

B. Answer the questions.

1. What is the main difference between youth sports today and 150 years ago?

_____

2. According to Mark Hyman, what are some steps we can take to improve youth sports today?

_____

LISTEN FOR DETAILS

CD 4
Track 18

Read the sentences. Then listen again. Circle the answer that best completes each statement.

1. The sports journalist describes an event in which a father ____.
   a. screamed at the team
   b. fought a referee
   c. got into a fight with another parent

2. According to the book, youth sports used to be run by ____.
   a. children
   b. parents
   c. educators

3. Mr. Hyman mentions that too much training can result in ____.
   a. bone fractures
   b. depression
   c. bad grades at school

4. When Mark Hyman's son complained about his shoulder, his father ____.
   a. forced him to stop playing
   b. encouraged him to keep playing
   c. talked to a doctor

5. Years later, when Ben injured his pitching arm, ____.
   a. he continued playing baseball
   b. he had surgery
   c. he quit playing for years

6. During games in one community, there's a rule banning ____.
   a. talking during games on Sundays
   b. eating food in the stands
   c. more than one parent from each family

Q WHAT DO YOU THINK?

A. Discuss the questions in a group.

1. Why do you think parents get their children involved in competitive sports at such an early age? Do you think they should wait until their children are older?

2. What can parents and coaches do to make sports a positive experience for kids? What specific things can be done to prevent the problems that the journalist and Mark Hyman describe?

B. Think about both Listening 1 and Listening 2 as you discuss the questions.

1. What do you think the young athletes in both China and the U.S. are learning from their involvement in competitive sports?

2. What are some similar pressures or challenges faced by young athletes both in the special schools in China and in youth sports leagues?

Vocabulary Skill | **Idioms** | web+

An **idiom** is a particular group of words that has a specific meaning different from the individual words in it. Idioms function as a separate unit, almost as if they were a single word.

To *make a point of* doing something means "to do something because you think it's important or necessary."

⌐ The coach **made a point of** congratulating all the players on the winning team.

In a nutshell means in "summary."

⌐ Sports can lead to injury, lower grades, and even tension in the family. **In a nutshell**, we must be very cautious when involving our kids in sports.

Because idioms have specific meanings, much like individual words do, it is useful to remember these "chunks" of language in the same way you memorize individual words.

There are thousands of idioms. Most of these idioms are not in the dictionary. For this reason, it is important that you notice them when they occur and use context clues to figure out their meaning.

Tip for Success

Idioms can be difficult to understand in a conversation. If someone uses an idiom that you are not familiar with, use a clarification strategy to ask him or her the meaning of the words.

A. Listen to the excerpts from Listening 1 and Listening 2. Then match each underlined idiom with its definition.

> a. left or quit
> b. pay for something
> c. defeated or overcame
> d. with and in front of other countries
> e. unexpectedly

_____ 1. First, I think we've all seen how the Chinese athletes have come <u>out of nowhere</u> in the last twenty years or so and have started to dominate in a number of sports.

_____ 2. In the United States, young athletes and their families have to <u>foot the bill</u>. Sometimes, if they're very good, the athletes can get funding from other sources, such as companies or individuals that want to invest in their athletic careers.

_____ 3. They are proud of their athletes and want their athletes to represent the country <u>on the world stage</u>.

_____ 4. But sometime in the middle of the last century, educators <u>bowed out</u>, and the parents took over, sometimes as coaches, but most often as very active spectators.

_____ 5. And their ambitions often <u>got the best of</u> them.

B. Write sentences using the five idioms in exercise A. Practice saying the sentences with a partner.

1. _____

_____

 **for Success**

Idioms are a type of collocation. Besides using context, another way to learn the meaning of an idiom is to use a collocations dictionary.

2. _____

_____

3. _____

_____

4. _____

_____

5. _____

_____

Real conditional sentences show a possible or expected cause and effect. Real conditional statements can give information about the present or the future.

Most real conditionals have a conditional clause containing *if* and a *simple present verb* connected to a main clause with a simple present or future verb.

> conditional clause   main clause
> If I **practice** every day, I **will improve** my skills.
> (I will improve my skills only by practicing.)

Conditional clauses can also begin with *when* or *whenever* to describe a general truth or habit.

> conditional clause   main clause
> When I **practice** in the afternoon, I **take** my soccer ball to school with me.
> (I only take my soccer ball to school on the days I practice in the afternoon.)

The *conditional clause* can come before or after the *main clause*. If the conditional clause comes first, there is a pause, shown by a comma, between the clauses.

**CD 4
Track 20**

> I will put on my uniform when I get there.
> When I get there, I will put on my uniform.

Real conditionals can be used to express many kinds of ideas.

Things that will become true

☐ If Brazil's team wins tonight, they will be in first place.

Predictions

☐ If we arrive early, we'll probably find a good parking space.

Habits

☐ I prefer to sit in the front row when I go to a game.

Deals, compromises, and promises

☐ If you can drive me to the game, I'll buy the tickets.

Advice

☐ When you throw the ball, remember to lean forward a bit.

Warnings

☐ You will not play in our next game if you show up late to practice.

Instructions

☐ When I pick you up from practice, remember to bring your equipment with you.

A. Read the sentences. Rewrite each one so that the conditional clause comes first. Then practice saying the sentences with a partner.

stopping a game due to rain

1. We can continue the game when the rain stops.

   _____

2. I can give you my tickets if you want to go to the game.

   _____

3. You should stay home if you're too sick to go to practice.

   _____

4. I don't like the noise of cheering when I have a headache.

   _____

5. I'll put on my uniform when we get to the baseball field.

   _____

6. We'll play again next week if the game is canceled.

   _____

7. You can't play if you don't show up to the team meeting.

   _____

8. My team wins if you miss this shot.

   _____

B. Write a conditional sentence for each situation. Then compare answers with a partner.

1. A team member keeps missing practice sessions. She might miss the next one, too. After that, you are going to suspend her from the team.

   Warning: _____

2. A friend is late for his baseball game. You can drive him there. In return, you would like him to buy gas for your car.

   Deal: _____

3. The next game is very important to your team. Winning the game will earn you all a prize.

   Prediction: _____

4. Your friend has trouble hitting a baseball. You notice he needs to hold the bat correctly. That might fix his problem.

   Advice: _____

Speakers don't talk in a steady, continuous stream of words. Instead, they say their words as **thought groups** to help listeners understand their ideas. Speakers separate thought groups with brief pauses.

A thought group may be a short sentence.

CD 4
Track 21

    Blake loves basketball.
    _____
        thought group

It may be part of a longer sentence.

    He plays every day   and watches every game.
    _____   _____
       thought group1   thought group 2

    Steve and Debbie,   on the other hand,   will not be going.
    _____   _____   _____
      thought group 1   thought group 2   thought group 3

It may be a short phrase or clause.

    Do you agree   or not?
    _____   _____
    thought group 1   thought group 2

The end of a sentence is always the end of a thought group.

    We're going out.   Do you want to come with us?
    _____   _____
     thought group 1   thought group 2

When speaking, think about how to form your ideas into thought groups to help your listeners understand your ideas.

CD 4
Track 22

A. Listen to the sentences. Draw slashes (/) between the thought groups.

1. In my opinion,/that's a bad idea.

2. Are they coming or not?

3. If I get home early, I'll go running. Want to join me?

4. Keep your head up as you kick the ball. It's important.

5. All week long these kids are so busy they have no time for fun.

6. If she wins this match, Ms. Williams will be in first place.

7. If you'd like to talk, call me at (555) 233-1157.

8. Here's my email address: goalkeeper100@global.us.

B. Practice reading the sentences in Activity A with a partner. Focus on separating thought groups.

Speaking Skill | Adding to another speaker's comments

One way to keep a conversation interesting is **to build on someone else's ideas**. Sometimes you want to communicate that you agree with another speaker or add other ideas related to the topic.

These phrases can be used to add to the conversation.

To show agreement	To build on an idea
I agree.	Plus . . .
That's a good point.	Furthermore . . .
That's true.	I would also add (that) . . .
Right.	Another important point is (that) . . .
Exactly.	To build on what you just said . . .
	Going back to what you said before . . .

Phrases of agreement can be combined with phrases that build on an idea.

I agree. I would also add (that) . . .
Exactly. I would also add (that) . . .

CD 4
Track 23

Listen to the conversation.

Sung-ju: I believe that organized sports are beneficial to kids. Sports are good exercise, and they give kids the chance to meet people they would never meet otherwise.

David: <u>That's true. And I would add that</u> sports help them learn to work as part of a team.

CD 4
Track 24

A. Listen to a discussion about payment for college athletes. Check (✓) the phrases of agreement and the building phrases you hear. Then work with a partner to summarize the main points.

☐ Another important point is that . . .

☐ And to build on what John said earlier, . . .

☐ And I would add that . . .

☐ That's a good point.

☐ Furthermore . . .

☐ Going back to what John said . . .

B. List at least four reasons why you think athletes should NOT be paid while they are in college.

1. _____

_____

2. _____

_____

3. _____

_____

4. _____

_____

C. Work in a group. Discuss the reasons you listed in exercise B. Agree with or add to the ideas you hear.

Unit Assignment **Share opinions about sportsmanship**

In this section, you are going to share your opinions about good sportsmanship—the way people behave while participating in sports. As you prepare to share your opinions, think about the Unit Question, "Is athletic competition good for children?" and refer to the Self-Assessment checklist on page 218.

For alternative unit assignments, see the *Q: Skills for Success Teacher's Handbook*.

CONSIDER THE IDEAS

Work with a partner. Discuss the questions about good sportsmanship.

1. How do team sports help children build social skills?

2. What do winning and losing teach children about life?

3. Does pressure from parents or coaches help children succeed? Why or why not?

4. What personality traits do children gain from sports participation?

5. How involved should parents be in their children's sports activities?

PREPARE AND SPEAK

A. **GATHER IDEAS** According to the American Academy of Child & Adolescent Psychiatry (AACAP), parents need to get involved in their children's sports and help their children develop good sportsmanship. In a group, brainstorm some ways that parents can follow this advice. Take notes about what you discuss.

Ways for parents to get involved:

_____

_____

_____

_____

_____

Tip for Success

When participating in a group discussion, write down ideas that you think of while others are speaking. This will help you to remember your ideas when you have an opportunity to take a turn.

Good sportsmanship means:

_____

_____

_____

_____

_____

Ways for parents to encourage good sportsmanship:

_____

_____

_____

_____

_____

B. **ORGANIZE IDEAS** Look over the results of your group's brainstorming session from Activity A. Choose the four ideas you think are the most important. Complete the chart.

Ways to get involved and to encourage good sportsmanship	Benefits to children
1.	
2.	
3.	
4.	

C. **SPEAK** Follow these steps. Refer to the Self-Assessment checklist below before you begin.

1. Conduct a group discussion on this topic: How and why should we encourage good sportsmanship in children?

2. Take turns expressing your ideas. Try to use conditional sentences to express your ideas. Also try to use some of the phrases you learned to add onto other speakers' comments. As you speak, use pauses to separate your thought groups.

CHECK AND REFLECT

A. **CHECK** Think about the Unit Assignment as you complete the Self-Assessment checklist.

Yes	No	SELF-ASSESSMENT
☐	☐	I was able to speak easily about the topic.
☐	☐	My partner, group, class understood me.
☐	☐	I used real conditional sentences.
☐	☐	I used vocabulary from the unit.
☐	☐	I added to another speaker's comments.
☐	☐	I spoke in thought groups.

B. **REFLECT** Discuss these questions with a partner.

What is something new you learned in this unit?

 Look back at the Unit Question. Is your answer different now than when you started this unit? If yes, how is it different? Why?

Circle the words you learned in this unit.

Nouns

ambition 🔑

apex

beneficiary `AWL`

burnout

era 🔑

funding `AWL`

intensity `AWL`

journalist 🔑

obsession

spectator

Verbs

collapse 🔑 `AWL`

conclude 🔑 `AWL`

dominate 🔑 `AWL`

escalate

invest 🔑 `AWL`

regret 🔑

Adjectives

brutal

former 🔑

fundamental 🔑 `AWL`

integral `AWL`

modest

reasonable 🔑

vulnerable

Adverb

ultimately 🔑 `AWL`

🔑 Oxford 3000™ words

`AWL` Academic Word List

Check (✓) the skills you learned. If you need more work on a skill, refer to the page(s) in parentheses.

LISTENING ●	I can listen for causes and effects. (p. 204)
VOCABULARY ●	I can understand idioms. (p. 209)
GRAMMAR ●	I can use real conditional sentences. (p. 211)
PRONUNCIATION ●	I can recognize and use thought groups. (p. 213)
SPEAKING ●	I can add to another speaker's comment. (p. 214)
LEARNING OUTCOME ●	I can participate in a group discussion about how to encourage children to exhibit good sportsmanship.

Audio Scripts

Unit 1: Power and Responsibility

The Q Classroom Page 3

Teacher: Today we are beginning Unit One. Every unit in Q starts with a question. As we go through the unit, we will continue to discuss this question. Our answers may change as we explore the topic. The question for Unit 1 is: "How does power affect leaders?" Think about some people in leadership positions, like executives of large corporations, or captains of sports teams. How does being a leader affect them? What do you think, Marcus?

Marcus: I think it can have a negative effect on some of them. You know, when some people get power, they start feeling that they are better than others, or that they don't have to follow the rules the way other people do.

Teacher: What do you think, Yuna? Do you agree that power has a negative effect on leaders?

Yuna: Hmm, maybe some leaders. But I think other leaders feel more responsible when they have power.

Teacher: You mean responsible for other people?

Yuna: Yes, they understand that their decisions affect a lot of people.

Teacher: How about you, Sophy? How do you think power affects people?

Sophy: Well, I agree with Yuna that not everyone is negatively affected by power, but I think it happens sometimes. When someone has a lot of power, maybe they think that they should be making all of the decisions, or that they don't really need to consider how other people think or feel.

Teacher: Felix? What's your opinion? We've heard about power giving people a strong sense of responsibility, and about it making them think they don't have to consider the advice of others. Are there any other ways that power affects people?

Felix: Well, sometimes powerful people are kind of isolated because everyone is looking to them to make the decisions, but at the same time everyone wants the decisions to go their own way. That's a difficult position to be in. I would say that power makes a person's life difficult in some ways.

LISTENING 1: Best of Both Worlds?
Listen for Main Ideas Page 6

Speaker: When Ginny Pitcher needed to hire a director of business development at her Westborough, Massachusetts marketing firm, she turned to her closest friend, Kate Massey.

Massey and Pitcher had talked money before, during the years they were roommates. Still, this is business. It brought up **issues** like **negotiating** salary and professional success, things most people want to keep separate from their friendships. Not to mention that Pitcher would be Massey's boss.

"I didn't jump on it immediately," says Massey. "I thought about it for a while."

It's been a year, and both women say their friendship is as strong as ever. Even better, they're both making money and succeeding professionally. That's likely because they handled it like **experts** from the beginning. They **acknowledged** there would be a change in their friendship and discussed potential challenges. Anything personal stays outside the office. Massey doesn't take **criticism** personally. Pitcher treats Massey no differently than she does her other employees.

Pitcher and Massey **exemplify** the best **aspects** of working with friends. "One of the tricky things when you interview someone is figuring out if their personality will fit with the culture of the office," says Pitcher, a co-founder of Kel & Partners. "When you know someone like I know Kate, you know the answer already."

Knowing someone will fit in doesn't alleviate other problems. Carly Drum had hired four trusted friends to work at her family's executive search firm in Manhattan, Drum Associates.

One of them had great **potential** but was bringing her personal problems to the office. It was affecting her work. "I knew going in that **addressing** it was going to be one of the more challenging things in my career," says Drum, the firm's managing director. "She expected me to be sensitive to her personal issues because we're friends. While I am, there has to be a line drawn when you're running a business. Even as soft as I tried to put it, her initial reaction was she was offended."

Two days later the employee came in and apologized to Drum. They openly discussed the matter and developed a plan of action so she could separate work from business.

While it was tough, that challenge was a good managerial experience for Drum. She learned that before hiring a friend you must **outline** for him or her exactly what an average day will be like. Part of that discussion should include the type of interaction you will have with each other and the fact that in a workplace it's all business. "Stuff that you do outside of the office together cannot be brought into the office," says Drum.

Managing friends isn't always a choice. Employees who get promoted may find themselves suddenly in charge of friends. The same rules for success apply. First, the new manager should be the one to tell the **staff** about the change, particularly if he or she will be in charge of friends. From there, it's important to acknowledge that things will change. Explain that it's not because the relationship isn't important or because you want to end your personal relationship. Rather, you now have a hand in the professional lives of a group of people.

Gena Cox, who runs the leadership coaching firm Human Capital Resource Center, suggests saying something like this: "I still want us to be friends. Can you support me and know that what happens at work doesn't have anything to do with you or our relationship?" As for the subordinate, he or she needs to understand that the boss can't show any **favoritism**.

That's precisely what Tory Delany had to deal with as she rose up the ranks at a restaurant company in Manhattan. She started as a coat checker at Maggie's Place in midtown and, after a series of promotions, eventually became general manager. "The staff becomes close-knit because it's a small restaurant. Most of our family is very far away," says Delany. "The owners have five places, so we all always knew there was a chance for promotion for everyone from within."

She says the key to successfully managing friends is developing rules and boundaries and enforcing them. For example, an employee who came in late was spoken to. If the employee was late again, he or she got a warning. The third time resulted in suspension. Delany attributes her success to that uniformity.

"If there's no structure, your whole team falls apart," she says.

She must be doing something right. She's a co-owner of a restaurant with the owners of Maggie's Place.

Listen for Details Page 7

[Repeat Main Ideas track]

LISTENING SKILL: Listening for main ideas
B. Page 9

Speaker: What do you need to start a new business and make it succeed? Many people would answer that what you need is a great idea. Others would say money. Of course, money and ideas are important. Unfortunately, when people think about starting a new business, they often ignore the single most important factor in the success of any company: people. Only people can make those great ideas happen. So, in order to start a successful business, you need to start with the right people.

But how do you identify the right people? That seems like a difficult question to answer because every business is different. Nevertheless, if you want to build a good team, there are some characteristics of the right people, no matter the business. We're going to focus on some of those characteristics and how to identify people who have what it takes to help make a new business a success.

First of all, your new business will need people who understand your vision and share your commitment to it. In other words, you need to build a team that truly understands what your goals for the business are.

Your new business will also need people who are creative, independent thinkers. You can't build a successful business based on your ideas alone. You want your business to be a place where people learn from each other and inspire each other to do their best work.

Lastly, your new business will need people who are willing to work hard. You need to find people who are ready to put in the long hours and all the hard work it takes to build a successful business.

No, starting a new business is not easy. Perhaps you've got a good business idea. Perhaps you have the money you need. But that's not enough to guarantee success. It's the people you hire that matter most. Remember that if you're going to find success, you need people who are creative, hardworking, and committed to seeing your dream become reality.

LISTENING 2: Myths of Effective Leadership
Listen for Main Ideas Page 11

Speaker: Podcasts from the *Leading Effectively* series are provided by the Center for Creative Leadership, an educational institution dedicated exclusively to leadership development and research worldwide. Information available at www.ccl.org. Today's topic: myths of effective leadership.

There's a difference between leadership and power. Successful **executives** know that difference and lead their teams more effectively because of it. Unfortunately, many executives on the rise in an organization forget the leadership skills and **contacts** that put their careers on track in the first place.

A study by the Center for Creative Leadership shows that as executives **advance** in a company, they begin to blur the lines between leadership, power, and influence. They see themselves as more intelligent and **capable** than those around them in the organization. They see people who agree with them as more capable, intelligent, and **ethical** than those who might disagree.

The result? Executives get affirmation from a small, expected group, which inflates their idea of how powerful and influential they are among the people who work with them. Their influence becomes constricted, and their leadership erodes. Some people overtly use power to accomplish their goals, says CCL's Pete Hammett, who is also the author of "Unbalanced Influence." He says others become used to having tools of power, such as the ability to dictate and set agendas.

Over time, that access to power distorts an executive's influence in the organization. They may have the **title** and power, but their disenfranchised team members won't see them as an **effective** leader. Those with different opinions choose to remain silent. Or they leave. With them, they take away a whole range of ideas.

CCL and Hammett recommend that executives calibrate their spheres of influence and see whether their team members perceive them as leaders or merely as suits with powerful titles.

Here are three ways to proceed:

Number 1: Find and listen to other voices. A leader should keep in touch with new ideas and fresh **perspectives**. If all you're hearing is one voice, then invite others to the conversation. And let them know you really want to hear them.

Number 2: Find a sparring partner. Find someone who's comfortable and capable of taking an opposing point of view. That doesn't mean you should seek out every malcontent in an operation. It means you should find someone who is intelligent, thoughtful, and open to tackling a discussion from an opposing view. Don't be seen as a leader who refuses to listen to different ideas. Or, worse, one who penalizes people for suggesting them.

Number 3: Leadership can be cultivated, but only in a self-aware person. Sign up for a leadership program. Get some feedback that **assesses** your leadership **style**. Make a point to hold a mirror up to your conversations and interactions within your organization. Only by seeing yourself through others' eyes can you go from someone who holds power to someone who leads.

Listen for Details Page 12

[Repeat Main Ideas track]

VOCABULARY SKILL: Understanding meaning from context
A. Page 13

1. The job didn't pay very well, but I loved the office and my co-workers. It was a great **environment** to work in.

2. It's impossible to **function** well when you don't get along with your co-workers. I can't work in a situation like that.

3. I'm sure you can **resolve** the conflict with your co-worker if you listen to each other's opinions.

4. James has great **aptitude**, but he needs more training. In a year or so, he'll probably be our best programmer.

5. The members of Emily's group are experienced and talented, plus they **exhibit** great teamwork.

B. Page 14

1. Managing friends isn't always a choice. Employees who get promoted may find themselves suddenly **in charge** of friends.

2. Part of that discussion should include the type of **interaction** you will have with each other and the fact that in a workplace it's all business. "Stuff that you do outside of the office together cannot be brought into the office," says Drum.

3. She says the key to successfully managing friends is developing rules and boundaries and **enforcing** them. For example, an employee who came in late was spoken to. If the employee was late again, he or she got a warning.

4. Find someone who's comfortable and capable of taking an **opposing** point of view. Don't be seen as a leader who refuses to listen to different ideas.

5. They may have the title and power, but their . . . team members won't see them as an effective leader . . . . CCL and Hammett recommend that executives . . . see whether their team members **perceive** them as leaders or merely as suits with powerful titles.

PRONUNCIATION: Syllable Stress
Page 16

neGOtiate

A. Page 17

1. excerpt
2. aspect
3. enforce
4. effective
5. leadership
6. acknowledge
7. perspective
8. opposing
9. promotion
10. interaction

B. Page 17

Listen again to Activity A.

SPEAKING SKILL: Checking for understanding
A. Page 18

Manager: OK guys, this project is huge, and it's going to be challenging. Here's what I need all of you to do. First of all, we all have to put in extra hours. That means long days for the next few weeks. It also means that we need to pull together and work extra hard as a team. That means all of us. Do you know what I mean?

Staff: Yeah / Sure / Yes.

Manager: OK. It also means that you need to drop all your other projects for now. Please focus on this project. It is our top priority. Does everyone understand?

Staff member: You mean stop working on every other project?

Manager: That's right. This account demands all our attention right now. Richard, please call the office in Tokyo, and let them know that we need all the information they have on this client. And we need the information by Friday at the latest. Are you following me?

Richard: Yep. Call Tokyo, get information on the client, tell them we need it by Friday.

Manager: Friday at the latest. Great! As for the rest of us, we'll be meeting again today at 3:00. Before that, read over the project description. If you have any questions, please bring them to the meeting. Got it? OK, let's get to work!

B. Page 18

Listen again to Activity A.

Unit 2: Appearances

The Q Classroom Page 23

Teacher: In Unit 2, we're going to talk about appearances. The Unit Question is "How does appearance affect our success?" Sophy, what do you think?

Sophy: Ooh, in lots of ways. Our appearance influences what people think of us.

Teacher: Can you give me an example?

Sophy: Sure. The way you dress, for example. If you dress well, people will think you're more successful or more competent. They'll treat you more respectfully and that will help you succeed.

Teacher: Yuna, do you agree? Does dressing well help you be successful?

Yuna: Yes, I agree. If you're careful about your appearance, people think you care about yourself.

Teacher: OK, what else? Marcus, how about the appearance of other things, for example, your desk or your bedroom? Does that affect your success?

Marcus: Well, it could. How people look at you is important. If they look at you and think you're disorganized or not in control of your life, they'll be less interested in working with you. That could affect your success.

Teacher: Anything else? Any other ways that appearance affects our success? Felix?

Felix: I agree with everyone else that appearances affect how other people react to you, but not everyone needs to be neat and well-dressed and good-looking to be successful. Your appearance also involves your style, and you can use that to help you fit into the group you want to be in. For instance, if I want to be a successful businessman, I would have a completely different kind of look than if I want to be a successful rock star.

LISTENING 1: A Perfect Mess
Listen for Main Ideas Page 27

Announcer: *A Perfect Mess* is a new book that explores the benefits of being messy. Our reviewer, Henry Rubins, finds reasons in the book to **embrace** his own habits of chaos.

Henry Rubins: Finally, in *A Perfect Mess* by Eric Abramson and David Freedman, I read the words I've been waiting for all my life: Neatness is not a virtue. It's OK to be a little disorganized. As someone who is frequently criticized for being messy, I now know I'm not such a bad person after all.

I've been messy since I was old enough to dress myself. As a child, I had the usual arguments with my mother about cleaning my room, putting my clothes and books away, and making my bed.

At college I was even worse. Books, papers, and dirty dishes were everywhere. Oh, part of it was because I was lazy, but I also felt so **stifled** in a neat, too-tidy room. I couldn't even think. I mean, I need a certain amount of chaos to feel comfortable.

But it wasn't until I got my first job that I found out how deep the world's **bias** toward neatness and order is. I mean, I didn't know I would be expected to have a neat desk in order to do my job. But after reading *A Perfect Mess*, I see I have had it easy at work compared to other people.

The book mentions a woman who worked at a post office in Australia. She was fined more than two thousand dollars at work. Why? Because she had four personal items on her desk. The post office only allowed her to have three. Maybe it was an extra photo of her kids—and for that she had to pay *two thousand dollars*? The police chief in a Pennsylvania town had it even worse. He was actually fired from his job because of a messy desk. At least I've never lost a job!

A Perfect Mess might help people like them, and me.

The book begins with a description of the National Association of Professional Organizers, or NAPO, conference. NAPO is a professional organization I could never join. Anyway, NAPO has thousands of members. Thousands. These are people who have gone to graduate school in business, or education, or even law, and now devote their lives to helping the rest of us get organized.

The authors, Eric Abramson and David Freedman, interview dozens of members of NAPO. And they **point out** that not once in any of the interviews does anyone answer the big question: What's wrong with being messy?

In fact, throughout the rest of the book, the authors show us that being **moderately** messy can actually be good for us. *A Perfect Mess* takes the reader on a tour of the various messy parts of our lives, starting with those messy desks. The book argues that a messy desk can actually help you find things more easily because they're right out in the open. And it can help people make connections between ideas in new ways.

Here's a great example. Leon Heppel was a researcher at the National Institutes of Health in Bethesda, Maryland, in the 1950s. One day, he was working at his desk. He **stumbled** upon letters written by two different scientists. The letters were in the piles of paper on his messy desk. If the two letters had been neatly put away he would never have looked at them side by side. But he did, and he suddenly **recognized** an important connection between the two scientists' research. This connection eventually led to a winning discovery and a Nobel Prize.

The book mentions he wasn't the only scientist like this. Albert Einstein was another great scientist who was known for having a very messy office.

Next the book looks at our messy homes. The authors say a messy home isn't so bad either. A very neat home can be impersonal and cold, but a home full of photos, personal items, and pieces of clothing strewn about shows others who we truly are.

Many people believe that an untidy house sets a bad example for children. Abramson and Freedman reassure us it's not true. In fact, children may learn better in a messy space. The book gets support from research suggesting that a **stimulating** environment full of clutter, movement, and noise may actually help children remember information. And it **turns out** that keeping your house too clean can actually be bad for children's health. Dirt and germs help children build up protection against diseases.

And the authors offer more evidence in favor of mess. It seems not only are messy people often more successful than neat people, they tend to be more creative and **open-minded**. Take, for example, the composer Johann Sebastian Bach. The authors describe his musical messiness. Apparently, each time he played a piece of music, he changed it. Bach would even take suggestions from the audience, and work them into the music as he played. He sometimes went in so many different directions when he was playing that he upset the other musicians and the audience. I'm sure Bach would be surprised to see how **inflexible** people are today about his music. Each piece is played the same way, note for note every time, all over the world.

As the authors Eric Abramson and David Freedman look into our messy lives, they show us how a little **chaos** can be good for us. They

tell us that mess may help us relax, be more creative, learn better, or even make an important scientific discovery. *A Perfect Mess* is a fascinating look at the unexpected benefits of mess. I'd recommend it to anyone—except possibly my kids.

Listen for Details   Page 27

[Repeat main ideas track]

LISTENING SKILL: Identifying details
A. Page 28

Ella Oskey: If you are one of the millions of people who just can't stay on top of your mess, don't worry, there is hope for you! Hi, and welcome to this workshop, Getting it Together. I'm Ella Oskey. I assume that you have come today because you feel like your life is too disorganized. If this is true, I have some suggestions that will help you organize yourself, both at home and in the workplace. OK, let's get started. How many of you have spent hours searching for an important document or paper? How long did you look for your car keys before leaving the house to come here today?

Ella Oskey: The first strategy I suggest is simple: put everything in its place. In other words, put everything into the room or space it belongs in after you use it. If it doesn't have a place, make one. This is not a radical idea, folks! If you always put your keys in the same box next to the door every night, they will always be there in the morning. How many of you think you can do that?

Ella Oskey: Great! Now, strategy number two is just as simple: follow a filing and organization system. Every time you find a piece of paper, decide which of these three groups it belongs in: now, later, or never. If it is a "now" item, like a bill that needs to be paid today, deal with it immediately. If it is a "later" item, like a magazine you still want to read, put it in its place, like I talked about in suggestion one. If it's a "never" item, throw it away in the garbage immediately. So remember: now, later, or never. This filing system requires immediate action, though. This is the key point; do something immediately with all papers and documents. OK? How would you feel if you never had to sift through piles of papers again?

Ella Oskey: Great! Now, on to the third strategy: Do a little at a time. Instead of trying to change your whole life in one afternoon, work on it step by step. One day, organize a drawer. The next day, organize something else. If you try to do too much at once, you might feel frustrated. Making this change little by little will not only ensure that you get organized, but will also help you stay organized.

LISTENING 2: The Changing Business Dress Code
Listen for Main Ideas   Page 31

Radio talk show host: My guests today are Andrew Park, from OPK Marketing, and Hana Nasser of Best Foot Forward Consulting. Thank you for being with us today.

Andrew Park: Glad to be here.

Hana Nasser: Thank you.

Radio talk show host: We're going to talk about the changing business dress code. Andrew, let me start with you. For the last ten or twenty years here in the United States, we've had a more relaxed attitude toward the clothing we wear at work, with some people working in jeans or even shorts. But is this relaxed attitude a thing of the past?

Andrew Park: Well, it's not over but I think it's fair to say it's on the way out and that more formal dress is definitely on the way in. Back in the 1990s, we really saw the **trend** of business casual catch on. Employees were allowed to ditch their suits and ties and formal skirts and blouses and wear more comfortable clothes in the office. For guys it might be an open-necked shirt and cotton slacks. Women might wear a sweater with a long skirt. And even businesses that didn't go all the way to business casual started allowing employees to dress informally at least one day a week. Casual Fridays became the **norm**. I remember everyone looking forward to getting to wear what they wanted to on Fridays. Most workers thought it was great, and for a while **morale** improved in many places. You know how it is with anything new. In the beginning there's a lot of **enthusiasm** for an idea.

Even employers liked the change. They thought of casual Fridays as a kind of **reward** to give their employees at the end of a long work week; dressing down on Friday would provide a bridge between the high-pressure work week and the weekend. They thought that if employees felt comfortable on Friday, it would increase productivity. But they found that this wasn't true. In fact, the opposite was true. Making employees more comfortable actually caused productivity to fall.

Hana Nasser: That's right. In fact, some supervisors noticed that on those casual Fridays, employees seemed to work less and relax a lot more.

Radio talk show host: Hmm. So, Hana, do you think casual Friday was a bad idea?

Hana Nasser: Well, of course, it varies from one workplace to the next. Certainly, some employees really enjoy a more casual dress code. One survey we **conducted** showed workers like casual Friday because they save money on clothes, and they like not having to worry about what to wear.

But in some companies, casual dress has had a negative effect. Maybe not so much on the work the employees do, but on the way customers and clients see them. Let's face it—clients don't always feel that casual clothes are **appropriate** in a business setting. They're looking for a sign that people are professional, like they know what they're doing.

And **investors** might be more **cautious** around casually dressed professionals. I recently heard an **anecdote** about a CEO who had a meeting with a possible investor. The CEO turned up in a T-shirt and shorts. The investor had been very interested in the company's products—really cool video games—but decided against putting up any money. Who wants to give their money to someone who looks like they could be hanging out at the mall?

Radio talk show host: OK, so business casual is on the way out because it's led to a fall in productivity and a lack of confidence from clients and investors.

Andrew Park: Yeah, that's a part of it. Some companies clearly saw they needed a more formal look to keep investors and customers happy.

But fashion trends always go in **cycles**. In the '50s and early '60s, the business uniform for men in the United States was a suit and tie. Working women wore a suit, or a dress and jacket. The look was professional. Then in the '60s and '70s, young people gave up that look. They connected the suit and tie with older people and older ways of thinking. They wanted a more natural, back-to-basics kind of lifestyle. The children who grew up during the '60s and '70s became managers in the '80s and '90s. They were the ones who accepted casual dress in the workplace. When one generation dresses formally, the next wants to be casual, and so on. That's the way fashion works.

Radio talk show host: So are you saying that this is all just part of regular fashion cycles? That what we wear at work doesn't really matter that much?

Andrew Park: Yes and no. Yes, there will always be cycles. And no, I think what we wear *does* matter. Because what we wear is not only about looks, it says something about who you are. For some people, a casual look is **associated** with a certain careless approach to other things.

Hana Nasser: I agree. To many people, a sloppy look indicates careless work, not just a style of dress. It's a matter of attitude. As Andrew said, the way we dress tells people who we are. What we're noticing is that nowadays many young professionals in their 20s or 30s want to look good and be taken seriously. They're the ones going back to suits and ties and formal skirts. They want a clean, professional look. The trend is toward a more grown-up form of dress.

Andrew Park: You're so right. In many places, casual Fridays are starting to fade and there's a move towards "dress-up" or "formal" Thursdays or Mondays. Formal as in employees showing up in tuxedos, dress slacks, fancy dresses, even wedding gowns! And this move is not coming just from the CEOs. It's coming from employees as well. Sometimes, looking good really is feeling good.

Radio talk show host: OK. That's all the time we have, so we'll leave it there. I'd like to thank my guests, who always look professional no matter what day of the week it is. Thanks for listening.

Listen for Details Page 31

[Repeat Main Ideas track]

PRONUNCIATION: Unstressed Syllables
Page 36

appearances

A. Page 36

1. pleasure
2. forgotten
3. successful
4. habit
5. business
6. allow
7. cautious
8. professional

B. Page 36

Listen again to Activity A.

SPEAKING SKILL: Confirming understanding
A. Page 37

1. **A:** Did you hear that starting next month, there won't be a "casual Friday" anymore?

   B: What? So you mean that they are getting rid of casual Friday completely?

   A: Yes, the email said no more casual Fridays.

   B: Oh.

2. **A:** More and more customers are looking for a sign of professionalism.

   B: Are you saying they prefer less casual dress?

   A: Yeah, that's right.

   B: Got it.

3. **A:** If my desk is too organized, I can't be creative.

    B: If I understand you, you need to be messy to work well?

    A: Yeah, I need a little mess.

    B: OK.

4. **A:** Most people can't get organized all at once.

    B: Does that mean it's better to work on it step by step?

    A: Yes, it does.

    B: I see.

Unit 3: Growing Up

The Q Classroom Page 43

Teacher: The Unit 3 question is: "When does a child become an adult?" What do you think, Felix? How would you answer this question?

Felix: I don't think we become adults at an exact age, but I think you start becoming an adult when you have to take care of yourself—pay your own rent, make your own meals, take yourself to the doctor when you're sick. Those are the things that make you grow up.

Teacher: It sounds like you associate adulthood with economic independence.

Felix: Yeah, I guess I do.

Teacher: What about you, Sophy? When do you think a child becomes an adult?

Sophy: I agree with Felix about it not being a specific age, but I think a lot of people don't really feel like adults until they get married and have children of their own. That's when you start to understand what life was like for your parents, and the kinds of responsibilities they had. That's when you're really an adult.

Teacher: What do you think, Yuna? Do you agree with Felix or Sophy?

Yuna: No, not really. I think of myself as an adult even though my parents help me financially and I'm not married. I manage my own life. I make decisions.

Teacher: Well, we have three completely different definitions! Where do you stand on this, Marcus? When does a child become an adult?

Marcus: I think I'm with Yuna. When you're in your early twenties, you're an adult, even if you still feel like a kid inside sometimes. Your body is done growing, your mind is developed, and your life is your responsibility, whether you're supporting a family or whether your family is supporting you.

LISTENING 1: Generation Next
Listen for Main Ideas Page 46

Robin Lustig: The sound of childhood: happy, energetic, **carefree**. We all know what it means to be young, and those of us who are adults, we also know what it means to be adult: commuting to work, earning a living, taking on financial responsibilities, feeding a family, **running** a home, and looking after babies.

So when do we become an adult? I still remember the exact moment that I grew up. It was the day I waved goodbye to my parents, got on a plane, and flew to Uganda, in east Africa, to spend a year there as a volunteer teacher. It was my 18th birthday, and from that day on, I was an adult. But not everyone can **pinpoint** the moment quite as precisely as I can.

Monika: In some ways I feel like an adult and some ways I don't. I'm definitely in between.

Robin Lustig: This is Monika, 17 years old, and the daughter of my American cousin. Monika's confused, just as millions of adolescents are around the world, and the American academic Cynthia Lightfoot, who studies the way children develop, and says we adults don't exactly help.

Cynthia Lightfoot: We don't do a very good job of defining an identity for them. We do a good job for kids, you know, kids are, they don't need to be responsible. Kids are playful; they are in school. So we have a fairly well-defined role for what it means to be a kid. We have a fairly well-defined role for what it means to be an adult, which is all the things that kids are not: responsible, not playful, you know, economically independent, um, **morally** independent and so on.

Robin Lustig: I asked my 21-year-old daughter the other day when she finally felt grown up. It was, she said, when she moved out of our house into a place that she's sharing with friends. She's now living an adult life, even if there was no formal ceremony to mark the **transition**. The academic, Cynthia Lightfoot again.

Cynthia Lightfoot: One of the things that often happens in traditional societies is that they have cultural supports for adolescents defining who they are and those cultural supports often come in the form of **initiation** ceremonies. So there are certain markers that are provided by the culture that allow kids to say "I am an adult now. I am separate from my family." In many industrialized societies, those **markers** aren't as clear cut, or they don't have the signal value that they do in traditional societies. So we do in fact have certain kinds of **milestones** such as getting a driver's license, being able to vote. But these don't have the same significance. One reason being that they're all spread out throughout adolescence.

John: I feel like I could do most of the things that adults do like right now. Like I have to wait two and a half years or so to be able to drive, and I think I could drive right now.

Robin Lustig: Most teenagers I've ever met think they could do just about anything. Rites of passage can help adolescents make the transition to adulthood; without them, we can sometimes get confused. So, there's a psychological element to growing up. It's when we decide who we are.

But ask the United Nations when in law you stop being a child, and they'll tell you it doesn't happen until a single, defined point in time, your 18th birthday. The United Nations Convention on the Rights of the Child **assumes** that anyone under 18 is a child and is **entitled** to be protected as such. Victor Karunan of the UN children's agency UNICEF explains why.

Victor Karunan: In most societies; you would be arriving at an age in and around 18, where that major shift would take place, from the period of adolescence to adulthood. However, we know in particular situations that children in a much earlier age would take on adult responsibilities, and that there you have a **contradiction** between the child exercising responsibilities, often adult, but legally not being given that recognition.

Robin Lustig: And if one turns that on its head in a developed society like Britain, for example, there are many, many hundreds of thousands of men and women in their 20s who are not yet self-sufficient economically, maybe living still with their parents. Are they still children?

Gerison Lansdown: Yes, interesting, isn't it? I think we define children very much in terms of emotional needs within the west. We see them as recipients of our love, our protection, our care, and so on. Whereas I think in many parts of the world, children are not just seen as recipients. They're seen as active **contributors** who play a socio-economic part in the family from really quite an early age, and that does affect the status of children within families.

Robin Lustig: No wonder we find adolescence so confusing.

Listen for Details Page 47

[Repeat Main Ideas track]

LISTENING SKILL: Making predictions
B. Page 49

1. **Lecturer:** Today's topic is "Proper Behavior in the Workplace." We'll be discussing several issues, including how to deal with a workplace disagreement, why it's important to be punctual, and how to dress appropriately in any work environment.

2. **Rudolph:** Ana, I can't keep up with the homework. I am just too tired after a long day at work.

    Ana: I know what you mean. I took an online business class last semester. It was tough getting all the work done at night. I had to come up with a plan.

    Robin Lustig: How did you do it?

3. **Yukio:** I'm excited about going to study in London for a year, but I'm going to miss you a lot, Tara.

    Tara: I know. I'll miss you, too. But . . .

4. **Maria:** Oh, thanks for stopping by. I'm trying to get all the employees together for a meeting. It's been very slow lately and morale is pretty low, but I want to share some important news with them. I just heard that our company won the Williams contract! That means we have a lot more business coming to us.

LISTENING 2: Growing Up Quickly
Listen for Main Ideas Page 51

Lecturer: Good morning. Today we're going to talk about the issues faced by children who have to take on adult responsibilities before they are 18.

First, let me tell you a story of a kid in this situation. Let's call him Bill. Bill's father died before he was born, and for a few years his mother was a single parent. Then his mom remarried and had another child. Bill worked hard in school, but he struggled to help his mother take care of his younger brother.

This is a common situation for children like Bill. They are forced to act like adults for a wide variety of reasons. In Bill's case, a young **sibling** gave him adult responsibilities. In other situations, a parent is sick, so the child has to take care of the sick parent. Sometimes, when parents divorce or one dies, a child takes on responsibilities such as cooking and cleaning. Or, in some immigrant families, a child may be the only family member who speaks the new language, so he or she has to translate for the parents at school or at the doctor's office. Although kids often want to help their families, too much responsibility can be a **burden** for them. They may feel they are giving up their childhoods.

An important term regarding these children is *parentification*. When we talk about parentification, we're saying that the child is taking on some of the duties and responsibilities of a parent. A ten-year-old who's making dinner every night, a 12-year-old who's **in charge of** getting her siblings ready for school every morning, a 16-year-old who picks the younger kids up from school, or who goes to the parent-teacher meetings for a sibling, all of these kids are parentified in a way.

However, some kids don't just act as parents to their younger brothers or sisters. Some take care of their mothers or fathers. They **reverse**

roles with their own parents. When you have this role reversal, the parents are so sick that they can no longer act in their parental role. The children cook for them, shop for groceries, even dress their parents, bathe them, and put them to bed. The children make the important decisions. The needs of the parents become more important than the needs of the child.

In less extreme cases, kids have to take care of their parents or another family member, but the parents are still in charge. So, for example, if a mother has a major illness and is too weak to get out of bed, the child may cook dinner or go to the grocery store, but the mother is still the parent in the relationship. She is the one who makes decisions and provides **guidance** to the child; she just can't physically do everything a parent does.

Okay, so kids are forced to grow up quickly for a variety of reasons. Is this a good thing or a bad thing? Well, it depends on the situation and on the child. As you might guess, the ones who suffer the most are the kids who reverse roles with a parent. Because role reversal happens in cases where the parents have the most problems and are the least **capable**, their children often feel more **isolation**. They may be embarrassed by the situation at home. They may feel **confusion** about how regular kids or teens are supposed to act. But many kids with adult responsibilities, not just those where the roles are reversed, **resent** their responsibilities, and see their duties at home as **barriers** to a happy social life. They can't go out and have fun. They feel a lot of **frustration**, and they have a lot of stress.

So which kids do the best? Probably the young care givers who take on responsibilities only for a short period of time and at an older age. Also, kids who feel supported by their families or who get support from school or other adults usually do much better. And there can be positive effects for children with some adult responsibilities. These kids often care more about others. They get **satisfaction** from helping people. Many of these kids grow up to become teachers, counselors, and health professionals. In fact, remember that kid Bill I told you about earlier? That was Bill Clinton, who later became president of the United States.

Listen for Details Page 52

[Repeat Main Ideas track]

GRAMMAR: Phrasal Verbs
A. Page 56

1. I can always count on my brother to help me with the chores.
2. I try to show up on time for school every day.
3. Once I tried to run away from home when I was a child.
4. Fortunately, I talked my son into cleaning the garage this weekend.
5. I didn't know what that word meant, so I had to look it up.
6. I decided to drop in on my father to see how he was doing.

PRONUNCIATION: Sentence Stress
Page 57

I <u>became</u> an <u>adult</u> when I got <u>married</u> and <u>started</u> a <u>family</u>.

A. Page 57

1. When you <u>become employed</u>, you can <u>call</u> yourself an <u>adult</u>.
2. I think it's <u>how much</u> you can <u>provide</u> for <u>yourself</u>.
3. <u>I</u> think it's when you get <u>married</u>.
4. I think you <u>become</u> an adult at <u>16</u>.

5. The <u>day</u> that I'm an <u>adult</u> is the <u>day</u> that I can <u>do whatever</u> I <u>want</u> to <u>do</u>.

6. The <u>age</u> at which you <u>become</u> an <u>adult varies</u>.

SPEAKING SKILL: Giving a Presentation
A. Page 59

Speaker: Uh, hi. Ummm, today my presentation is about an important turning point in my life. Umm, okay. So, when I turned 16, I got my driver's license. I was really, really excited. Uhh, on my birthday, my mom and dad also gave me a new car.

The car was a red sports car and really fun to drive. Uh, I used to go really fast on the highway. I felt like a real adult when I was in my car. But, one day, I drove past a police officer, and he, uh, he stopped me for driving over the speed limit.

Uh, where was I? Oh, yeah, uh, I got a ticket and a fine, and I had to tell my parents about it. Um, I didn't feel like an adult when I had to tell them. Because of the ticket, they took away my car until I could prove to them that I was more responsible. Umm, that's it.

UNIT ASSIGNMENT: Consider the Ideas
A. Page 60

Speaker: Hello. I'm Trish, and today I'd like to tell you about an important turning point in my life. When I was 18 years old, I went to Europe for a long vacation. I had a lot of interesting adventures, and I grew up a lot on that trip. However, one event sticks out in my mind as a moment in my life when I really left childhood and entered adulthood. I was traveling in Russia at the time. My father's voice sounded so far away on the phone when he called. I couldn't believe his news: my mother had a problem with her brain, and the doctors didn't know if she was going to live.

I got on a plane the next day and hurried across the planet hoping that my mom would still be alive when I got back home. When I walked into her hospital room, she recognized me, but couldn't talk. She got better, bit by bit, and, one day, I was allowed to take her outside in the hospital garden. As I pushed her wheelchair, I realized that my mom would need me for a while. I understood that even though traveling was my dream, it was more important to stay home and take care of my mom. I guess that I learned that being an adult means putting other people's needs first. I think I grew up a little more as my mom and I enjoyed the flowers in the hospital garden.

Unit 4: Health Care

The Q Classroom Page 65

Teacher: Today we'll discuss the Unit 4 question: "How is health care changing?" Let's start with Sophy. First of all, do you think health care *is* changing?

Sophy: Oh, of course.

Teacher: How?

Sophy: Well, for one thing, technology. There's new technology all the time. Nowadays, doctors can perform surgeries with lasers that leave hardly any scar. And there are lots of new technologies for detecting illnesses.

Teacher: OK, technology is one aspect of health-care change. What else? Yuna?

Yuna: There are more specialists now. You can find doctors who focus on your particular problem.

Teacher: That's true. As the field of medicine grows, more people need to specialize, don't they? What else? How else is health care changing? Felix?

Felix: I think there is more emphasis on prevention now. They used to wait until people got sick and then try to cure them, but now we know about nutrition and the importance of a healthy lifestyle, and they can do tests to see if someone has a high chance of getting a particular illness.

Teacher: So, we've got technology, more specialists, more emphasis on prevention. Is there anything else? What do you think, Marcus? How else is health care changing?

Marcus: Hmm. People live longer now. That must be changing health care. There's probably more focus on diseases you can get when you're older.

Felix: That's true. Also, because people are living longer and older people need more health care, it means that health-care systems are costing governments more than they used to.

LISTENING 1: Vacation, Adventure, and Surgery?
Listen for Main Ideas Page 68

Bob Simon: Thailand—an exotic vacation land known for its Buddhas, its beaches, the bustle of Bangkok. But for people needing medical care, it's known increasingly for Bumrungrad Hospital, a **luxurious** place which claims to have more foreign patients than any other hospital in the world. It's like a United Nations of patients here.

They're cared for by more than 500 doctors, most with international training. The hospital has **state-of-the-art** technology, and here's the clincher: the price. Treatment here costs about one-eighth what it does in the United States. That's right, one eighth. Curt Schroeder is the CEO of Bumrungrad.

Simon: This place where we're sitting right now is the number one international hospital in the world?

Mr. Curt Schroeder: I haven't heard anybody yet who's told us that they take more than 350,000 international patients a year.

Simon: One of them is Byron Bonnewell, who lives 12,000 miles away in Shreveport, Louisiana, where he owns and runs a campground for RVs. A year and a half ago, he had a heart attack, and his doctor told him he really needed bypass surgery.

They told you that you were going to die.

Mr. Byron Bonnewell: Yeah, they did tell me I was going to die.

Simon: You did not have insurance.

Mr. Bonnewell: Did not have insurance, no.

Simon: He estimates he would have had to pay over $100,000 out of his own pocket for the operation he needed, a complicated quintuple bypass.

And did you actually decide not to do it?

Mr. Bonnewell: Yeah, yeah, I did. I guess I'd rather die with a little bit of money in my pocket than live—live poor.

Simon: He says his health was **deteriorating** quickly when he read about Bumrungrad Hospital.

Mr. Bonnewell: I was in my doctor's office one day having some tests done and there was a copy of *Business Week* magazine there. There was an article in *Business Week* magazine about Bumrungrad Hospital. And I came home and went on the Internet and made an appointment, and away I went to Thailand.

Simon: He made that appointment after he learned that the bypass would cost him about $12,000. He chose his cardiologist, Dr. Chad Wanishawad, after reading on the hospital's website that he used to **practice** at the National Institutes of Health in Maryland.

Mr. Bonnewell: That's where he practiced for a number of years.

Simon: Right.

Mr. Bonnewell: Every doctor that I saw there has practiced in the United States.

Simon: You never called him.

Mr. Bonnewell: No. Never talked to him.

Simon: But three days after walking into the hospital, he was on the operating table. Two weeks later, he was home.

How was the nursing? How was the treatment?

Mr. Bonnewell: I found it so strange in Thailand because they were all registered nurses. Being in the hospital in the United States, you see all kinds of orderlies, all kinds of aides, maybe one RN on duty on the whole floor of the hospital. In Thailand, I bet I had eight RNs just on my section of the floor alone. First-class care.

Simon: That's what the hospital prides itself on, its first-class medical care, which it can offer so cheaply because everything is cheaper here, particularly labor and malpractice insurance. You can get just about any kind of treatment, from chemotherapy to plastic surgery.

The rooms look more like hotel rooms than hospital rooms, and that's no accident. The idea was to make the whole hospital look like a hotel, and a five-star hotel at that. Take a look at the lobby: boutiques and restaurants to suit every taste and nationality.

Mr. Schroeder: Part of the concept was to create an **environment** when people came in, they didn't feel like they're in a hospital.

Simon: What's wrong with—I mean, this is a hospital. What's wrong with looking like a hospital?

Mr. Schroeder: Because nobody really wants to go to a hospital.

Simon: India wants to become the world leader in medical tourism and might just make it. Alongside the familiar **images** of the country: teeming, dusty streets, poverty, you can add gleaming, new private hospitals.

. . . The hospital boom in India was fueled by India's growing middle class, who demanded **access** to quality health care. Now, the country known for **export**ing doctors is trying hard to import patients.

The most important player is the Apollo Group, the largest hospital group in India, third largest in the world.

Anjali Kapoor Bissell is a director of Apollo's international patient office.

Why is it important to get foreign patients here?

Ms. Anjali Kapoor Bissell: It makes sense to establish India as sort of like the world destination for health care.

Simon: That's the ambition—that India should become the world . . .

Ms. Bissell: Destination for health care, that's right.

Simon: But why should foreigners come here? Well, it's even cheaper than Thailand for most **procedures**, with prices about 10 percent what they would be in the U.S.

Stephanie Sedlmayr didn't want to spend the tens of thousands it would have cost her for the hip surgery she needed, and she didn't have insurance. So with her daughter by her side, she flew from Vero Beach, Florida, to the Apollo Hospital in Chennai. . . . But she didn't come here just to save money. She came for an operation

she couldn't get at home. It's called hip resurfacing, and it's changed people's lives.

It hasn't been approved yet by the FDA, but in India, Dr. Vijay Bose has performed over 300 of them.

Simon: What did it cost you?

Ms. Stephanie Sedlmayr: $5,800.

Simon: Including food, service, nurses, the works?

Ms. Sedlmayr: Private nurse after surgery, and, feeling always that they were just totally attentive. You—if you rang the bell next to your bed . . . somebody was there immediately.

Simon: By the time she left India, she was into the tourism part of her treatment, convalescing at a seaside resort an hour's drive from the hospital.

Is this **standard**, that when somebody gets surgery at a hospital here, they come to a resort like this afterwards?

Ms. Sedlmayr: Yeah, they suggest it.

Simon: This, too, is not very expensive, is it?

Ms. Sedlmayr: $140 a day, including . . .

Simon: For you and your daughter.

Ms. Sedlmayr: For myself and my daughter, including an enormous, fabulous breakfast that they serve until 10:30.

Simon: I think a lot of people seeing you sitting here in what's usually called post-op, and hearing your tales of what the op was like . . .

Ms. Sedlmayr: Uh-huh.

Simon: . . . are going to start thinking about India.

Ms. Sedlmayr: Yeah, and combining surgery and paradise.

Listen for Details   Page 69

[Repeat Main Ideas track]

LISTENING SKILL: Listening for reasons
Page 70

Harrison is flying to Brazil <u>because</u> his mother is sick and he wants to see her.

I decided to delay the surgery. <u>Here's why . . .</u>

Harrison is flying to Brazil. His mother is sick and he wants to see her.

I decided to delay the surgery. It's too expensive. Plus I want to find a better doctor.

A. Page 70

Excerpt 1:

Simon: He estimates he would have had to pay over $100,000 out of his own pocket for the operation he needed, a complicated quintuple bypass.

And did you actually decide not to do it?

Mr. Bonnewell: Yeah, yeah, I did. I guess I'd rather die with a little bit of money in my pocket than live—live poor.

Excerpt 2:

Simon: He says his health was deteriorating quickly when he read about Bumrungrad Hospital.

Mr. Bonnewell: I was in my doctor's office one day having some tests done and there was a copy of *Business Week* magazine there. There was an article in *Business Week* magazine about Bumrungrad Hospital.

And I came home and went on the Internet and made an appointment, and away I went to Thailand.

Simon: He made that appointment after he learned that the bypass would cost him about $12,000. He chose his cardiologist, Dr. Chad Wanishawad, after reading on the hospital's website that he used to practice at the National Institutes of Health in Maryland.

Excerpt 3:

Mr. Bonnewell: I found it so strange in Thailand because they were all registered nurses. Being in the hospital in the United States, you see all kinds of orderlies, all kinds of aides, maybe one RN on duty on the whole floor of the hospital. In Thailand, I bet I had eight RNs just on my section of the floor alone. First-class care.

Simon: That's what the hospital prides itself on, its first-class medical care, which it can offer so cheaply because everything is cheaper here, particularly labor and malpractice insurance. You can get just about any kind of treatment, from chemotherapy to plastic surgery.

Excerpt 4:

Simon: The rooms look more like hotel rooms than hospital rooms, and that's no accident. The idea was to make the whole hospital look like a hotel, and a five-star hotel at that. Take a look at the lobby: boutiques and restaurants to suit every taste and nationality.

Mr. Schroeder: Part of the concept was to create an environment when people came in, they didn't feel like they're in a hospital.

Simon: What's wrong with . . . I mean, this is a hospital. What's wrong with looking like a hospital?

Mr. Schroeder: Because nobody really wants to go to a hospital.

Excerpt 5:

Simon: Stephanie Sedlmayr didn't want to spend the tens of thousands it would have cost her for the hip surgery she needed, and she didn't have insurance. So with her daughter by her side, she flew from Vero Beach, Florida, to the Apollo Hospital in Chennai. . . . But she didn't come here just to save money. She came for an operation she couldn't get at home. It's called hip resurfacing, and it's changed people's lives.

It hasn't been approved yet by the FDA but in India, Dr. Vijay Bose has performed over 300 of them.

Simon: What did it cost you?

Ms. Stephanie Sedlmayr: $5,800.

Simon: Including food, service, nurses, the works?

Ms. Sedlmayr: Private nurse after surgery, and, feeling always that they were just totally attentive. You—if you rang the bell next to your bed . . . somebody was there immediately.

LISTENING 2: Medical Travel Can Create Problems
Listen for Main Ideas   Page 73

Reporter: Medical tourism is now a huge industry all over the world, especially in Asia and the Middle East. Medical tourists are people who travel to other countries to get medical care they cannot get at home . . . or for care that they would have to wait too long for at home . . . or they would have to pay too much for at home. Many countries are eager to gain customers in this healthcare market—about $40 billion a year and growing. A recent study showed that in 2008 the Middle Eastern country of Jordan had over 210,000 patients from some 48 foreign countries, bringing in around a billion dollars. And the list of countries providing these services keeps growing and growing, and now includes Turkey, Costa Rica, Argentina, South Africa, Hungary, India, Thailand, and Brazil.

But is there a downside as well? Some critics point to the difference between the care provided to the medical tourist, and the care provided to the **typical resident** of the country.

Maria Torres represents World Health Focus, a nonprofit agency working to promote better health across the globe.

Ms. Torres, why is World Health Focus studying this growing trend of medical tourism?

Maria Torres: Well, we know there are many financial advantages for the host countries. Medical tourism clearly brings in a lot of money. Developing countries like Thailand and India **benefit** not only from the income, but from the added jobs and more advanced medical equipment and technology. However, we're becoming concerned about the quality of medical care available to the people who live in these countries. And right now, we're **focusing** on problems medical tourism might cause for the poorer residents of these countries.

Reporter: If medical tourism brings in new technology and creates jobs for **skilled** professionals, like doctors and nurses, it seems like this would help the local people. So, what do you see as the problems?

Maria Torres: Well, the main problem is for the people with low incomes. They go to public hospitals and clinics for medical care. . . . Let me give you an example. In India in 2003, 75% of the total amount spent on health care was in the **private sector**. But most of India's population—much of it is **rural**—is served by government-run health facilities. And less than one in three of these public health **facilities** has enough doctors and nurses, equipment, and medicine to provide good medical care. In other words, millions of people in rural India have difficulty getting the basic medical care they need.

This is in stark contrast to the medical facilities in cities that provide care to medical tourists. In these facilities, they have plenty of medicine, state-of-the-art equipment, and many highly skilled doctors and nurses. About 80% of the specialists in India are in large cities. World Health Focus is concerned that doctors and nurses will choose to take jobs in these modern, urban hospitals rather than in the public hospitals in the rural areas. So, as we see it, the basic medical care available to people who go to government-run health facilities, especially in rural areas, could get worse if medical tourism continues to grow.

Reporter: As Maria Torres mentioned, the amount of money available for public health is not the only problem. And India is not the only country where there is a concern that medical tourism may create a **shortage** of doctors who are willing to work in public health care. Thailand is facing a similar problem.

Siriraj Hospital, in the center of Bangkok, is the largest public hospital in Thailand. More than a million patients go there each year for medical care under the national health insurance system. It's the oldest hospital in Thailand, **founded** in 1888 by the king, who established the hospital after the death of his son, Siriraj. He wanted to have a hospital that would serve the basic medical needs of the people of Thailand, as well as provide training for doctors. Every day, 365 days a year, Siriraj Hospital is crowded with patients seeking medical care.

On our visit to Siriraj Hospital, we met with Dr. Pan Chittarong, who has worked at Siriraj Hospital for more than ten years. We asked him how medical tourism is affecting the hospital.

Dr. Pan Chittarong: Well, right now, our main problem is we have trouble keeping doctors. Doctors leave public hospitals like Siriraj Hospital to practice in the private sector hospitals. And I can't blame them, really. The private hospitals are modern, with all the technology. And the doctors can make more money in the private hospitals.

Unfortunately, doctors sometimes have to make a difficult choice between taking care of people at a public hospital, or making good money at a private hospital. Just last week, the head of surgery at our hospital **resigned** to go to work at Bumrungrad Hospital, a private hospital.

Reporter: So the main reason doctors are leaving is for more money?

Dr. Pan Chittarong: Yes, but that is not the only reason. Medical tourists usually come here for some kind of surgery. So these private hospitals need more surgeons and other specialists. They don't need primary care doctors. And many surgeons and specialists would rather work in these private hospitals where they can focus on one medical problem. This is easier and much less stressful than dealing with a lot of people's health problems all day in a public health facility.

Reporter: We asked Maria Torres if World Health Focus is concerned about more doctors choosing to work as surgeons and specialists.

Maria Torres: Certainly. We have found that when a country becomes a medical tourism center, priorities can change. There is a shift away from primary, basic care toward greater specialization. Primary care doctors are the ones who see people when they are sick. They are the ones who take care of children and keep average people healthy. But medical tourists need specialists like surgeons more than anything else. Medical tourism may be encouraging more and more medical students to choose to focus on these specialties, rather than the general practice that local people are most likely to need.

Reporter: Although medical tourism can cause problems, there may be solutions, according to Dr. Chittarong and Maria Torres.

Dr. Pan Chittarong: Many of our doctors want the best of both worlds. They feel an **obligation** to take care of the local people, but also want to have the advantages of working in the private sector. As a result, some work at Siriraj full-time, and part-time at Bumrungrad. So I feel encouraged. I see the doctors using their training and experience in both places.

Maria Torres: I think, in time, countries like India and Thailand will find a balance between serving the medical tourist and the local population. Obviously, medical tourists bring in money to a country, but countries want to take care of their own citizens, too.

Listen for Details Page 74

[Repeat Main Ideas track]

VOCABULARY SKILL: Collocations with verbs and nouns
B. Page 76

1. This new trend is creating several <u>problems</u>.

2. Every winter, the Reyes family takes a <u>trip</u> to South America.

3. If I do enough <u>research</u>, I can find the best doctor.

4. Remember that you have to see the <u>doctor</u> on Monday.

5. Mrs. Blake can walk much more easily ever since she had hip <u>surgery</u>.

6. Although the problem was complicated, we found a <u>solution</u>.

7. We're not sure if we should go, but we have to make a <u>decision</u> soon.

8. The man went to the hospital to have some <u>tests</u> done.

PRONUNCIATION: *can* and *can't*
Page 79

I can go. I can't go.

A. Page 79

1. The nurses can speak Thai and English.

2. Patients can stay as long as they want.

3. You can make an appointment online.

4. His doctor can't see him today.

5. Patients can usually spend time at a beach resort.

6. I can't return for a checkup this month.

7. I can't find the address of the doctor's office.

8. Most patients can get the care they need.

9. Patients can visit the hospital before they have surgery.

10. Sometimes a patient can't choose which doctor to have.

SPEAKING SKILL: Asking open-ended questions
B. Page 81

1. **Simon:** What's wrong with . . . I mean, this is a hospital. What's wrong with looking like a hospital?

   Mr. Schroeder: Because nobody really wants to go to a hospital.

2. **Simon:** This place where we're sitting right now is the number one international hospital in the world?

   Mr. Schroeder: I haven't heard anybody yet who's told us that they take more than 350,000 international patients a year.

3. **Simon:** Why is it important to get foreign patients here?

   Ms. Bissell: It makes sense to establish India as sort of like the world destination for health care.

Unit 5: Art Today

The Q Classroom Page 87

Teacher: The Unit 5 question is " What makes a work of art popular?" What do you think, Marcus?

Marcus: One thing that makes a work of art popular is if the artist is popular. What I mean is, when artists draw attention to themselves in some way—by being controversial or beautiful or getting a lot of publicity for any reason, then people get more interested in their art and buy it.

Teacher: Interesting point. What else makes a work of art popular? Sophy?

Sophy: I think that a work of art becomes popular when it expresses something that is true for a lot a people; for example, when it expresses a feeling that everybody has or if it's about an experience that many people have had.

Teacher: What do you think, Yuna? What makes a work of art popular?

Yuna: Maybe it depends on the art. Popular books and movies are usually exciting.

Teacher: Hmm, so maybe they're not necessarily about experiences we've had, but about experiences we would like to have?

Yuna: Yes. Or about things we'd rather watch or read about than experience ourselves, like mysteries and thrillers.

Teacher: What's your opinion, Felix? What makes a work of art popular?

Felix: I think I agree with Yuna that it depends on the art. Popular music is usually music with a catchy beat that people can easily sing with or dance to.

Sophy: That's right. And popular visual art is art that people think is pretty—the kinds of things they like to put on walls in their homes. Sometimes critics like art that is disturbing or thought-provoking, but I think most people just like things that look nice.

LISTENING 1: Manga's New Popularity
Listen for Main Ideas Page 91

Reporter: It's possible that you haven't yet heard of the Japanese comic-book style called manga. But don't worry, you soon will. Manga is known for its distinctive artistic style, in which the youthful-looking heroes have big round eyes. It's been popular in Japan since the 1950s. The U.S. and Europe started to pay attention in the late '80s and early '90s, and now you'll see the comic books in unexpected places like bookstores and your local library. So what's the big deal about manga? We visited the recent Planet Comic **convention** and asked around.

John Abrams is a buyer for a major bookstore chain. Abrams says all the major bookstore chains have **taken note of** the rise in manga's popularity. The comics I **recall** from my childhood were about superheroes battling bad guys. But manga is different. John Abrams says that manga is not like the old comics.

John Abrams: Our **generation** grew up reading about heroes fighting to save the world, but manga tells all kinds of stories. I think that attracts different readers. And each manga story is longer, the length of a book. Once a reader becomes interested in a story or a character, he or she can usually read a whole **series** of books about that same character. And that means that bookstores are paying attention—if someone is buying a series of books, we want that person to be our customer.

Reporter: Abrams says there's greater variety in the types of stories manga tells.

John Abrams: Just about everything, from science fiction to high-school dramas to sports stories. And I think another factor is the art itself. Manga looks a lot like video games, and that attracts many younger readers.

Reporter: Manga, unlike earlier American comics, appeals to a different **breed** of reader: girls. Sixty percent of manga readers are female. Fourteen-year-old Tina Roberts is one of the young readers at the convention. We met her and her mother at a booth that specializes in *shoju*, manga written especially for girls.

Tina Roberts: Manga is really great. I really like the characters and the stories. I used to think comics were all about fighting, but manga has stories about regular girls like me.

At Planet Comic last year, I saw Rumiko Takahashi. I couldn't believe it! She writes *InuYasha*, a really good story about a girl who goes back in time. These conventions are really cool because sometimes you get to meet the artists.

Reporter: Although many people believe true manga still comes from Japan, a lot of manga or manga-style books are now produced in North America, many by female artists. And this may be contributing to its increased popularity. After our **encounter** with Tina, we attended a session about North American manga, and about an American manga company called Tokyopop. Colin Baxter, a UCLA graduate student who's studying manga, explained Tokyopop's success.

Colin Baxter: Yeah, this guy Stuart Levy founded Tokyopop in L.A. in 1997, after working over in Japan, and he's had amazing success. And he broke all the Western comic book rules. For one thing, he published all his books from right to left, just like they do in Japan, but the opposite of traditional American comics. And he printed them in black and white, like most manga, not color, like most American comics. And every single book sold for less than ten dollars. They must be doing something right. In 2005, they reached a thousand titles and are bringing in more than forty million dollars in yearly sales. They're on all the social networking sites. And they sell video games, produce films, and hold contests. No wonder manga is so popular.

Reporter: Margaret Brown, a librarian from Topeka, Kansas has a different take on manga's popularity. She's part of a **panel** that will talk later today about manga and its new role in libraries. I asked her if her library included manga among its titles.

Margaret Brown: Oh, my goodness, yes. We've got a whole section devoted to manga in the children and young adult categories. Manga is incredibly popular. On any given day, I'd say at least three-quarters of our manga titles are in **circulation**, so we plan to **expand** that section of the library. That's why it's so exciting to come to conventions like these to see all of the great new titles.

Reporter: According to Brown, there's a connection between manga and more traditional forms of literature.

Margaret Brown: I think anything that helps young people have an **appreciation** for reading is terrific. And because manga looks like television shows and video games, it can get kids to turn off the TV and actually read. And like all literature, good manga shows the **development** of characters and plot over time. We're even starting a manga discussion group at our library so younger readers can talk about these important parts of any story.

Listen for Details Page 91

[Repeat Main Ideas track]

LISTENING SKILL: Making Inferences
Page 92

Tina Roberts: At Planet Comic last year, I saw Rumiko Takahashi. I couldn't believe it! She writes *InuYasha*, a really good story about a girl who goes back in time. These conventions are really cool because sometimes you get to meet the artists.

A. Page 93
Excerpt 1:

Margaret Brown: I think anything that helps young people have an appreciation for reading is terrific. And because manga looks like television shows and video games, it can get kids to turn off the TV and actually read.

Excerpt 2:

Reporter: Abrams says all the major bookstore chains have taken note of the rise in manga's popularity.

Excerpt 3:

John Abrams: Our generation grew up reading about heroes fighting to save the world, but manga tells all kinds of stories. I think that attracts different readers. And each manga story is longer, the length of a book.

B. Page 93
Excerpt 1:

Margaret Brown: Oh, my goodness, yes. We've got a whole section devoted to manga in the children and young adult categories. Manga is incredibly popular. On any given day, I'd say at least three-quarters of our manga titles are in circulation, so we plan to expand that section of the library.

Excerpt 2:

Colin Baxter: Yeah, this guy Stuart Levy founded Tokyopop in L.A. in 1997, after working over in Japan, and he's had amazing success. And he broke all the Western comic book rules. For one thing, he published all his books from right to left, just like they do in Japan, but the opposite of traditional American comics. And he printed them in black and white, like most manga, not color like most American comics. And every single book sold for less than ten dollars.

LISTENING 2: Thomas Kinkade
Listen for Main Ideas   Page 95

Morley Safer: OK, a little test for you: Who is the artist who's sold more canvases than any other painter in history, more than Picasso, Rembrandt, Gauguin, Monet, Manet, Renoir, Van Gogh combined?

If you didn't say Thomas Kinkade, then you've been shopping in the wrong places. He is America's—the world's—most collected living artist.

He produces paintings by the container-load. He is to art what Henry Ford was to automobiles. Ford said of his Model T, "You can have it in any color, as long as it's black." Thomas Kinkade might say, "You can have it in any color, as long as it's in every color."

Thomas Kinkade: Everyone can **identify with** a fragrant garden, with the beauty of sunset, with the quiet of nature, with a warm and cozy cottage.

Safer: Cottage. He is a one-man cottage industry. There's *Candlelight Cottage, Twilight Cottage, Cottage by the Sea, Sweetheart Cottage, Foxglove Cottage, Teacup Cottage*. For variety, there are lighthouses, old-time street scenes and gardens by the gazillion. If you like six sugars in your coffee, these are the paintings for you.

While some art lovers might head for New York or Paris or Florence, Kinkade fans make their pilgrimage to quaint and cozy Placerville, California, where the master grew up.

Mr. Kinkade: There's been million-seller books and million-seller CDs, but there hasn't been, till now, million-seller art.

We have found a way to bring to millions of people an art that they can understand.

Safer: Art and the power of **marketing** and multiplication. The cottage industry is now traded on the New York Stock Exchange under the name Media Arts Group. Last year alone, it sold over $100 million worth of **reproductions**. Last summer, Craig Fleming, then CEO of the company, took us through the **unique** Kinkade **cloning** process.

A few dabs of paint and—*Presto*—each canvas: $1,000 to $50,000, framed. The **operation** is huge. More than 400 employees work in this vast artist's garret, where forklifts and power tools and assembly lines push the artist's vision out the door to the more than 350 Kinkade **galleries** in the U.S. and **overseas**; more than 600 more are being planned.

Is there any concern that as this thing just gets bigger and bigger, people might be concerned that it's the result of a process and a factory floor, but there's no Kinkade in the Kinkade?

Mr. Craig Fleming: Uh-huh. Well, Tom paints every single painting that—that we produce, and it's still an original Kinkade, as far as we're concerned, of his image.

Safer: Picasso, that titan of 20th century art, was a rank **amateur** when it came to marketing. How do you regard Picasso?

Mr. Kinkade: I don't believe, in time, that he will be **regarded** as the titan that he is now. He is a man of great talent who, to me, used it to

create three Picassos before breakfast because he could get $10,000 each for them.

Safer: You may not create three Kinkades before breakfast, but you may sell 30,000 before lunch.

Mr. Fleming: There's over 40 walls in the average American home, and Tom says our job is to figure out how to populate every single wall in every single home and every single business throughout the world with his paintings.

Listen for Details   Page 96

[Repeat Main Ideas track]

PRONUNCIATION: Basic Intonation Patterns
A. Page 101

1. How much do these paintings cost?
2. Is the library open?
3. We're looking for Broadway.
4. Walk north for two blocks.
5. Are you sure?
6. Please sign on the dotted line.
7. Call me tomorrow at six.
8. Have you read her new book?

B. Page 102

Alex: Did you watch *Gravity* yet?

Lee: Yeah, Jae and I watched it last weekend.

Alex: What did you think of it?

Lee: The special effects were great.

Alex: That's it? Come on. Tell me what you thought.

Lee: Well, the plot was ridiculous. I mean, it was hard to believe.

Alex: It's science fiction. It's not supposed to be realistic.

Lee: I know. I guess sci-fi isn't me. Jae thought it was pretty good. Did you like it?

SPEAKING SKILL: Avoiding answering questions
A. Page 103

1. **A:** How old are you?
    B: I'd rather not say.
2. **A:** What did you think of that book?
    B: What did you think of it?
3. **A:** Hello. Is Nico there?
    B: Who's calling?
4. **A:** Is Joseph doing a good job?
    B: Joseph is a very hard worker.
5. **A:** Can I have your address please?
    B: I'm sorry, but I don't give out that information.
6. **A:** Where were you on Friday?
    B: Why do you need to know?
7. **A:** Where do you want to have dinner?
    B: Where would you like to go?
8. **A:** How much did you pay for that car?
    B: It was affordable, and we're happy with it.

Unit 6: The Science of Food

The Q Classroom Page 109

Teacher: In Unit 6 we're going to talk about the science of food, so let's start off with the Unit 6 question, "How has science changed the food we eat?" Yuna, what do you think?

Yuna: Science has changed packaged food a lot. They add vitamins because they're good for us, and they use less fat and things that aren't good for us.

Teacher: What do you think, Felix? How has science changed the food we eat?

Felix: Well, I think it's because of science that people eat so much packaged food. They've discovered ways to create food that people like, usually by adding a lot of salt or sugar. It's not healthy at all.

Teacher: How else has science changed the food we eat? Marcus?

Marcus: They've learned to make all kinds of things out of corn. They use corn syrup to sweeten sodas and candy, and corn oil for frying. Corn is cheap to grow, so a lot of food is less expensive, like fast food. But I agree with Felix—it's not healthy.

Teacher: Sophy, do you have any other answers to this question? How else has science changed the way we eat?

Sophy: Well, science has changed the plants and animals we eat. A long time ago, corn was a small plant, but now it's a huge one. And the animals are bigger, too, because they've figured out just the right diet to feed them to make them larger.

Teacher: Some of you feel that science has made food less healthy. Do you think science has done anything good for our diets?

Sophy: Absolutely. Because of science, we're able to grow more food and feed more people. Less hunger in the world is a very good thing.

LISTENING 1: Food Additives Linked to Hyperactivity In Kids

Listen for Main Ideas Page 112

Reporter: The **controversy** about food additives and children's behavior continues, this time with a study linking food additives and a common preservative to hyperactivity. But not everyone is convinced this latest research is definite. Certain **artificial** food colorings and other additives can worsen hyperactive behaviors in children aged 3 to 9, UK researchers report. Tests on more than 300 children showed **significant** differences in their behavior when they drank fruit drinks mixed with food colorings and preservatives, say Professor Jim Stevenson and colleagues at the University of Southampton.

"These findings show that **adverse** effects are not just seen in children with extreme hyperactivity but can also be seen in the general population," the researchers write. Stevenson's team, which has been studying the effects of food additives in children for years, made up drinks to test in a group of 3-year-olds and a second group of children aged 8 and 9. Children received ordinary fruit juice or a drink **identical** in look and taste that contained common additives. Some children were given a drink containing colorings typically found in a couple of

50 gram bags of candy. Others were given a higher level of colorings, equal to **consuming** the additives in four of these bags. Parents, teachers, and the researchers then studied the children's behavior.

Both mixtures significantly affected the older children, when compared with the regular drink.

"Although the use of artificial coloring in food might seem **superfluous**, the same cannot be said for sodium benzoate, which has an important preservative function," the researchers write. "The changes to food additive rules could be **substantial**."

The issue of whether food additives can affect children's behavior has been controversial for decades. Dr. Benjamin Feingold has written books arguing that not only do artificial colors, flavors, and preservatives affect children, but so do natural chemicals found in some fruits and vegetables.

Several studies have contradicted this notion. And some have only found an effect of food additives on the behavior of children diagnosed with extreme hyperactivity. In this latest research, children generally reacted poorly to the mixtures.

"We have found an adverse effect of food additives on the hyperactive behavior of 3-year-old and 8- to 9-year-old children," the researchers write.

Stevenson has this message for parents: "Parents should not think that simply taking these additives out of food will prevent all hyperactive disorders. We know that many other influences are at work, but this at least is one a child can avoid," he says.

Dr. Sue Baic says that the study is well-designed and "potentially very important."

"It supports what scientists have known for a long time: that feeding children on diets that mainly **consist of** heavily processed foods which may also be high in fat, salt, or sugar is not **optimal** for health."

Others disagree.

"The paper is not a demonstration of cause and effect," says Dr. Paul Illing.

Listen for Details Page 113

[Repeat Main Ideas track]

LISTENING SKILL: Understanding bias in a presentation
A. Page 114

Speaker: Don't Believe the Organic Hype.

For too many people, eating healthier means buying organic food. People think that just because the label says "organic" that the food is better for them. However, a quick look at the list of ingredients of many organic products shows that they can be just as high in salt, calories, and fat as normal foods. Just because some potato chips are made from organic potatoes doesn't mean it's a healthy choice to eat the whole bag. Furthermore, research shows that the dangers associated with eating too much high-calorie food are worse than eating food with additives or artificial coloring.

B. Page 114

Excerpt 1:

As the sale of fast food increases internationally, people's weights are increasing, too. Several important international organizations, including the World Health Organization, are very concerned about the growing rate of obesity around the world. Scientists believe that fast food restaurants play a substantial role in more and more people becoming overweight.

Excerpt 2:

Can it really hurt your heart to drink one soda a day? A recent study published by the American Heart Association says it can. The report suggests that drinking even one soda a day can increase your chances of getting heart disease.

Excerpt 3:

Tea is one of the world's oldest and most popular drinks. In spite of the recent popularity of fancy coffee in parts of Asia, most people in China still look forward to the peace and calm they associate with the ancient practice of drinking tea.

Excerpt 4:

Can we believe what the food labels claim? Labels say things like "all-natural" or "helps build healthy bones" or "made with real fruit" or "contains real chocolate," or "helps burn fat." But research shows that food labels can often be confusing. Or they try to make you believe something that isn't quite true.

LISTENING 2: The "Flavr Savr" Tomato
Listen for Main Ideas Page 117

Announcer: Turning now to the world of science, genetically **altered** food may soon be available at your local vegetable stand. The "Flavr Savr" tomato is already on sale in the United States. It's supposed to stay riper, fresher, and more flavorful than an ordinary tomato. It's also one of the first foods to be produced by biotechnology. But not everyone is a fan. As Nina Winham reports, **consumers** often have an uneasy **reaction** to scientifically improved food.

Nina Winham: At the Kensington Fruit Market in Toronto, tables are piled high with everything from rutabagas to radicchio. People are picking through the produce, comparing prices and freshness. Ask them about genetically engineered vegetables.

Speaker 1: Oh, no. No, I wouldn't go for genetically altered. I wouldn't go for it.

Winham: Yeah, and if it . . .

Speaker 1: If it would be sweeter and maybe more tastier, but I wouldn't go for it.

Speaker 2: I guess, to begin with, you would want to know what goes into it, to see whether it is going to affect us.

Speaker 3: I feel that if you tamper with nature, there's bound to be a rebound.

Speaker 4: I think most people are scared of what, if something can be altered that much, is it really going to be good for them in the long run?

Winham: Genetic engineering is when scientists alter the chemical blueprint of an organism. They can make it develop the **traits** they want, sometimes by adding a part of the blueprint from a completely different species. To some, the process seems fantastic, but to others, it's **disturbing**. Professor Robert Strong studies the **ethics** of biotechnology at the University of Redding.

Robert Strong: People think that um, certain, many aspects of our modern lifestyle are unnatural, and that is, sort of, colored with moral overtones. Because it's unnatural, it must be bad.

Winham: But society has already accepted some genetic engineering, especially for medical uses. Insulin for diabetics, human growth hormone for underdeveloped children are two widely used products of biotechnology. It's when the science lab produces food that people start to back away. Steven Burke is vice president of the North Carolina Biotechnology Center.

Steven Burke: With food biotechnology, the issues are, in many cases, **compounded**. Not only are we concerned, or at least interested in the application of the techniques and in the movement of different genes between different organisms, we are doubly interested because we are, ourselves, ingesting the result.

Winham: Burke says the biotechnology industry is realizing people have moral and cultural reactions to food, and so this very personal **commodity** may be the area where the **debate** over the ethics of biotechnology comes to a head. Susan Harlander is director of research with Land o' Lakes Dairies. She says the key for food producers will be to underline the benefits of biotechnology, such as higher-quality foods. And she says that people need to see the science done in a lab as a continuation of the science that has long been a part of farming.

Susan Harlander: I think most people don't understand breeding and selection and how much **modification** of the food supply has gone on with traditional agriculture, and how little we can actually control what's happening in a traditional breeding experiment versus what we can control with genetic engineering.

Winham: Back at the Kensington Market, Linda Arugio is busy helping customers at the checkout counter. She says genetically engineered foods aren't that different from other hybrid products she's sold in the past. She remembers a lettuce, a cross between two varieties, that people just wouldn't buy. But she says watermelon with no seeds has caught on and has loyal fans.

Linda Arugio: Most people get used to trying different things, and they start thinking that it's all right or even accepting that it's all right, or knowing that it's all right, they'll start buying it and getting more into it.

Winham: The uncertain reaction of consumers is only part of the **hurdle** faced by food producers. Genetically engineered foods are expected to cost considerably more than their old-fashioned counterparts, and people here will tell you that may be the **ultimate** turn-off.

Listen for Details Page 117

[Repeat Main Idea track]

PRONUNCIATION: Other common intonation patterns
Page 122

This tomato is genetically altered?

You eat five hamburgers a day!

I ate eggs, bacon, and cereal.

Would you like coffee?

Would you like coffee or iced tea?

A. Page 122

1. What? You've never eaten a tomato?
2. Do you prefer water or juice?
3. My favorite foods are rice, yams, and pizza.
4. What did you say? You don't like ice cream?
5. Are you hungry? Do you want some bread and cheese?

SPEAKING SKILL: Expressing interest during a conversation
A. Page 123

Noriko: Hey, Marc. Is this seat free? Do you mind if I sit here?

Marc: Not at all! How are you doing?

Noriko: I'm absolutely starving!

Marc: Really? Why?

Noriko: I went to the gym this morning before school, and by 11:00, my stomach was growling in class.

Marc: Wow, that had to be embarrassing.

Noriko: Definitely. So, what did you get for lunch?

Marc: Well, they're serving French onion soup today, so I got some of that. It's not bad, but not like home!

Noriko: Yeah! French food is famous around the world, but I've never had it.

Marc: Well, I am from Provence, in the south of France. People take food very seriously there.

Noriko: Mm-hmm.

Marc: People buy fresh fruit and vegetables from the market every day.

Noriko: Every day!

Marc: Yeah, and the cheese is amazing! It tastes nothing like what we buy in the grocery stores here.

Noriko: That's interesting. I feel that way about Japanese food here, too. It's not quite the same.

Unit 7: From School to Work

The Q Classroom Page 129

Teacher: Today we're going to talk about the Unit 7 question, "Is one road to success better than another?" Marcus, what do you think? Is there a best road to success?

Marcus: I think that in most cases it's better to take a non-traditional road. If you have a different kind of experience than other people in your career, then you'll have a different perspective. You might know things other people don't know.

Teacher: Good point. What do you think, Sophy? Is one road to success better than another?

Sophy: I guess I'd say no, that there are many different ways of reaching your goals. The best way for one person might not be the best for someone else. Maybe a non-traditional road works for Marcus but a more traditional one works for someone else.

Teacher: What do you think, Felix? Marcus feels it's best to find your own unique path, and Sophy feels that while that might work for some people, it won't work for everyone. What do you think?

Felix: I agree with Sophy in the sense that everyone is different and everyone needs to find their own way. But one argument for a more traditional path to success, say studying hard, getting a degree, getting an entry-level job, and working your way up, is that you gain a lot of work experience along the way. If you take a less traditional path, you might miss out on that valuable work experience.

Teacher: OK. How about you, Yuna? Would you say that one road to success is better than another?

Yuna: No. I agree that there are advantages and disadvantages to every choice.

LISTENING 1: Changing Ways to Climb the Ladder
Listen for Main Ideas Page 132

Professor: How many of you are **currently** working? Right. Now, how many of you would like to be in exactly the same jobs five or ten years

from now? None? Well, I assume that one of the main reasons you are continuing your education is so that eventually you can get your dream job. Of course, the right education or training is important, but take a minute to think about the answer to this question. Say you want to be the next CEO of a giant company. What steps, other than getting a strong education, should you take to reach that goal? The answer you give to that question today is probably **radically** different than the answer that students sitting in those seats gave twenty-five or thirty years ago. In fact, today's **career path** is very different from the one that was common even a few decades ago. Today, I'm going to talk about these two different models of career advancement. First, let's focus on the more traditional **model** for **advancement**. A good picture of this model would be a businessperson climbing up a single ladder, one step at a time. In this situation, a worker would start at a large company, just out of high school or college. The worker would stay with the company, receiving promotion after promotion and rising from the bottom of the ladder, perhaps working in the mail room, to working in an office, to managing, and so on. Are there any questions? Yes?

Student 1: So, these workers would just stay at the same companies for their entire careers?

Professor: Exactly. Traditionally, workers were usually **loyal** to their companies. They **devoted** their entire working lives to the same company. This is true about both office work and physical work, like working in a factory. The workers stayed at the company and **climbed the ladder** as far as they could, at which point, they would simply stop moving up. In return, the company was **stable** and protected the workers. The workers **counted** on the company to pay them during their working lives and take care of them once they were too old to work. Yes?

Student 2: I think this model is similar to the business cultures in other countries.

Professor: Absolutely. Many countries in Asia follow this business model. In fact, a popular CEO in Japan recently said in an interview that he views his workers as his family. He feels responsible for them, just as they feel a responsibility to the company. Not surprisingly, this model works best in cultures that have more traditional family structures. Specifically, this model works well when the father can devote a lot of time to work, and the mother is able to stay at home with the family. This traditional model is very different from the second model that I want to talk about today.

The second model is one that you will probably be more familiar with. In contrast to the single ladder model, try to picture a person climbing several different ladders, stepping from one step on one ladder to a step on another ladder. In other words, instead of staying at one company, hoping for a promotion, these workers move from one company to another. Sometimes the move is sideways. By that, I mean sometimes the person leaves one position at a company for a similar position in a different company, maybe for better pay or for the promise of a quick promotion. On the other hand, often the worker is able to move to a position one, two, or even three steps higher than their previous position. In fact, jumping up a few steps at a time, something that would be almost impossible in a traditional career path, is actually quite common in this model, and now business leaders are getting to the top an average of four years faster than in the days of the traditional model. In the new model, workers are starting their careers at smaller companies rather than bigger ones. They move in and out of companies as positions open, and they can move faster or more slowly toward their goal, depending on their personal situations. Questions?

Student 3: I can see why someone would want to move quickly up the ladder. But why would someone want to move more slowly?

Professor: That's a great question, and it moves us into the final part of this lecture. Why *would* someone want to slow down their career path? Well, now that the traditional family **structure** has changed and women are a major part of the workforce, the needs of the workers to balance career and family have changed. Men often want to spend more time with their children than they were expected to spend in the past. This social change is definitely a main reason for the change from a traditional single-ladder model to a many-ladder model.

Another reason many companies no longer take care of their workers the way they did in the past is because of economic change. Workers can no longer count on continuing to receive money from their employer after they turn sixty-five and retire. As a result, workers usually don't feel the same sense of loyalty that they used to. Their **attitude** is to learn as much as they can at one company before moving on to another. Although this model might make some more traditional workers uncomfortable, it has become very common in North America. In fact, this year approximately 87% of all workers will be engaged in the new model as they climb to the top of their professions.

Listen for Details Page 133

[Repeat Main Ideas track]

LISTENING SKILL: Listening for contrasting ideas
A. Page 134

Mr. Doshi: Bob Quintero and Susan Miyamoto are the final candidates for the marketing position at our company. Bob has a degree from Harvard University in the U.S.A., **whereas** Susan has a degree from Keio Business School in Japan.

Ms. Stanz: Bob and Susan both have good work experience. Bob has worked for five years at a small marketing company, **but** Susan has worked for eight years at our company.

Mr. Doshi: Susan speaks more languages. Bob speaks Arabic and Spanish. **However**, Susan speaks French, Spanish, and Japanese.

Ms. Stanz: Bob has a lot of sales experience. **On the other hand**, Susan has a lot of experience at our company.

Mr. Doshi: Hmmm. This is going to be a tough decision!

B. Page 134

[Repeat Main Ideas track]

LISTENING 2: Life Experience Before College
Listen for Main Ideas Page 137

Announcer: In many parts of the world, students often take time off before heading to college. In Great Britain, it's known as the "Gap Year," and in Australia it's called a "Walkabout." It's still a foreign **concept** for most Americans, but a growing number of our young people are **daring** to be different.

Reporter: Antonia House is about to graduate from high school in Manhattan, but as her **peers** are picking out dorm room furniture, she's preparing to go globetrotting.

Antonia House: I'm going to Madrid, where I'll take Spanish lessons. I'm going to Berlin, where I'm going to take German lessons and then I'm probably going to travel on my own a little bit around Central and Eastern Europe.

Reporter: After spending a summer in France, Antonia became interested in international relations.

Antonia House: A lot of people in Europe take time off. I'm not getting that sort of American college experience, but, I **figure,** you know, I'm getting my own thing, and that's really what I want.

Reporter: While few students are as brave as Antonia, taking a year off between high school and college can mean a brighter future. According to a recent survey of 350 students, 55 percent of those that had taken time off say the experience had a positive effect on their grades. Fifty-seven percent said their job search after graduation benefited from their experiences away from the classroom.

Ron Lieber: Most of the deans of admissions, at most of the best colleges in the country, absolutely believe that their schools would be better off if every single student took time off.

Reporter: Ron Lieber is the co-author of *Taking Time Off*. He says the hard part is convincing your parents that your gap year will not be a slack year.

Ron Lieber: Taking time off is almost like school in the sense that you need to plan every day, every month. You need a lesson plan. You need a syllabus. It's not something you figure out as you go along because the **point** of the exercise is to create a year for yourself that's better, that's more valuable than being at college at that **particular** moment.

Reporter: That's just what Trudee Goodman did. Four years ago, she was graduating from high school and was burned out on books.

Trudee Goodman: I was at the same school for 10 years. It was really very **rigorous**, academically. I was ready for a different type of challenge.

Reporter: So she took a gap year and moved from Houston to Boston, where she joined a domestic Peace Corps, offering her services in troubled schools and neighborhoods.

Trudee Goodman: I was in Boston, often until, you know, 7 or 8 at night, and then, made the hour-long **commute** back to the suburbs. But I felt like, you know, this is much more real, if you will, than what my friends are experiencing.

Reporter: **Logging** 1,700 hours of community service provided plenty of life lessons.

Trudee Goodman: Well, I lived with my grandparents for the year. My grandmother had more of a social life than I did that year, so. . . .

Reporter: And after one year, Goodman was ready to dive back into academia at Trinity College, in Hartford, Connecticut.

Trudee Goodman: I had some experiences to share as examples in classes that I never would have had, had I not had this experience.

Reporter: Just three weeks ago, Trudee graduated from Trinity. And while most of her peers are **facing** the real world for the first time, she can say she's been there, done that.

Trudee Goodman: You'll realize how quickly a year goes by, if anything, that's what I learned. And just make the most of all the little moments, all the experiences you have within that year, because it'll **serve you well** into the future.

Reporter: Did it work? Trudee's gap year worked for her. She's already taken a job as an elementary school teacher, and she says her gap year experience really **stood out** on her resume. The author of *Taking Time Off* had some tips. He says talk to people who've taken a gap year doing the same thing you'd like to do. You can also ask your college if it has grants available to students who are traveling or doing community service.

Listen for Details Page 137

[Repeat Main Ideas track]

PRONUNCIATION: Highlighted words
Page 143

Colleges say a gap year doesn't have to be costly.

Colleges say a gap year doesn't HAVE to be costly.

COLLEGES say a gap year doesn't have to be costly.

A. Page 143

1. I would LOVE to take a gap year to work in India.

2. If I had to pick just ONE place to go, it would be Turkey.

3. When CARLOS was there, they didn't have the volunteer program.

4. Chris and Ilona are going, too? Hassan told me they're NOT going.

5. You'll learn a LOT while you're there, and you'll have SO much fun!

B. Page 143

1. I would like to get a job in Africa taking care of wild animals.

2. I change jobs often. My father's career path was more traditional.

3. I think I can build skills for this career if I take a year off to study.

4. The best reason to take a gap year is the chance to learn about yourself.

5. No one ever told me that the group would leave before school is over.

SPEAKING SKILL: Changing the topic
A. Page 145

A: I've had a very long day. I just came from my job.

B: That reminds me. I need to get your resume. My company is hiring and you would be perfect for the position.

A: Really? That's great! You make your job sound fun.

B: It is most of the time. We all get along well at work.

A: Oh, I wanted to ask you if you have time to help me with my homework.

B: Sure I can. We'll do it after class.

A: Anyway, I'd love to give you my resume. I've been looking for a new job.

B: I know. Speaking of which, my boss says she's interviewing people next week. Are you free in the morning?

A: I'll make sure I'm available if she calls me.

B: Hold that thought. I have to get to my next class. We'll talk about this later.

A: See you.

UNIT ASSIGNMENT: Consider the Ideas
Page 147

Susan Jones: I was a housewife for most of my life, but after my divorce, I decided I wanted to travel and see the world. For 11 years, I've taught outside of the U.S.—in Poland, Thailand, and Peru, where I've learned so much about other cultures. Sometimes, I think my students have taught me more than I taught them!

My son just had a baby, and I want to come back to the U.S. so that I can be closer to my family. I still want to travel, though. And I want to have a job where I can help students and inspire them to have some new experiences in other countries! I speak Spanish, Polish, and a little Thai.

Doug Orman: I have taught history at a university for my entire career. I wanted a promotion, but it didn't happen, and I can see that my career is going nowhere. So now I am ready for a complete change. I've spent most of my summers traveling around the world, visiting historical sites and museums. I have studied Russian and French, but I don't speak either very fluently.

Narayan Tej: I just finished college, and I'm ready to start my career. I'm from India originally, so I would bring a multi-cultural element to your team. In addition, I love to travel. I went to Europe, Brazil, and Ecuador when I was in school, and I traveled all over Asia with my family when I was a child. I speak English and Hindi, and a little Spanish and French.

Teresa Lopez: I took a gap year when I finished high school, and I think it really helped shape who I am. It broadened my world, and made me aware of so many things. I'd like to help students have the same experience. Encourage them to stretch themselves a little. I don't speak any other languages, but I would love to learn!

Unit 8: Discovery

The Q Classroom Page 151

Teacher: Here we are at Unit 8. The question is: "How can chance discoveries affect our lives?" Yuna, what do you think? Has a chance discovery ever affected your life?

Yuna: Yes. I learned about this school by chance. I was at a café back home, and I ran into an old acquaintance from high school. She told me about this school, so I went home and looked it up on the Internet.

Teacher: So if you hadn't run into your friend, you might not be in this class today.

Yuna: That's right.

Teacher: Well, I'm glad you made that discovery! So a chance discovery can affect where you go to school. How else can chance discoveries affect our lives? Sophy?

Sophy: They can also affect your career. My brother happened to sit next to a man on an airplane who owned an import/export company. The man and my brother got along really well—they spent the whole flight talking and getting to know each other. Now my brother works at the man's company.

Teacher: Another lucky chance meeting! Felix, do you have any other examples of how a chance discovery can affect our lives? Maybe a discovery that doesn't involve meeting someone?

Felix: Well, I discovered the guitar by chance. I was in this shopping mall with my parents when I was a kid, and I wandered off into a music store. They were looking all over for me, and when they found me I was playing with a guitar. Pretty soon I was begging them to buy me one and get me lessons. The guitar has been a big part of my life ever since.

Teacher: It seems like everybody has discovered some important things by chance. How would you answer the question, Marcus? How can chance discoveries affect our lives?

Marcus: I think it's clear they can affect just about everything in your life. That's why it's important to keep learning and having new experiences, because the more you do, the more likely you are to have one of these good chance discoveries.

LISTENING 1: The Power of Serendipity
Listen for Main Ideas Page 155

Martha Teichner: Nothing like starting off with a bang. In 1867 Alfred Nobel accidentally discovered dynamite after putting a popular but **flammable** salve on a cut finger. Call it serendipity.

Rubber, indispensable today. Before Charles Goodyear mixed it with sulfur and accidentally dropped it on a hot stove, it was a smelly, **unreliable** mess. Again, serendipity.

The list of serendipity stories is as long as the history of discovery.

Dr. Morton Meyers: Serendipity refers to looking for one thing and stumbling over something else that proves to be of greater value.

Teichner: Radiologist Dr. Morton Meyers accidentally figured out how stomach cancer metastasizes by watching where dye he injected for X-rays would spread and then collect. He has written *Happy Accidents* about serendipity in medicine.

Dr. Meyers: What serendipity means is misadventure, an **inadvertent** observation that a sharp, open mind can **exploit** to find its true benefit.

Teichner: In other words, having the brains to recognize an "aha!" moment. We have Horace Walpole, an 18th-century English writer and politician, to thank for the word serendipity. Walpole was inspired by a fairy tale called "The Three Princes of Serendip." The princes travel far and wide turning every potential disaster into a **triumph**. Serendip is the old Persian name for what is now Sri Lanka, aka Ceylon, as in tea. Which brings us to coffee.

Mr. Andrew Smith: So, the story goes that Caldi, who happened to be a goat-herder, stood back and watched his goats eating coffee in—coffee beans in Ethiopia. Wild coffee beans. And he sound—saw that they really engaged in some strange behavior afterwards, because of the caffeine.

Teichner: Animals, according to food historian Andrew Smith, played an important role in early food serendipity. You like cheese? Think dead camel stomachs. Nomads filled them with milk and hung them like sacks from live camels' saddles.

Mr. Smith: . . . so you got the shaking motion of the camels . . . you got the rennet of the stomach, you got the milk in the stomach, and that really is the beginning of cheese.

Teichner: My favorite serendipity story, for **obvious** reasons? Post-it notes. In 1968, a scientist at 3M made an **adhesive** that wasn't sticky enough. Eventually, somebody else at 3M thought maybe that adhesive would keep his bookmark from falling out of his hymnal at church. A thousand Post-It products later, a world without them seems **inconceivable**. After the fact, serendipity seems so obvious.

If there ever was a place literally in the serendipity business, the MIT Media Lab is it.

Mr. Frank Moss: The whole idea is to bring together people with **vastly** different backgrounds—artists, scientists, engineers, designers, biologists—and have them **interact** in open play-like environments, to experiment, not to be afraid of failure, and to build.

Teichner: Which is how PhD student Adam Boulanger found himself working on software that allows Dan Elsey—who has cerebral palsy, who cannot move anything but his head, who can barely talk—not only to compose, but to perform symphonies.

Can serendipity change the world?

Mr. Moss: I think only serendipity can change the world. I think serendipity is **mandatory**. It's not—it's not a luxury.

Teichner: But it can be fun. During World War II, GE tried to make **synthetic** rubber. It failed. Nobody could figure out what to do with it until a marketing genius put it in a little plastic egg and sold it as a novelty toy. More than 300 million little eggs have been sold.

Here's the best part: When Silly Putty turned 50 in the year 2000, it got the white glove treatment as it was solemnly installed in the Smithsonian Institution.

Serendipity enshrined.

Listen for Details Page 155

[Repeat Main Ideas track]

LISTENING SKILL: Listen for signal words and phrases
A. Page 157

Professor: Many people use a microwave oven every day. How many of you know that the microwave oven was the result of an accident?

During World War II, scientists invented the magnetron, which is a kind of electronic tube that produces microwaves. We're all familiar with microwave ovens, but what is a microwave? Well, it's a very short electromagnetic wave.

Anyway, in 1946, an engineer named Dr. Percy Spencer was standing close to a magnetron he was testing. He suddenly noticed something unusual. He felt something warm in his shirt pocket. He reached in and discovered that the candy bar in his pocket was a hot, chocolaty mess. In other words, the candy bar had melted. Dr. Spencer was so excited because he realized that microwaves could raise the internal temperature of food. In other words, microwaves were able to cook food from the inside out! And do it very quickly.

Dr. Spencer saw the possibilities here. His next step was to build a metal box into which he fed microwave power that couldn't escape. He put various foods inside the metal box and tested cooking them. In time, he invented something that would revolutionize cooking—the ubiquitous microwave oven. By that I mean that we see microwave ovens just about everywhere.

LISTENING 2: Against All Odds, Twin Girls Reunited
Listen for Main Ideas Page 159

Hannah Storm: Over the past 14 years, 45,000 Chinese children have been **adopted** by American families. So what are the **odds** that sisters, separated at a very early age, could actually find each other again half a world away? Some might call it a **miracle**, and they wouldn't be far off. To see Renee Surrey now, a happy eight-year-old who loves gymnastics, dancing, and horseback riding, you would never know she was once a sad and scared orphan in China.

Eileen Surrey: She was crying so hard she was turned all red. She was very scared. She'd never seen anyone who looked like us.

Storm: Eileen and her husband, David, brought Renee back to their home in Florida to shower her with love, but they could tell her heart still **ached**.

Eileen Surrey: Her sense of loss was just so big, and she was just so afraid to be alone. And at first I thought it was because in the orphanage she wasn't alone, but it—it seemed bigger than that.

Storm: Meanwhile, just outside Philadelphia, Annie Bernstein, almost eight, loves her new home a world away from the orphanage in China. Her parents, Andrea and Craig, remember their daughter as a bright little girl.

Andrea Ettingoff: She was very **alert** and bright. She was very aware—she was looking around, and she was very aware of what was going on.

Storm: But Annie also seemed very **deprived**, because they noticed she ate as if she'd never eat again.

Andrea Ettingoff: She wouldn't want to leave the table. All the other kids seemed to eat and be satisfied, but all this food was around her and she wasn't stopping.

Storm: Andrea sought help from a support group on the Internet, and one of the many who responded was a mom named Eileen.

Andrea Ettingoff: Her answer was the best answer, which was to try sharing a plate in the middle of the table, and we'd both eat from the same plate. It was incredible. It was—stopped it immediately.

Storm: These two moms, who lived 1,000 miles apart, noticed their daughters were from the same orphanage and decided to exchange pictures.

So, when you opened up her email, do you remember that moment of what that was like when you saw her daughter's picture?

Andrea Ettingoff: I—I—I—I was shocked.

Storm: The girls had the same hairline, same nose, same chin, same mouth. After exchanging more pictures, they just had to bring their two-year-olds **face to face**.

Eileen Surrey: It was . . . it was . . .

David Surrey: Amazing!

Eileen Surrey: Amazing. That's the word, yeah.

David Surrey: It was like a miracle!

Storm: What did you think?

Eileen Surrey: I thought they were twins. Yeah.

Storm: Andrea didn't believe it, but she did notice the girls seemed to have a special connection.

Andrea Ettingoff: We have pictures where Renee has her hand on Annie's stroller, and Annie would never let even us, like tou—touch the rim of her stroller, but she seemed like there was some kind of comfort level there.

Storm: But it would be four more years before Renee and Annie saw each other again, in July 2004, at a **reunion** of families who had **adopted** children from the same orphanage.

David Surrey: And they never left each other the whole time.

Eileen Surrey: When Renee came back to the room she would say things like, "Please don't tell my best friend at home, but Annie's my best friend."

Annie Bernstein: Best, best friends.

Renee Surrey: Sisters!

Storm: Since the reunion, the families have met three more times. We brought them together again for another visit.

Renee Surrey: Sometimes me and Annie trade places.

Storm: What? You play tricks on people?

Annie Bernstein: Yeah.

Renee Surrey: Sometimes I say I'm An—I'm Annie, and sometimes Annie says I'm Renee.

Storm: Do you wish you guys lived closer together?

Annie Bernstein: Yeah. I would like to live next door to—to—to play together, like—or have play dates, like, right after school.

Storm: Four months ago the families tested their daughters' DNA.

Andrea Ettingoff: They were really beginning to consider themselves to be sisters, and I didn't want them to have false hopes that this was, you know, a relationship that had a **biological** root and it didn't.

Storm: The DNA results: the girls are almost certainly sisters, which means, because they're the same age, Renee and Annie, **in all probability**, are fraternal twins.

Eileen Surrey: Renee, she just started jumping up and down and squealing, "Yes, we're sisters, we're sisters. Yeah, we're sisters!"

Storm: Finally, Eileen and Dave understood why their daughter Renee never liked to be alone.

Eileen Surrey: She was never alone, not even in the womb. So for her, she needed Annie.

Mr. Craig Bernstein: Since it's important to Annie, I think it's important to all of us.

Storm: OK, you tell me why—why you love Renee.

Annie Bernstein: Because we hardly ever fight and we agree on a lot of things.

Storm: And why do you love Annie?

Renee Surrey: Because she's my sister, and I just love her.

Eileen Surrey: My daughter has—has not asked me a single question about her birth family or searching for them since she's got Annie in her life.

Listen for Details Page 160

[Repeat Main Ideas track]

VOCABULARY SKILL: Collocations with prepositions
A. Page 162

1. She was looking around and she was very aware of what was going on.
2. Since it's important to Annie, I think it's important to all of us.
3. Because we hardly ever fight, and we agree on a lot of things.
4. My daughter has not asked me a single question about her birth family or searching for them since she's got Annie in her life.

GRAMMAR: Indirect speech
A. Page 164

1. Ellen said she was excited about the reunion.
2. She said, "I can't wait to get there."
3. Tonya shouted, "I haven't seen you in so long!"
4. She told me she was glad I could come.
5. Ray called to tell me he would be late.
6. He said he had missed his bus.
7. I told Teresa I was bringing dessert.
8. She said, "I hope it has chocolate in it."

PRONUNCIATION: Linked words with vowels
Page 166

She always wants to say it.

Tell me why it's important to be early

Can she go out with us?

Please show us your new invention.

A. Page 166

1. early age
2. very alert
3. stay awake
4. fly out
5. you opened
6. know about
7. go over
8. how interesting

B. Page 166

1. Annie also seemed very deprived, because they noticed she ate as if she'd never eat again.

2. After the fact, serendipity always seems so obvious.

3. Because we hardly ever fight, we agree on a lot of things.

4. Eventually somebody else at the company thought maybe it would keep bookmarks from falling out of his hymnal at church.

5. Try and spot the next big thing.

6. So after you opened the file, can you recall how it felt?

SPEAKING SKILL: Using questions to maintain listener interest

A. Page 167

1. And in 1879, Thomas Edison finally created a working lightbulb. What's the main reason this invention is so important? It changed the way we live today.

2. Why did Henri Becquerel leave dangerous chemicals in his desk drawer? Well, he didn't know they were dangerous. But that helped him to discover what we call *radioactivity*.

3. **Teacher:** Does anyone know who invented the first plastic? Over there, in the front.

   Student: Leo Baekeland, right?

   Teacher: That's right. Mr. Baekeland was looking for a new kind of material to use on wires and he accidently created the first plastic.

4. **Teacher:** William Perkin accidentally created the first artificial color for clothing. What was he really trying to make? Yes, Colin?

   Student: I think it was a medicine.

   Teacher: Correct. Mr. Perkin was trying to create an artificial medicine that people needed.

B. Page 168

Speaker: The Popsicle™ is a popular summertime treat in the United States. Kids have been enjoying them for decades. But most people don't know that the Popsicle was invented by an 11-year-old.

In 1905, Frank Epperson filled a cup with water and fruit-flavored "soda powder," a mix that was used to make a popular drink. Frank left his drink outside on his porch with a stir stick in it. He forgot all about it, and went to bed. That night, the temperature dropped to below freezing in San Francisco, where Frank lived. When he woke up the next morning, he discovered that his fruit drink had frozen to the stir stick. He pulled the frozen mixture out of the cup by the stick, creating a fruit-flavored ice treat.

In 1923, Frank Epperson began making and selling his ice treats in different flavors. By 1928, Frank had sold over 60 million Popsicles™, and his business had made him very wealthy. Nowadays, over three million Popsicles™ are sold each year.

Popsicles aren't the only invention made by accident. But they might be the tastiest.

Unit 9: Humans and Nature

The Q Classroom Page 173

Teacher: The Unit 9 question is: "How can we maintain a balance with nature?" What do you think, Sophy?

Sophy: Well, we have to work on waste disposal. We throw so much away and create so much pollution with our trash. I think if we just had fewer packages and recycled more, it would help a lot.

Teacher: What do you think, Felix? How can we maintain a balance with nature?

Felix: We need to think about the environmental effects of everything we do. In the old days, people used to just put up buildings and destroy forests without thinking about it. Nowadays we consider the risks to the animals in the area, the pollution that might be caused and all that. So I think we're on the right track.

Marcus: We've got a long ways to go, though.

Teacher: Why do you say that, Marcus?

Marcus: We're still using a lot of energy and water and creating a lot of pollution. I think we focus too much on growing, on having more stuff. People don't have to live in gigantic houses and drive huge cars, but that's what everyone wants now. I think we need to focus more on having good communities and good lives and less on buying things.

Teacher: So, we've got to buy less, pollute less, consider risk to animals and the environment before we build, what else? Yuna, how can we maintain a balance with nature?

Yuna: We need to preserve wild areas. Parks, forests, places in the ocean. We need some areas that are completely protected.

LISTENING 1: Polar Bears at Risk
Listen for Main Ideas Page 176

Narrator: Here on Wrangel Island, a team of scientists watches three polar bears that **grip** the edge of the ice. To these scientists, the polar bears' **fragile** hold on the ice is a symbol of their slipping hold on a disappearing world. Wrangel Island is part of Russia, and is located in the Arctic Ocean. It is home to one of the largest concentrations of polar bears in the world. This team of scientists has been doing research on the polar bears in this area for more than a **decade**. They hope to gain knowledge from their research that will help the polar bear in the future.

The information they have gathered so far is **alarming**. Their research suggests that not only is the population of polar bears decreasing, but the size of the bears themselves is also **decreasing**. The scientists have concluded that the polar bear is facing a **crisis** as a result of climate change. Their research shows that climate change is having a **devastating** effect on the polar bear habitat—the ice.

Most people have read that the ice caps are melting because of climate change, but for most of us, this problem feels very distant. But it is not for the polar bear. The polar bear is a creature of the ice. The ice is its home. Its body is specially **adapted** to the cold, with a double layer of fur and hollow hairs that work to trap the animal's body heat to keep it warm in the freezing temperatures. Pregnant polar bears build dens in the ice, often far from dry land.

Polar bears also hunt on the ice, usually for ringed seals. Polar bears do not truly hibernate. They are active year round. However, they can only hunt while there is plenty of sea ice, during the winter and early spring. To hunt, the bear usually finds an active breathing hole, a gap in the ice used by seals to take a breath. The bear crouches above the breathing hole, and as soon as a seal surfaces, the bear dashes to the hole and drags the seal out of the water with its powerful claws. Although polar bears are excellent swimmers, they are not fast enough to catch the seals in open water. They have to stay on the ice, and move quickly as soon as the seal shows its head. During the late summer and early fall, when the ice is melted, they cannot hunt, and so they have to live off their fat reserves and the **meager** supply of food that is available.

But the ice is not as stable as it once was. As temperatures rise, the ice is melting earlier in the year. This means that the bears have a shorter hunting season. They enter the summer thinner and less prepared to survive. And as the ice melts, it **retreats**, creating greater distances between one hunting area and another. A well-fed polar bear can swim at least 50 miles. But as the distance between hunting areas increases, and as the bears get thinner, they sometimes drown trying to reach a distant food source.

At the moment, the polar bear population is around twenty to twenty-five thousand worldwide. In some places the number of polar bears has gone down significantly over the last 15 to 20 years. Why are there fewer bears? One reason is that the birth rate is decreasing. Polar bears used to have two or three cubs at one time, and two-thirds would survive. Now one cub is the norm, and not as many of the cubs survive to adulthood.

Polar bears are also smaller than they used to be. In the past, an adult male polar bear might weigh up to 1,800 pounds. Now most weigh less than 1,000 pounds, about half the size. Females might be only three to four hundred pounds. So both males and females have become much smaller. This could be because the bears are thinner, losing weight as their food becomes harder to find. But their skull sizes are smaller too, suggesting the changes are more permanent, not simply a result of a short-term change in food supply.

The problems facing the polar bear are **potentially** disastrous. Scientists are working to better understand the role humans are playing in climate change, and what actions can be taken to address its impact. Conservationists are also trying to come up with ways to help the bears survive despite the shorter winters. A short-term solution may be to create land **refuges** for them, because their survival at the moment depends on the availability of ice and food. If people can provide these magnificent animals with a safe place to live and find food for a short while, hopefully the polar bear can adapt to its changing environment.

Listen for Details   Page 177

[Repeat Main Ideas track]

LISTENING SKILL: Listening carefully to an introduction
A. Page 179

Professor: Hello! Um, today, I want to continue our discussion about the impact of human behavior, specifically pollution, on the environment. I want to draw your attention to the effect humans are having on one of the smaller animals with which we share the planet: honeybees. You might be thinking, "Why should we care about honeybees?" Well, in the first part of this lecture, I'll explain the important role honeybees play in our daily lives. You might be surprised to find out just how vital their health is to you!

In the second half of the lecture, I'll review some recent research on how pollution in the environment is causing flowers to lose their smell. I'll also talk about how the bees are confused by this lack of smell. Finally, we'll finish up today with my predictions for the future for bees and, consequently, for humans. OK, let's get started . . .

LISTENING 2: The Effects of Oil Spills
Listen for Main Ideas   Page 182

Lecturer: Good morning. Today we'll continue to look at the way humans affect the environment. This class will focus on the *Exxon Valdez* oil spill, one of the largest oil spills in U.S. history. The *Exxon Valdez* was an oil tanker, a ship that carries large amounts of oil. It ran aground in Prince William Sound in Alaska in 1989. It released about

11 million gallons of oil into the water and onto the beaches. Many oil spills around the world have been bigger, but the *Valdez* oil spill has **emerged** as among the most serious in terms of its environmental impact. I'll explain why.

I'm also going to talk about some methods used to deal with oil spills. The oil spill in Prince William Sound has been particularly difficult to clean up, and efforts to restore the environment there are expected to continue **indefinitely**. We continue to learn a great deal about the different approaches to this problem from those efforts.

All right. So, first some background on the spill. On March 24, 1989, the *Exxon Valdez* oil tanker hit a rocky area called Bligh Reef in the northeast part of Prince William Sound. The reef tore open the ship, spilling oil into the water. When the oil spilled, the weather was calm. But after three days, a storm moved in and the wind started to **disperse** the oil down the shoreline. As the wind blew the oil and water together, the oil changed into a thick **substance** called mousse—that's M-O-U-S-S-E— which is very sticky and very difficult to remove from the water and the beaches. The oil continued to spread and move along the shoreline, and it gradually affected about 1,300 miles of beach altogether.

If you look at a map of Prince William Sound, you see that there are several islands there. Some of these, like Cordova Island and Green Island, have small communities in which many people work in businesses related to fishing, especially salmon fishing. The Sound is also home to other **species** of fish, such as herring and pollack, and to sea otters, seals, and many species of seabirds.

So, why did this spill have such a serious environmental impact?

The features of Prince William Sound are big factors. The Sound is very cold and relatively **enclosed**. It has a very rocky shoreline and a narrow opening out to the open waters of the Pacific Ocean. The very cold water caused the oil to stay in the Sound and sink into the rocks and sand, and below the surface of the water. The enclosed area kept the oil from spreading into the open ocean water. This kept the damaging effects of the oil in a small area. In addition, the water in Prince William Sound is very calm most of the time. We know that ocean waves can break down oil so it's not so **toxic**, but there aren't usually big waves in the Sound.

Now let's look at the short-term environmental impact. What happened right after the oil spilled? Thousands of oil-coated birds, seals, and fish began dying on the blackened beaches and in the oil-covered water. Volunteers rushed in to try to save the birds and animals by cleaning them. But in the days that followed the spill, it's estimated that 250 bald eagles, 250,000 seabirds, 2,800 sea otters, 300 harbor seals, and billions of salmon eggs died.

One reason the animals died was from the cold. When oil gets onto animals and birds, their fur and feathers cannot keep them warm. Their body temperatures drop, and they die. As the days went on, many more birds, seals, and sea otters suffered **injuries**. And oil is very toxic. Many animals died or became ill from swallowing oil as they hunted for food.

The people there were deeply affected as well. For example, the shores of Green Island were covered in crude oil. **Individuals** who fished for a living were hit especially hard. So many fish died that some fisheries had to close.

Now let's look at the long-term environmental impact. Hundreds of studies have been conducted since 1989. Scientists are starting to understand how complicated the recovery of Prince William Sound is. Although the Sound looks beautiful again, the environment there is still in deep trouble. A recent report **presented** some of the continuing problems.

One big problem is that there is still a large amount of oil there. As much as 20,000 gallons of the *Exxon Valdez* oil is still trapped in the Sound, deep in the water and on the beaches. Researchers have dug holes on the shore between 5 inches and 1 foot—that's between 10 and 30 centimeters—below the surface. They have found layers of oil still in the sand. Some species, such as the sea otter, dig in the sand for food. The sea otters often come into contact with the toxic oil even now, many years after it was released.

Another problem is the large number of animals still suffering the consequences of the spill. Killer whales, salmon, herring, and other species were all injured by the oil spill. Scientists are **tracking** these animals. They've found that the salmon are recovering, but salmon born from eggs exposed to the oil are smaller than salmon born before the spill. The Sound's commercial herring fishery completely collapsed within a few years. Many of the **inhabitants** of the Sound are still feeling the impact. The herring and salmon populations still haven't returned to what they were before the spill, and some of the fisheries still haven't reopened.

And the killer whale has been hit especially hard. Killer whales live in groups called pods. At the time of the oil spill, one pod had twenty-two members. The spill killed nine whales within the first year, and five more died after 1990. Since then, there have been no births in the pod—zero. This pod is in serious trouble. Another pod, fortunately, is beginning to slowly recover. Scientists think most of the dead whales died from breathing in toxic fumes from the oil, or from eating harbor seals that were covered in oil.

Thousands of harbor seals died right away, but their numbers have finally started to increase again.

So, it's clear that the environmental impact of the *Valdez* oil spill, both short and long-term, was serious. Thousands of animals suffered immediately following the spill, and some species are still feeling the effects more than two decades later.

Now let's consider how to deal with oil spills. A lot of research has been done on ways to clean up an oil spill. We know it's important to respond as soon as a spill occurs. Oil can spread quickly and cause a lot of damage in a short time. There is a variety of equipment that can be used to keep the oil from spreading, and to remove it from the surface of the water. There are also chemicals that can be used to treat the oil and remove it.

We also know that animals can die quickly from an oil spill, and that washing the oil off affected birds and animals can improve their odds of survival. I mentioned earlier that right after the *Exxon Valdez* spill, thousands of people went to the nearby beaches to try to rescue the birds and other animals.

With the *Exxon Valdez* oil spill, the first clean-up response was to use a chemical mixture to try to disperse the oil. This didn't work because there weren't enough waves to mix the water and the chemicals—remember the water in Prince William Sound is often calm—and so they had to try something else. Next they tried to use very hot water to remove the oil from the shoreline. However, they learned that this was a bad idea because the hot water killed bacteria on the shore that could have actually helped break down the oil. They went on to try other methods. The clean-up effort was huge: it lasted for four summers. There were about 10,000 workers in 1,000 boats. The cost? About $2.1 billion.

Since the *Valdez* spill, researchers have been trying to develop better methods for dealing with oil spills. For example, they have developed a chemical that promotes the growth of the bacteria that help break down the oil. To me, this is a positive step because it's a way to use what we know about how nature works to repair the damage we as human beings have caused.

Of course, the best way to stop the damage caused by oil spills is to stop the spills from happening in the first place. Next time we'll talk about some of the improvements that have been made to oil tankers and the way they are used. But right now, does anyone have any questions?

Listen for Details Page 182

[Repeat Main Ideas track]

PRONUNCIATION: Reduced forms
Page 188

Most people have read that the ice caps are melting because of climate change, but for most of us this problem feels very distant.

Their research shows that climate change is having a devastating effect on the polar bear habitat—the ice.

I want to help the animals because they are all affected by the oil spill.

A. Page 189

Sasha: People are doing many things that are helping the environment.

Brian: Yeah, I'm trying to do my part. For instance, I started walking more places.

Sasha: Yeah, but I can't worry about everything at once . . . like all the animals that are endangered.

Brian: What do you mean? That's serious.

Sasha: Don't get me wrong. I'm concerned about them. I just mean climate change is big. It's global—bigger than you or me.

Brian: So, what's your solution?

Sasha: Start at home. I've started recycling and turning off the lights when I leave a room. I'm doing what I can to save energy and resources.

Brian: Yeah, Akbar is trying to remember to unplug laptop cords and phone chargers. They use electricity even when he isn't using them.

Sasha: That's a good idea.

Brian: It's something. We have to start somewhere.

SPEAKING SKILL: Using persuasive language
A. Page 190

Amir: Wait! What are you doing?

Isabel: Huh?

Amir: Are you throwing that can away?

Isabel: Uh, yeah.

Amir: Aren't you worried about the environment?

Isabel: Well, I have to say that I don't really think what I do has that much effect on the world. I mean, I'm just one person.

Amir: Even one person can make a difference.

Isabel: Yes, but I heard that climate change isn't even real. You know, almost 20,000 scientists signed a petition saying that they don't believe that climate change is caused by humans.

Amir: You can't believe that!

Isabel: Well, why not? And many people believe that climate change is something recent. But, actually, there has been warming in the past. So, climate change is nothing new—and nothing to worry about.

Amir: Well, there might be 20,000 scientists that aren't worried about climate change, but tell that to the polar bears!

Isabel: The polar bears?

Amir: Yeah, think about the polar bears that can't find food because the ice at the North Pole is melting so fast.

Isabel: Really? That's terrible!

Amir: Whether climate change is man-made or not, I think you should recycle that can, just to be safe!

UNIT ASSIGNMENT: Consider the Ideas
Page 193

Speaker: It is no secret that our town, Spring Hill, is facing a major budget crisis. Ever since the paper factory closed, people have been out of work, and many have moved out of the area. Income from taxes is down, so the city is looking to the area around Clear Lake as a source of income. Fifty years ago, the Smith Paper factory was built on the shores of Clear Lake. The factory was helpful to the town. It provided jobs and brought people to Spring Hill. However, its impact on Clear Lake was not very positive. The factory polluted the waters of the lake during the thirty years it was in operation. The animals in the lake suffered from this pollution, and one species almost went extinct. Since the factory closed, the environmental situation has improved, thanks to the hard work of a group of scientists from Spring Hill Community College.

Spring Hill is now making plans for developing the land around Clear Lake. They don't want to repeat the problems of the paper factory. The mayor of Spring Hill is now asking for input at a town meeting. The meeting is open to anyone who wants to share ideas about the best way to develop land around the lake.

Unit 10: Child's Play

The Q Classroom   Page 199

Teacher: The Unit 10 question is: "Is athletic competition good for children?" What do you think, Marcus?

Marcus: Of course it is. Kids need to exercise. Childhood obesity is a growing problem, and exercise helps with that. It gets kids off the sofa and away from their computers and TVs.

Teacher: That's true. But why athletic competition and not just exercise?

Marcus: Because competition is motivating. Kids are more likely to play if they're trying to win at something.

Teacher: What do you think, Felix? Do you agree? Is athletic competition good for children?

Felix: Not necessarily. I agree that some kids find it motivating, but for other kids it's too much pressure. They're so focused on winning that it takes all the fun out of the sport. They do need exercise, but if they're under too much pressure, it's just adding stress to their life instead of helping them.

Teacher: Sophy, what's your opinion about this? Is athletic competition good for children?

Sophy: I think Felix and Marcus both made good points. But there's something else in favor of competition besides exercise. Kids in competitive sports learn sportsmanship, they learn how to work together toward a goal, and they learn self-discipline. I think there are a lot of benefits.

Teacher: How about you, Yuna? Do you think athletic competition is good for children?

Yuna: Mostly yes. Some adults get too extreme and push their kids too hard. But if you don't put too much pressure on the kids, I think it's good for them.

LISTENING 1: Training Chinese Athletes
Listen for Main Ideas   Page 202

Host: Good morning. Welcome back to Topic Talk. I'm Ben Irwin and my guest today is Jacinta Muñoz, a writer currently working on a book about youth sports. She's just returned from several months in China, investigating what made the athletes on the Chinese Olympic team so good so quickly. Is there something American athletes could learn from their example? If you've competed in a sport, if you are the parent of an athlete, or if you are just interested in this topic, we'd love to take your calls later in the show.

So, Jacinta, why did you decide to learn more about the Chinese training system?

Jacinta Muñoz: A couple of reasons. First, I think we've all seen how the Chinese athletes have come out of nowhere in the last twenty years or so and have started to **dominate** in a number of sports. Just look at the 2008 Olympics, where their gymnasts won so many medals. But I have a personal interest as well. When I was younger, I was a pretty good gymnast myself, and I wanted to see how the Chinese training methods differed from the ones I used.

Host: *"Pretty good?"* You're much too **modest**. You made the Olympic team in 1996, didn't you?

Muñoz: I did, but unfortunately, I was badly injured the month before the Games began, so I never actually competed in them.

Host: It was a knee injury, wasn't it?

Muñoz: Yes, I was coming off the balance beam, and I injured my knee. I just **collapsed**. The doctors couldn't fix it well enough to compete again, so I had to retire from gymnastics altogether.

Host: Hmm. That must have been so disappointing, to really be at the **apex** of your athletic career and have to retire.

Muñoz: It really was. I had trained for years with that one goal in mind—making the Olympic team—and I gave up a regular childhood, so it was a crushing blow at the time.

Host: It seems to me that training for any sport at the highest level is pretty tough, but gymnastics is particularly **brutal**.

Muñoz: Well, I think at that level of competition in any sport it's probably the same: long hours, the **intensity** of the schedule, and many sacrifices. For example, I think I missed out on a lot of the fun activities most high school students participate in. But I think gymnastics is a little different because competitors are so young.

Host: So gymnastics is probably similar around the world in that the athletes start very young. But in China, you found out athletes in many other sports are also starting their training at a young age, didn't you?

Muñoz: Yes. What's interesting about the Chinese system is it's a bit like the old Soviet system in that talented athletes are identified when they are small children, and they are usually sent to train at a special school provided by the government. As a result, they often don't see their parents for months or even years. Their counterparts in the United States, on the other hand, are often encouraged by their parents to stick with a sport. The parents are usually the ones making it happen, by taking their kids to practice, paying a lot of money for special trainers, and so on.

Host: Living away from home and family at such a young age must be very hard on the athletes. Why do they do it?

Muñoz: There are many benefits of this system. The Chinese children have all of their physical needs met, from housing to food and clothing to training costs to medical care—it's all paid for by the government. In the United States, young athletes and their families have to foot the bill. Sometimes, if they're very good, the athletes can get **funding** from other sources, such as companies or individuals that want to **invest** in their athletic careers. In general, though, it's up to the parents to pay for everything. But in China, there's no need for private investment. Government funding is **integral** to the whole system.

Host: Why is training athletes so important to the government?

Muñoz: Susan Brownell, an anthropologist who has lived and studied in China off and on for several decades, has **concluded** that for the Chinese, sports have been a way to open up. Sports are the first areas in which the Chinese provided incentives, or rewards, for performance. They are proud of their athletes and want their athletes to represent the country on the world stage. They want to their athletes to excel.

Susan Brownell says that in the U.S. we raise our children to excel—to try to be number 1—and we teach them to share. So in our sports training, athletes need to learn how to work together. Picture a child in the U.S. playing with a ball in the schoolyard. We often have to teach the child that it's important to share the ball.

On the other hand, in China, they raise their children to share, and so they train them to excel. Humility is very important in Chinese culture. It's not good to stand out. But when athletes compete, they need to be better than others. They need self-confidence. So much of their training is focused on building self-confidence and on becoming faster, stronger, and better.

As part of this process, individual provinces start selecting potential athletes from the elementary schools, and they train them to compete. Only about 80,000 of the hundreds of thousands of children selected will make it to the national training center. And that will take them years.

Host: How are the children selected? Is it on the basis of their performance in the sport so far?

Muñoz: Not really. The recruiters are usually looking for body types. For example, children with small hips and flexibility are chosen for gymnastics and diving, whereas tall children are selected for basketball and volleyball. Some children are sent for training before they've ever even played the sport. But once they get there, they train for six hours a day, six days a week. As a result, they can get very good, very fast.

Host: Is it worth it?

Muñoz: Many athletes think so, since they get a chance to go to school, travel, and compete. Remember, often these children come from rural communities where they don't have as many options as those in larger cities. But the real **beneficiary** of the system may be China itself. In just 20 short years, China has gone from winning five medals in 1988 to one hundred in 2008, the second highest total. It's really the beginning of a new **era** for Chinese sports.

Host: Now we'll open the phones to take some of your calls. We've got James from Madison on the line. Hi, James. What's your question?

Listen for Details Page 203

[Repeat Main Ideas track]

LISTENING SKILL: Listening for causes and effects
Page 204

Many athletes are driven by the hope of winning medals at the Olympics.

The athlete won two gold medals as a result of years of hard work.

Due to bad weather, the baseball tournament was canceled.

The kids live far from home and practice very hard. Therefore, they only see their parents every few months.

Some kids start playing some sports too young. The result is they often get injured before they even reach high school.

A. Page 205

1. Our team won the tournament as a result of that goal.

2. Amy trained too hard and didn't get enough sleep. Because of this, she didn't compete well on the day of the race.

3. Due to the snow, our game had to be canceled.

4. Olympic athletes in China receive government payment and do not have to support themselves financially. The result is that they can concentrate fully on their training.

5. Coach Zheng has won several gold medals. Therefore he is respected around the world.

6. I can practice more often since we live closer to the gym.

LISTENING 2: *Until it Hurts* Discusses Youth Sports Obsession
Listen for Main Ideas Page 207

Host: It's now 8:45 on Monday morning—which is the time we turn to sports writer Jim Butler for his take on the sporting world.

Jim Butler: Maybe you heard the story last week: Yet another parent jumped onto the field at his kid's soccer game to yell at the referee. And just like too many other times, the yelling **escalated**, ending up with the father fighting with the referee. What a sad reflection on youth sports today, and the role of adults in them.

Which brings me to a book I read recently, about our **obsession** with youth sports, called *Until It Hurts*. The author, Mark Hyman, is a sports **journalist** who has written for *Sports Illustrated* and *The New York Times*. He's also a dad, a coach, and a **former** athlete.

Mr. Hyman's book is about many things—how youth sports have changed over time, and how they should change in the future—but it's also a personal story about what he's proud of—and what he **regrets**—about his decisions as a father and a youth sports coach.

When we first began organizing youth sports, say, oh, 150 years ago, the teams were guided by schools and educators. They were designed to be fun, teach skills, maybe build a little character. But sometime in the middle of the last century, educators bowed out, and the parents took over, sometimes as coaches, but most often as very active **spectators**. And their **ambitions** often got the best of them.

Parents wanted to see their kids do as well as possible at a sport, and so some big changes happened in the way children play sports. One change is that children started to play competitive sports at very young ages, when they're more **vulnerable** to certain kinds of injuries, like bone fractures. Mark Hyman says that kids now commonly start playing organized sports at four or five years old.

Another change is that instead of playing a variety of different games, many children now concentrate on only one, which they play year-round. Again, injuries and **burnout** are more likely, because they're doing the same thing over and over again, straining the same muscles.

Mark Hyman knows more than most about this problem. In 2004, he wrote an article about how overuse of the pitching arm in baseball can result in an injury so crippling that you need a major surgery to repair it. In the article, he criticized the parents and coaches who failed to keep the young players safe.

Then at age 18, Mr. Hyman's son Ben, a baseball player, found that he needed the very same surgery because of overuse of his pitching arm. This encouraged Mr. Hyman to think about his own role in his son's athletic career. He recalled an incident when Ben was 14. Ben complained that his shoulder was tired and sore, but Mark encouraged him to play again a few days later. **Ultimately**, the decision to play was Ben's. He played because he wanted to, and he enjoyed it. But Mr. Hyman still wondered if he had made the right decision in encouraging Ben to play.

Mark Hyman suggests we take some **fundamental** steps to get youth sports back to where they used to be. We should listen to doctors, which will mean educating coaches about overuse injuries. We should also discourage kids from playing just one sport year-round. We should listen to children and help them decide if and when they want to play. And most of all, we need to restore perspective—encourage parents to be the **reasonable** people they are off the field. In some communities, parents sign contracts about their behavior. In the contract, they agree to follow rules about fighting with one another and arguing with the referee. One such rule introduced Silent Sunday, a day when parents are banned from yelling or even talking at the game. If only that father at the game last week had signed such a contract. He might not have made such a fool of himself, and maybe, just maybe, the kids playing the game would have had more fun.

Listen for Details Page 208

[Repeat Main Ideas track]

VOCABULARY SKILL: Idioms
A. Page 210

1. First, I think we've all seen how the Chinese athletes have come out of nowhere in the last twenty years or so and have started to dominate in a number of sports.

2. In the United States, young athletes and their families have to foot the bill. Sometimes, if they're very good, the athletes can get funding from other sources, such as companies or individuals that want to invest in their athletic careers.

3. They are proud of their athletes and want their athletes to represent the country on the world stage.

4. But sometime in the middle of the last century, educators bowed out, and the parents took over, sometimes as coaches, but most often as very active spectators.

5. And their ambitions often got the best of them.

GRAMMAR: Uses of real conditionals
Page 211

I will put on my uniform when I get there.

When I get there, I will put on my uniform.

PRONUNCIATION: Thought groups
Page 213

Blake loves basketball.

He plays every day and watches every game.

Steve and Debbie, on the other hand, will not be going.

Do you agree or not?

We're going out. Do you want to come with us?

A. Page 213

1. In my opinion, that's a bad idea.

2. Are they coming or not?

3. If I get home early, I'll go running. Want to join me?

4. Keep your head up as you kick the ball. It's important.

5. All week long these kids are so busy they have no time for fun.

6. If she wins this match, Ms. Williams will be in first place.

7. If you'd like to talk, call me at (555) 233-1157.

8. Here's my e-mail address: goalkeeper100@global.us.

SPEAKING SKILL: Adding to another speaker's comments.
Page 214

Sung-ju: I believe that organized sports are beneficial to kids. Sports are good exercise, and they give kids the chance to meet people they would never meet otherwise.

David: That's true. And I would add that sports help them learn to work as part of a team.

A. Page 215

John: In my opinion, college athletes should be paid a salary for playing. Here's why: We all know that college sports are a big business. Universities make a lot of money when their teams perform well. And I think the athletes should receive a part of that profit. That would be fair.

Lisa: Another important point is that these athletes have to work really hard. They practice every day. They travel around the country. And they have to attend classes just like everyone else. Basically, they work like employees of the university. And if they are employees, they should be paid a salary.

David: That's a good point. And to build on what John said earlier, if universities really want to succeed in sports, they should be happy to pay their athletes. If they do agree to pay them a salary, these athletes will play better, and they'll be more likely to stay in school longer, instead of leaving school to become professionals before they graduate.

Sung-ju: John and Lisa are both right. And I would add that, as a college athlete, I could definitely use the money!